The Perception of Women
in Spanish Theater
of the Golden Age

Saint Margaret of Antioch, by Francisco de Zurbarán. Courtesy of the Trustees, the National Gallery, London.

The Perception of Women
in Spanish Theater
of the Golden Age

Edited by Anita K. Stoll
and Dawn L. Smith

Lewisburg
Bucknell University Press
London and Toronto: Associated University Presses

Associated University Presses
440 Forsgate Drive
Cranbury, NJ 08512

Associated University Presses
25 Sicilian Avenue
London WC1A 2QH, England

Associated University Presses
P.O. Box 39, Clarkson Pstl. Stn.
Mississauga, Ontario,
Canada L5J 3X9

The paper used in this publication meets the requirements
of the American National Standard for Permanence of Paper
for Printed Library Materials Z39.48-1984.

Library of Congress Cataloging-in-Publication Data

The Perception of women in Spanish theater of the golden age / edited by Anita K. Stoll and Dawn L. Smith.
   p. cm.
  ISBN 0-8387-5189-X (alk. paper)
  1. Spanish drama—Classical period, 1500–1700—History and criticism. 2. Women in literature. 3. Sex role in literature.
I. Stoll, Anita K. II. Smith, Dawn L.
PQ6105.P46 1991
862'.309352042—dc20   89-46402
                                        CIP

This volume is dedicated
to the understanding families
and friends of the essayists
who facilitated its creation,
and to Everett Hesse,
who was there at the beginning.

Contents

8 Contents

Acknowledgments

The editors wish to express their appreciation to the members of the Editorial Board, Frederick A. de Armas and Shirley B. Whitaker, for their assistance in preparing this volume.

The frontispiece, *Saint Margaret of Antioch,* by Francisco de Zurbarán, is reproduced by courtesy of the Trustees, the National Gallery, London. It depicts the saint in seventeenth-century rustic costume holding a book and a shepherd's crook (references both to her Christian and her rustic upbringing). In the background stands the dragon in which the devil disguised himself and appeared to her in prison. According to the legend, she overcame him with the sign of the cross. It is thought that Zurbarán may have modeled his subject on the figures he saw in religious processions in his native Seville; it is also possible that he was influenced by the lively presentation of saints such as Tirso's Santa Juana in the popular *comedias de santos* of his time (see *Zurbarán: Catalogue of the Exhibition held at the Metropolitan Museum of Art, New York, 1987,* ed. Jeannine Baticle [New York: Metropolitan Museum of Art], p. 248).

Contributors

THOMAS E. CASE is professor of Spanish and chair of the Department of Spanish and Portuguese at San Diego State University. He has published three books on Lope de Vega and many articles on Golden Age literature, Latin American literature, and Spanish and Latin American culture.

MARÍA MARTINO CROCETTI was born in Italy and educated in Argentina. She is a Ph.D. candidate at Yale University specializing in Spanish Golden Age Drama and the picaresque. Crocetti is also continuing research on the women's role in the *comedia.*

DANIEL L. HEIPLE has published on the history of medicine and science in Golden Age literature and on seventeenth-century music and is the author of *Mechanical Imagery in Golden Age Poetry.* He is currently chair of the Department of Spanish and Portuguese at Tulane University and is completing a book on the poet Garcilaso de la Vega.

MARGARET RUTH HICKS received the doctoral degree in comparative literature from the University of North Carolina and is on the faculty of Duquesne University. She has published articles on Spanish Golden Age drama and is pursuing her interest in the staging practices of the period.

CATHERINE LARSON is currently on the faculty of Indiana University (Bloomington). Her book-length study of the relationship between language and the *comedia* has been published by Bucknell University Press. She has also published a number of articles on Golden Age and contemporary Latin American drama, has served as a Golden Age reader for several scholarly journals and is a member of the Board of Directors of the Association for Hispanic Classical Theater, Inc.

RUTH LUNDELIUS teaches Spanish at the University of Georgia. Her area of specialization is the Spanish Golden Age drama, particularly the depiction of women characters. She has published articles in this area, and is currently studying the seventeenth-century dramatist Ana Caro.

MICHAEL D. MCGAHA is professor of Romance Languages and chair of the Department of Modern Languages at Pomona College. He is currently Editor of *Cervantes* and Associate Editor of *Hispania*. His publications include a critical edition of Lope de Vega's *Perseo* (1985) and translations of Lope's *Lo fingido verdadero* (1986) and Antonio Mira de Amescua's *El esclavo del demonio* (1989) as well as numerous articles on seventeenth-century Spanish literature.

THOMAS AUSTIN O'CONNOR is professor of Spanish and chair of Romance Languages and Literature at the State University of New York at Binghamton. He has published numerous articles on Golden Age literature and his book, *Myth and Mythology in the Theater of Pedro Calderón de la Barca,* was published in 1988.

DAWN L. SMITH earned the doctoral degree in Spanish and French from Oxford University and has been on the faculty of Trent University in Peterborough, Ontario, since its inception. She has published a critical edition of *La mujer que manda en casa* by Tirso de Molina as well as a number of articles on Golden Age drama. She is currently engaged in research on performance studies and in translating Cervantes' *entremeses* for performance.

TERESA S. SOUFAS is associate professor of Spanish at Tulane University. She has a book-length study, *Melancholy and the Secular Mind in Spanish Golden Age Literature* (1990) and has published articles on Golden Age literature in *Hispanic Review, Journal of Hispanic Philology, Forum for Modern Language Studies,* and *Romance Quarterly,* among others.

ANITA K. STOLL is professor of Spanish at Cleveland State University. Reflecting her interests in Golden Age drama and women's literature, she has edited an anthology of materials on the twentieth-century Mexican writer Elena Garro, also published by Bucknell University Press, and *A Study and Critical Edition of Lope de Vega's La noche de San Juan.*

MATTHEW D. STROUD is professor of Foreign Languages at Trinity University in San Antonio. His research deals exclusively with

Spanish Golden Age theater, and he has published numerous articles, an edition and translation of Calderón's *Celos aun del aire matan*, and a monograph, *Fatal Union: A Pluralistic Approach to the Spanish Wife-Murder Comedias*.

MARCIA L. WELLES is professor of Spanish at Barnard College. Principally committed to research in the Golden Age, Welles has published *Style and Structure in Gracián's 'El Criticón'*, *Arachne's Tapestry: The Transformation of Myth in Seventeenth-Century Spain*, as well as essays on María de Zayas y Sotomayor and the female picaresque. She is also co-author of *From Fiction to Metafiction: Essays in Honor of Carmen Martín Gaite* and has an essay on Latin American women writers in *Women in Hispanic Literature: Icons and Fallen Idols*.

CONSTANCE WILKINS is professor of Spanish at Miami University in Oxford, Ohio. She has published a monograph, *Pero López de Ayala*, in the Twayne World Authors Series and, in collaboration with Heanon Wilkins, an edition and study of Ayala's *Chronicle of Pedro I*. She has written a number of studies on the Golden Age *comedia*, concentrating mainly on the work of women dramatists and on the portrayal of women characters in the drama.

AMY R. WILLIAMSEN, of the faculty of the University of Arizona, specializes in sixteenth and seventeenth-century Spanish literature. Her research includes work on Cervantes, the *comedia*, and women writers of the period. She is particularly interested in humor and irony and their subversive function in Golden Age discourse.

The Perception of Women
in Spanish Theater
of the Golden Age

Introduction: The Perception of Women in the Spanish *Comedia*

DAWN L. SMITH

The radical changes that have been taking place in critical theory since the beginning of this century have helped to revitalize our way of looking at the literary texts of earlier times. The critical study of the Spanish *comedia* of the sixteenth and seventeenth centuries, while initially slow to reflect these changes, has been making up for lost time in the past few years. In particular, it has benefited from the example of Shakespearean studies, as well as from the influence of Marxist and Structuralist theory. More recently, criticism of the *comedia* has reflected other perspectives: for example, the upsurge of feminist criticism has brought about a special scrutiny of texts in which women feature prominently. This, in turn, has given rise to new hypotheses concerning both the dramatists themselves, who were usually male, and the ideas and attitudes prevalent in the society for which they wrote.

At the same time, the interest in semiotics has increased our awareness of the special nature of theater, not only as text, but also as performance—as an experience shared between actors and spectators. This conjunction of critical perspectives serves to make the subject of women in the *comedia* both timely and fascinating. We should not forget that the plays were written to be performed by acting companies that included women and for a public composed of a large number of women. These sociological factors undoubtedly had an influence on shaping the repertoire.

It has long been recognized that the Spanish *comedia* of the sixteenth and seventeenth centuries contains an astonishing abundance of female characters—some of whom offer remarkable theatrical possibilities. For a long time, however, scholarly criticism was more concerned with describing the phenomenon than with analyzing it. An examination of the Modern Language Association critical bibliography since 1965 clearly indicates the change taking place in recent years under the influence of new theoretical approaches. The bibliography also shows that, while the subject has always provided ample material for articles and doctoral theses, to date it has prompted relatively few book-length studies.

Nevertheless, three of these longer studies deserve special mention for their contribution to the developing awareness of the importance and complexity of the feminine presence in the *comedia*. In 1955 Carmen Bravo-Villasante published a pioneering study of the transvestite woman in Golden Age theater,[1] but it was not until nearly twenty years later, in 1974, with Melveena McKendrick's book, *Woman and Society in the Spanish Drama of the Golden Age*[2] that a more comprehensive attempt was made to analyze the various types of women who appear in the Spanish classical theater. McKendrick subtitled her book "A Study of the *mujer varonil*" (i.e., the equivalent of what Natalie Zemon Davis has called "the virtuous virago"), thereby emphasizing the potentially subversive role of women in the *comedia*.

Within six main categories of female types, McKendrick identified women who rebel against society and become bandits; women who become scholars and even, in a sense, "career women"; those who show their independence, either by simply playing hard to get, or by dazzling their male admirers with their beauty, courage and strength, and by their skill as huntresses—qualities which, in an extreme form, are embodied in the figure of the Amazon.

While McKendrick's study has long provided the benchmark for Hispanists looking at feminine aspects of the *comedia,* her conclusions now seem somewhat tentative insofar as they are based on an unquestioning view of the monolithic solidarity of the patriarchal system in seventeenth-century Spain. She saw the theme of the "virtuous virago" as one that was principally exploited and popularized by Lope de Vega, "both as a box-office draw, and as a fertile source for serious investigation of social responses to one of the subjects that fascinated him most—women" (313). She touched briefly on the titillating effect that these fantasies of dominant women may have had on the male theatergoers of the time (320–21), but was more inclined to see the theme as part of the baroque fascination with contradiction, particularly between appearance and reality. For McKendrick, the male dramatists who created these female characters were feminists only in the sense that they believed in the ability of women as human beings to challenge, equal, and even get the better of men in many situations. At the same time, however, she argued that they accepted the reality of a society that assigned a circumscribed role to women. These dramatists were "prepared to uphold woman against society but never against nature" (328). McKendrick suggested that the seventeenth-century belief in Neoplatonic order and harmony had a good deal to do with this view (172–73) and nine years later, she returned to this theme in an essay titled "Women Against Wedlock."[3] While reaffirming the dramatists' attitude as one of benign feminism, she concluded "they would not emancipate woman from man, but neither would they emancipate man from woman. For them, love was the greatest equalizer of all" (145).

Several years after the appearance of McKendrick's book, Frederick de Armas explored another aspect of feminism in the Spanish Golden Age in his book *The Invisible Mistress*.[4] He looked at the Spanish treatment of an old myth—that of a young man's encounter with a mysterious woman who refuses to reveal her identity and who exercises a power over him which may be magical, demonic or angelic. De Armas argued that women resort to artifice (and especially the *burla,* or trick) because they are obliged to create a world of fantasy and deception for themselves in order to escape "and halfway attain their wishes" (51). He concluded that the persistence of this theme in the *comedia* shows it to be a fantasy created by women as a means of expressing their wish "to be free and equal with man, but only to perform (their) 'proper' role" (190).

Another Hispanist who has attempted to map the movement of feminism in the *comedia* is Everett Hesse. Although he has not been specifically feminist in his approach, he has consistently looked to psychoanalytical theory (especially to Freud and Jung) in his analysis of plays.[5] Henry Sullivan has moved closer to a feminist stance in his application of Lacanian theory to the plays of Tirso de Molina. He has examined Tirso's views on love, matrimony, and desire and concluded that, for this dramatist, the criterion of equality between the sexes was based, not on love, but on "the compatibility of moral grandeur."[6]

The women who appear in the *comedia* fit into a number of categories that go beyond those suggested by Melveena McKendrick for identifying the "virtuous virago." As a first step, it may be useful to consider these women within the framework of the patriarchal setting: that is to say, in relation to the men who control and shape their lives in the world of the *comedia*. Since, almost by definition, the plots of the *comedia* involve conflict, all of the female protagonists in these plays in some way challenge male authority as represented by fathers, husbands, brothers, and even sons, or by suitors, whether encouraged or not. It is significant, perhaps, that the literary hierarchy includes few mother figures; where a mother does play a dominant role, she is either idealized (like Tirso's queen

in *La prudencia en la mujer* [Prudence in Women], or condemned
for her overweening ambition (for example, Semiramis as portrayed
by Virués—Calderón's interpretation is more complex).[7] Mothers
rarely appear in comic plays, although Lope created the figure of a
mother who is ridiculed for believing that she is being courted by
her daughter's suitor (as in *La discreta enamorada* [*In Love But
Discreet*].

There are many portrayals of wives (especially in Calderón's
plays) and probably even more of daughters and sisters whose
virtue provides the central issue of the play (for example, Lope's
Peribáñez or Calderón's *El médico de su honra* [*The Surgeon of His
Honour*], and *El alcalde de Zalamea* [*The Mayor of Zalamea*].
Some, like those in the three plays just mentioned, are relatively
passive in their relationship with the opposite sex; however, by far
the greatest number of female protagonists in the *comedia* are out
to manipulate men for their own ends—which almost invariably
lead to marriage and a conventionally happy ending (Tirso's *Don
Gil de las calzas verdes* [*Don Gil of the Green Breeches*] and Lope's
El perro del hortelano [*The Dog in the Manger*]). While the importance given to the fact that these women are also daughters or
sisters varies from play to play (note, for example, the differing
situations in Calderón's *La dama duende* [*The Phantom Lady*],
Tirso's *Marta la piadosa* [Pious Martha], and Lope's *El perro del
hortelano),* the nature of the framework is always dictated by the
codes and mores of seventeenth-century Spain. The playwrights
sometimes appear to escape from this framework into the world of
mythological fantasy, yet even here the codes remain unchanged:
ultimately the Amazon warriors, the willful queens and the elusive
huntresses must conform to the incontrovertible laws of society and
biological nature.

Although powerful women dominate in these fanciful constructs
it is usually in comedy that they achieve their fullest development
as complex personalities. As de Armas has shown, the figure of the
unattainable, mysterious woman has a long history in Western
literature and art. It can also be seen as yet another aspect of male
fantasy: a provocative and sometimes erotic version of the world-
upside-down topos, which expresses the essential contradiction of
the male view of women.

On the other hand, the female characters who arouse their husbands' jealous suspicions, or who otherwise become tangled in the
unyielding meshes of the honor code, generally become tragic
victims (although both Lope and Tirso notably avoid this equation

in such plays as *Peribáñez* or *El celoso prudente* [Jealous but prudent]). A fallen woman is not often allowed a second chance in the *comedia:* if the man who wrongs her is not prepared to marry her (assuming, of course, that she is not already married) she must pay the price of infamy (real or imagined) by death or by banishment to a convent, or she may sometimes be redeemed through divine intervention (as in Mira de Amescua's *El esclavo del demonio [The Devil's Slave]*. In this case the social code is reinforced by the teachings of the Church.

While at one end of the spectrum we find the woman whose rebellion against nature, society, and perhaps even against God, has turned her into a bandit (the symbolic outlaw), at the other end we find the figure of the saint. In his well-known essay, "Bandits and Saints in the Spanish Drama of the Golden Age," A. A. Parker showed how close the relationship between these two types can be in the *comedia.*[8] The symbolism takes on a special significance when it is applied to women. Like the female bandit [la bandolera] the saint places herself outside the usual constrictions of society as well as beyond the importunings of men. As Tirso's Santa Juana demonstrates, she can count on divine powers to come to her rescue (most often by means of a timely apparition, or by causing her to levitate out of reach of her male assailant).

Nevertheless, whatever degree of freedom a woman may enjoy for the duration of the play, by the end of it she will be (re)integrated into the social status quo; even the rebel is obliged to conform or be effectively eliminated (as in *El esclavo del demonio*). In Tirso's *La ninfa del cielo* [The Nymph of Heaven] the rebellious heroine is redeemed by a mystic union with Christ, a reward which parallels that received by her saintly counterpart in the *Santa Juana* trilogy. Thus marriage, either in the spiritual or earthly sense, provides the ideal ending in the *comedia*. There are rare exceptions to the rule, although Lope occasionally allows us a glimpse of this possibility in enigmatic comedies like *El perro del hortelano* or, as Anita Stoll suggests in this volume, *El anzuelo de Fenisa* [Fenisa's Hook].

While the perception of women as presented in the *comedia* generally conforms to the traditional male view of women as angel or devil (based on the antithetical models of the Virgin Mary and Eve), there is room for considerable variation in the ways the different dramatists handle this perception. It would be wrong to suggest that their view of women was monolithic, just as it would be risky to believe that with the tools of modern criticism one can somehow find infallible answers to the riddles they have left us. The

complexity of the problem is exemplified by the fact that for every
critic who assures us that Tirso was a feminist, another can be
found who supports the opposite view.

This collection of essays, by fourteen American Hispanists—all
of whom are known for their work on the Spanish *comedia*—
reflects both the richness of the theme and the variety of critical
approaches to which the theme lends itself. The title of the collection is appropriately ambiguous so as to indicate many possible
interpretations: these include the perceptions of women of both
male and female writers; society's view of women in sixteenth- and
seventeenth-century Spain; and our view of those perceptions as
critics living in the twentieth century. The essays are divided into
three main groups: 1) Theoretical Approaches; 2) Taking the
Woman's Part; and 3) Rape, Politics, and Sexual Inversion.

Theoretical Approaches

Calderón's comedy of intrigue, *La dama duende,* is one of the
quintessential examples of the mysterious lady who successfully
dominates her male antagonists in order to procure the husband of
her choice. In this collection the play is the subject of two essays.
Catherine Larson takes a feminist and semiotic approach that aims
at complementing, rather than contradicting, existing critical views
of Calderón's attitude towards women. She argues that Calderón
goes beyond sexual stereotyping in creating a complex character
who stands outside the conventional norms of her society and, by
so doing, both subverts and reaffirms them. María Crocetti explores
the use of space in *La dama duende* and suggests that its staging
can be seen as an analogical structure whereby Doña Angela's
room represents the internal feminine area separated from the
external masculine area by a hymen/cupboard. Doña Angela attempts to control the masculine space, as well as the access to her
own internal area, by manipulating the hymeneal barrier. Like
Larson, Crocetti also sees subversion in the play; she interprets
Angela's manipulation, together with her open criticism of the
traditional role assigned to women in her family and society, as acts
of rebellion against the patriarchal establishment.

Matthew Stroud uses Lacanian theory in his study of sex and
gender in Tirso's comedy, *Don Gil de las calzas verdes.* Proposing
that Doña Juana's transvestite adventures are an allegory of the
feminine search for identity, he takes Reichenberger's formula for
the *comedia* (that is, the movement from "order disturbed to order

restored") and equates it with the reconciliation between Lacanian concepts of the Imaginary and the Symbolic.

Taking the Woman's Part

Teresa Soufas examines the female writer's point of view in seventeenth-century Spain in her study of Ana Caro's treatment of the *mujer varonil* theme. Soufas sees Caro's stance in the play *Valor, agravio y mujer* [Courage, Grievance and Woman] as a means of subtly undermining the accepted norms, a challenge from within the traditional patriarchal culture. This she achieves through the expedient of temporary inversions which, as in many male-authored texts, draw on the familiar topos of the world-upside-down; unlike her male counterparts, however, she unequivocally champions the right of the abused woman, while exposing the double standards of the honor code enforced by males.

Like Larson, Crocetti, and Soufas, Connie Wilkins also considers the theme of subversion. Taking the view that the gender of the author influences the perspective of a literary work, Wilkins asserts that Sor Juana Inés de la Cruz and María de Zayas make use of comedy as a means of subverting the literary genre and of questioning the political and social status quo. Within the conventional framework of the *comedia,* they impose significant shifts of perspective and emphasis that reflect their views as writers who are marginalized by gender. Wilkins concludes that the dramatic worlds they create are very different from those created by their male contemporaries: "In their references to intellectual pursuits of women, female friendships, sexual repression by both sexes and rejection of the restrictive forces of the honor code and of public opinion, these women interrogate the dominant notions of gender difference and of societal standards for behavior."

Daniel Heiple argues that both María de Zayas and Lope de Vega are proponents of feminism by examining what he believes to be their reactions to the overt misogyny of Huarte de San Juan in his popular *Examen de ingenios* [Study of Wits]. Huarte's insistence on the influence of the humors leads him to find women severely lacking in intellectual abilities—a view Lope rejects in a play significantly titled *La prueba de los ingenios* [The Test of Wits]. Heiple sees a similar rebuttal in María de Zayas' preface to her *Novelas amorosas y ejemplares* [Exemplary stories of love] in which she blames the apparent deficiency of intellect in women on their education rather than on their physiological makeup.

A complementary view of Lope's attitude towards women is provided by Ruth M. Hicks's study of *La boba para los otros y discreta para sí* [Foolish for others and clever for herself]. In this play the female protagonist is principally matched with a female opponent who is also her cousin. In order to assert her claims both to the dukedom, which is hers by inheritance, and to her chosen mate for marriage, she adapts a clever strategy of incompetence whereby she deliberately misrepresents herself as a country bumpkin. Hicks shows how Diana uses her natural wit to manipulate linguistic and social conventions as a means of outmaneuvering her well-educated rival. The comic metamorphosis both exploits the conventional prejudices against women at the same time that it apparently holds them up to ridicule.

Rape, Politics, and Sexual Inversion

Four contributors have looked at the role of women in plays that are either based on, or affected by, mythological and historical themes. In each case the theme is seen to be a pretext for reflecting on other issues.

Michael McGaha traces the source of Lope's *Las mujeres sin hombres* [Women without men], a play about Amazons—those quintessentially androgynous constructs who were objects of such fascination in seventeenth-century Europe. It would seem that Lope took most of his material from Boccaccio, but that he was also influenced by his relationship with Marta de Nevares, to whom he dedicated the play. McGaha notes that Lope changes the source, creating an equality between the sexes which, he argues, shows the dramatist's "genuine sensitivity to the feminist viewpoint." Here, too, as with María de Zayas, it is suggested that by denying women an education men are to blame for many of what they view as feminine shortcomings. Is this play merely an example, as some would argue, of Lope's propensity for ironic fantasy? Or is it representative, as McGaha proposes, of his more critical attitude towards the society in which he lived and wrote?

Thomas O'Connor also raises the question of authorial attitude in his study of the politics of rape in Calderón's mythological plays. He identifies four ways in which Calderón uses the theme and suggests how they reveal some of the deep structures of the dramatist's comic and tragic theater. At the same time, O'Connor argues "his varied dramatizations of the rape motif reveal fissures in solidly sexist seventeenth-century Spain."

Rape is also the theme of Marcia Welles's essay on Calderón's *Pintor de su deshonra* [*The Painter of his Dishonor*]. She poses the question of whether the play requires the audience to view Serafina as a willing victim of her seducer and, if so, how viewers should interpret Calderón's attitude towards the honor code. In seeking answers to these questions, Welles examines the function in the play of a painting depicting the mythological story of the Rape of Deianeira. She finds in it an iconic significance that is rich in implications for understanding the play and, as well, the society it served.

If mythology acts as one catalyst for transforming human relationships into suitable material for the *comedia,* historical tradition undoubtedly acts as another. In his essay, "A Time for Heroines in Lope," Thomas Case looks at the role of women in two of Lope's historical plays, *Las almenas de Toro* [The battlements of Toro] and *Las famosas asturianas* [The famous Asturian women]. He concludes that the characterization of the two female protagonists (both of whom are typical "virtuous viragos") not only provided good entertainment for the seventeenth-century *corral de comedias,* but probably also served a didactic purpose; on the one hand appealing to the audience's national pride, and on the other, providing exemplary models of leadership that contrasted with the troubled realities of Philip III's Spain. In Case's view, the choice of women as the chief protagonists is significant because "heroines are especially optimistic figures in a male-dominated structure . . . a sort of reserve of additional resources when all else fails."

Ruth Lundelius finds a very different view of women in Vélez de Guevara's *La serrana de la Vera* [The peasant girl from Vera]. Gila, the larger-than-life protagonist, is a *mujer varonil* who carries the characteristics of the genre to the limit. So disturbing is this portrayal of gender reversal that Gila finally dies unrepentant and unredeemed—a social anomaly that has to be destroyed in order to preserve and affirm the values of the establishment. Lundelius sees this play as an example of the *comedia* as an instrument of social control that was all the more effective for being unconscious and because it also provided very entertaining theater.

The last two essays in this section return to the theme of female subversion within the patriarchal society by exploring aspects of the upside-down topos. Anita Stoll's study of comic inversion in Lope's *El anzuelo de Fenisa* also takes into account three later versions of the play that, in themselves, are indicative of the subtly shifting views of woman's place in society. In the original version the theme of the *mujer varonil* is intertwined with picaresque ele-

ments so that, contrary to the usual pattern, the rebellious protagonist is not brought to heel at the end of the play. Instead, by
shunning marriage, she remains an outcast from society and, by
implication, is free to continue her picaresque adventures. Although the dominant group, male and aristocratic, ostensibly triumphs and the social status quo is restored, Fenisa's continuing
independence is an ironic reminder of what Stoll calls "the picaresque nature and carnivalesque spirit of the underside of society,
which serves as a renewing force for the audience."

Amy Williamsen also looks at the carnivalesque aspects of sexual
inversion in two plays by Mira de Amescua, finding in them further
examples of a subversive element in the *comedia* that appears to
question the social equilibrium of seventeenth-century Spain.

*   *   *

Although the essays in this collection range widely in their treatment of the subject of women in the Spanish *comedia,* one theme
clearly dominates: women are perceived as an essentially subversive force. Yet while, on the one hand, their presence is unsettling,
even disruptive, they are also cast in the role of restorative angels,
the repository of the enduring values of the hierarchical status quo.

It is hardly surprising that in the context of drama, which depends on an element of conflict, the subversive note is dominant. It
is instructive, however, to note how this subversive theme is dealt
with in the *comedia*. In the comic mode, as the majority of these
essays show, the woman is finally reduced to accepting the yoke of
matrimony as the price of remaining within the accepted bounds of
the social pale. On the other hand, the comic treatment of the
theme does not diminish the woman's power within the microcosm
created for the duration of the play. Today, we appreciate the rich
ironies of these plots and suspect that at least some members of the
seventeenth-century audience looked beyond the diverting entertainment and conventional happy endings to a more sobering truth.
The world-upside-down topos reaches back into Antiquity and has
long been a satirical as well as a merely comic image.[9] In particular,
it makes a clear statement about sexual politics; namely, that men
are forever intrigued by the power of women and, at the same time,
fearful of their own vulnerability. The paradigm of the world-upside-
down carries the assurance that, no matter how successful the
woman may be in her manipulations of the male sphere, in the end
the world will turn right side up again, the comedy will end in
marriages, the laws of society will be reimposed. In the *comedia*
woman may sometimes be portrayed as a wild animal [una fiera],

but she is safely contained in a gilded cage whose existence is acknowledged and maintained by the dramatists themselves, both male and female. Nevertheless, despite the acceptance of this ultimate sanction, the *comedia* suggests to us that even in her most flattering role—in the theater, as in life—woman is, at best, perceived as a "troublesome helpmate,"[10] a challenge and an enigma. She may be relegated to the margin, but her presence and her power cannot be ignored.

As this volume serves to show, Hispanists are participating—with their counterparts in other disciplines—in what Mary Beth Rose has recently described as "the excitement of discovery generated by asking new questions of familiar material."[11] These questions offer us the opportunity to change our perceptions of the ethos and structure of the *comedia*. The issue of feminine identity in the *comedia* is especially open to new interpretations. Nor is it necessary to adopt an overtly feminist stance in order to share in this change of perspective. It is part of the present climate of ideas that pervades our daily lives and conditions our thinking about the past. We hear those feminine voices with new interest and understanding. The challenge facing the critic, the scholar and the reader/ spectator—in the Spanish *comedia* as in other areas of Renaissance literature—is to search out and interpret those voices so that what they have to say can be clearly heard and understood today.[12]

Notes

1. Carmen Bravo-Villasante, *La mujer vestida de hombre en el teatro español: siglos XVI–XVII* (Madrid: Revista de Occidente, 1955.)

2. Melveena McKendrick, *Woman and Society in Spanish Drama of the Golden Age* (Cambridge: Cambridge University Press, 1974).

3. McKendrick, "Women Against Wedlock," in *Women in Hispanic Literature: Icons and Fallen Idols,* ed. Beth Miller (Berkeley: University of California Press, 1983).

4. Frederick de Armas, *The Invisible Mistress* (Charlottesville: Biblioteca Siglo de Oro, 1976).

5. See various essays in *New Perspectives on Comedia Criticism* (Potomac, Md.: Studia Humanitatis, 1980); *Essays on Spanish Letters of the Golden Age* (Potomac, Md.: Studia Humanitatis, 1981); and *Theology, Sex and the Comedia* (Potomac, Md.: Studia Humanitatis, 1982).

6. "Love, Matrimony and Desire in the Theatre of Tirso de Molina," *Bulletin of the Comediantes* 37 (1985): 98. See also "Sibling Symmetry and the Incest Taboo in Tirso's *Habladme en entrando*," *Revista Canadiense de Estudios Hispánicos* 10 (Invierno, 1986): 261–79; "The Sexual Ambiguities of Tirso de Molina's *Don Gil de las calzas verdes*," in *Proceedings of the Third Annual Golden Age Spanish Drama Symposium* (El Paso, 1983), ed. Richard Ford (El Paso: University

of Texas at El Paso, n.d.), 107–21; "Tirso de Molina: Dramaturgo andrógino," in *Actas del Quinto Congreso Internacional de Hispanistas,* ed. Maxime Chevalier et al (Bordeaux: Université de Bordeaux, Instituto de Estudios Ibéricos e Iberoamericanos, 1977), 811–18.

7. Cristóbal de Virués, *La gran Semíramis:* Calderón de la Barca, *La hija del aire.*

8. Reprinted in Pedro Calderón de la Barca *Comedias,* vol. 19, ed. J. E. Varey (London: Tamesis, 1973), 151–68).

9. See E. R. Curtius, *European Literature and the Latin Middle Ages,* trans. Willard R. Trask (New York: Harper and Row, 1963), 94–98. Bruce Wardropper referred to the role of women in relation to this topos in his study of the *comedia* written as long ago as 1968 (republished in *Teoría de la Comedia,* ed. Elder Olson; trans. S. Oliva and M. Espín [Barcelona: Ariel, 1978], 226–27). While noting that in the comedies women are usually the winners, he argued that this subversive view of the world is offered as a subtle corrective, rather than as a satirical attack on social institutions. At the same time, however, he also noted that Golden Age comedies were preludes to potential tragedies (227). Edward Friedman also explores this line of thinking in " 'Girl Gets Boy': A Note on the Value of Exchange in the Comedia," *Bulletin of the Comediantes* 39 (1987): 75–83. I would go further than either Wardropper or Friedman in stressing the satirical implications of these comedies, although the full force of those implications is undoubtedly more evident today than it was in the seventeenth century.

10. This suggestive term comes from the title of a book by Kathleen M. Rogers, *The Troublesome Helpmate: A History of Misogyny in Literature* (Seattle: University of Washington Press, 1966).

11. Mary Beth Rose, *Women in the Middle Ages and the Renaissance* (Syracuse, N.Y.: Syracuse University Press, 1986), xiv. Another important collection of essays that take the feminist perspective has been published in *Rewriting the Renaissance: The Discourses of Sexual Difference in Early Modern Europe,* ed. Margaret W. Ferguson, Maureen Quilligan, and Nancy J. Vickers (Chicago: University of Chicago Press, 1986).

12. Unless otherwise noted, all translations in this volume are provided by the individual essayists.

Works Cited

Bravo-Villasante, Carmen. *La mujer vestida de hombre en el teatro español: siglos XVI–XVII.* Madrid: Revista de Occidente, 1955.

Curtius, E. R. *European Literature and the Latin Middle Ages.* Translated by Willard R. Trask. New York: Harper and Row, 1963.

De Armas. Frederick A. *The Invisible Mistress.* Charlottesville: Biblioteca Siglo de Oro, 1976.

Ferguson, Margaret W., Maureen Quilligan and Nancy J. Vickers, eds. *Rewriting the Renaissance: The Discourses of Sexual Difference in Early Modern Europe.* Chicago: University of Chicago Press, 1986.

Friedman, Edward. " 'Girl Gets Boy:' A Note on the Value of Exchange in the Comedia." *Bulletin of the Comediantes* 39 (1987): 75–83.

Hesse, Everett. *Essays on Spanish Letters of the Golden Age.* Studia Humanitatis. Potomac, Md.: Studia Humanitatis, 1981.

————. *New Perspectives on Comedia Criticism*. Studia Humanitatis. Potomac, Md.: Studia Humanitatis, 1980.

————. *Theology, Sex and the Comedia*. Studia Humanitatis. Potomac, Md.: Studia Humanitatis, 1982.

McKendrick, Melveena. *Woman and Society in the Spanish Drama of the Golden Age*. Cambridge: Cambridge University Press, 1974.

Miller, Beth, ed. *Women in Hispanic Literature: Icons and Fallen Idols*. Berkeley: University of California, 1983.

Parker, Alexander A. "Bandits and Saints in the Spanish Drama of the Golden Age." In Pedro Calderón de la Barca, *Comedias*. A Facsimile Edition prepared by D. W. Cruickshank and J. E. Varey. Vol. 19, "Critical Studies of Calderón's *Comedias*," edited by J. E. Varey. London: Tamesis, 1973.

Rogers, Kathleen M. *The Troublesome Helpmate: A History of Misogyny Through Literature*. Seattle: University of Washington Press, 1966.

Rose, Mary Beth, ed. *Women in the Middle Ages and the Renaissance*. Syracuse, N.Y.: Syracuse University Press, 1986.

Salstead, M. L. *The Presentation of Women in Spanish Golden Age Literature: An Annotated Bibliography*. Boston: G. K. Hall, 1980.

Sullivan, Henry W. "Love, Matrimony and Desire in the Theatre of Tirso de Molina." *Bulletin of the Comediantes* 37 (1985): 83–99.

————. "The Sexual Ambiguities of Tirso de Molina's *Don Gil de las calzas verdes*." In *Proceedings of the Third Annual Golden Age Spanish Drama Symposium*. El Paso, 1983. Edited by Richard Ford. El Paso: University of Texas at El Paso, n.d.: 107–21.

————. "Sibling Symmetry and the Incest Taboo in Tirso's *Habladme en entrando*." *Revista Canadiense de Estudios Hispánicos* 10 (1986): 261–79.

————. "Tirso de Molina: dramaturgo andrógino." in *Actas del Quinto Congreso Internacional de Hispanistas,* edited by Maxime Chevalier et al. Bordeaux: Université de Bordeaux. Instituto de Estudios Ibéricos e Iberoamericanos, 1977: 811–18.

Wardropper, Bruce. *La comedia española del Siglo de Oro*. In Elder Olson, *Teoría de la comedia,* and B. W. Wardropper, *La comedia española del Siglo de Oro*. Translated by Salvador Oliva and Manuel Espín. Barcelona: Ariel, 1978.

Part 1
Theoretical Approaches

La dama duende and the Shifting Characterization of Calderón's Diabolical Angel

CATHERINE LARSON

As feminist literary theory and criticism establish themselves as determinant ideological and methodological forces, the articulation of feminist issues in the theater of the Golden Age is very much open to textual explication. Critics interested in the ways a male writer presents his female characters will find that we can learn more about the ways those characters were portrayed. In the seventeenth century, an era in which the characterization of women in the *comedia* tended to follow rather conventionalized modes of expression, female characters were presented within a generally limited range of types, including the standard, beautiful *dama* [lady], the *mujer esquiva* [disdainful woman], the religious woman, the *mujer vestida de hombre* [woman dressed as a man], and the married woman and victim of the wife-murder plays. Calderón, a product of seventeenth-century attitudes concerning women, was undoubtedly influenced by the mores of his age. Yet, recent discussions have led to new readings of Golden Age drama; feminism has entered the critical arena of *comedia* studies, even if rather belatedly. This essay addresses Calderón's constantly-shifting characterization of one of his most famous female characters, Doña Angela from *La dama duende* [*The Phantom Lady*]. Calderón's depiction of this woman reveals a signifying process that both upholds and subverts the tradition of which he is a part.

The first issue raised here is how to integrate a feminist reading into plays written by dramatists who were male and who wrote in a time in which male-female relationships would have to be judged as extremely unliberated by today's standards. A sociofeminist approach, which examines images of women in literature, would emphasize what Toril Moi has called "the way in which writers constantly *select* the elements they wish to use in their texts."[1] Yet, in addition, Moi observes that "no criticism is 'value-free'" (43): we always make critical assessments of an author's decisions based on the tradition from which we come, one that is still inherently patriarchal. Elaine Showalter has been a leading proponent of the notions that women approach texts differently than men and that male writers always operate from within the bounds of a patriarchal system. Showalter observes that "One of the problems of the feminist critique is that it is male-oriented. If we study stereotypes of women, the sexism of male critics, and the limited roles women play in literary history, we are not learning what women have felt and experienced, but only what men have thought women should be."[2] In that context, I would like to suggest that we need to explore how discussions of women in the *comedia* can move beyond mere attacks on the sexism of androtexts in order to lead us to new levels of interpretation. I am positing a revision of the critical canon, but from within a kind of feminist perspective that allows new thought on how Calderón depicts his women to join with, rather than to supplant completely, traditional critical approaches to his plays.

When applied to *La dama duende,* these traditional views often reveal a great deal about what happens when male critics confront texts written by men, but about women. Robert ter Horst's work with *La dama duende* is a useful example: ter Horst states that "in *La dama duende,* the dominant masculine order intrudes upon a feminine chaos and masters it. . . ."[3] He further observes that the central issue of *La dama duende* is not, as Edwin Honig had suggested, "a woman's rebellion against the [honor] code's autocratic male principles";[4] rather, ter Horst contends that the main character of the play is Don Manuel, "whose masculine hierarchy is superior in the art of life and civilization to Angela's chaos" (72). This view of Don Manuel as a *paterfamilias,* as a tamer of "his splendid shrew" (72), clearly proffers a phallocentric reading of the play. I do not, however, mean to suggest a wholly negative response to that point of view; rather, I see ter Horst's article as exemplary of the patriarchal critical tradition in which we all have been trained, one that focuses, as in this case, on androcentric issues of superiority and dominance and on the opposition of order to chaos.[5] I would, however, suggest a counter reading, one that illuminates the precarious position that defines the essence of the title character. To do so, I will examine Calderón's signifying practices in the classification and representation of his diabolical angel.

As a typical *comedia de capa y espada* [cloak and sword play],

La dama duende deals with disguise, plot complications, and problems of determining identity. The use of disguise is central to any examination of the role of women in the *comedia* and in this play in particular, since it implies that women often must resort to disguises and masks when they can't get what they want in more socially acceptable ways. In *La dama duende,* these disguises are both physical and linguistic. In semiotic terms, we could describe Doña Angela as the referent; she is an object, the mystery woman who is pursued early in the play by her brother, Don Luis, and, later, by Don Manuel. The signs pointing toward that referent consist of signifieds (that is, the men's concepts or images of the woman) and signifiers (all of the words representing her). Both the signifieds and the signifiers function on different levels for the male characters of the play and for Angela, herself. Further, because signs cannot express a one-to-one correspondence with the referent, but can only signal or point toward it, countless numbers of signs endlessly defer to the future the possibility of determining absolute truth in identity; they can never reveal it completely.[6] In this play, the signifieds and signifiers, the concepts and language describing the woman, frequently emerge as contradictions that impede the exact revelation of the referent: Calderón presents his unknown woman as both devil and angel. The signs that Calderón uses to describe Angela, however, are constantly shifting, for she is neither an angel, nor a devil, and is, at the same time, both—although, even more importantly, by the end of the play, the principal sign used to characterize her is "woman." In that sense, we might suggest that the mystery woman is both disguised and illuminated throughout the play, as the signs describing her converge and separate simultaneously.

Frederick de Armas explains this curious combination of elements, *ángel, demonio y mujer* [angel, demon, and woman], as characteristic of what he describes as the Invisible Mistress plot: "most works dealing with this theme present us with a woman of great (angelical) beauty, whose *burlas* [tricks] are so elaborate that supernatural powers are often attributed to her—be it as a witch, an enchantress, or a *duende* [spirit]."[7] Susan Fischer, on the other hand, surveys not the "Invisible Mistress" but the "Invisible Partner" in *La dama duende;* she views Angela and Manuel as Jungian analogues of each other in which the male, Manuel, finds his own inner female side in the anima, Angela, who leads him through a journey of self-discovery.[8] Both of these readings suggest a bipartite division (man/woman, angel/devil, *dama/duende,* anima/animus) that ultimately foregrounds a complex, Baroque vision of the

characterization in *La dama duende*.[9] By focusing on the interplay
of these opposing elements—and their synthesis in the concept of
woman—one may better appreciate how a male writer such as
Calderón fashioned a character like Doña Angela, who is both
independently strong and stereotypically weak, successful and un-
successful in achieving her goals, beneficent and maleficent.

There are apparently two Angelas in this play, the character who
is the widowed sister of Don Juan and Don Luis and the woman
who appears as the disguised object of Don Manuel's desire, the
dama duende seen by Don Manuel and his servant. They are one
and the same woman; yet, even these two apparently different
women can be subdivided into two opposing aspects: angel and
devil. The first Doña Angela, the widowed sister, has a scheming
side; she possesses a number of qualities that link her to the
licentiousness and machinations associated with the devil—at least
within the scope of seventeenth-century culture and religion. First,
she defines herself when she describes flirtatious women, saying
that such a woman is "una mala mujer . . . una mujer tramoyera"
[an evil woman . . . a scheming woman; literally, *tramoya* means
stage machinery] (1.515, 517). Angela is witty and deceitful; Calderón's choice of the word *tramoyera* indicates that Doña Angela
understands well the stagecraft needed to pull off the theatrical
illusions of her own dramas with the male characters, dramas that,
from a theatrical point of view, self-consciously involve going in and
out of the secret doorway that is hidden behind the cupboard in
Don Manuel's bedroom.[10] Calderón details the reasons for that
characterization when a maid explains why widows have such a bad
reputation:

> este estado
> es el más ocasionado
> a delitos amorosos;
> a más en la Corte hoy,
> donde se han dado en usar
> unas viuditas de azahar.
>
> (1.405–11)

> [this state
> is the most given
> to amorous offenses;
> even more so at Court today,
> where certain little perfumed widows
> have surrendered themselves for
> use.]

From the seventeenth-century male-dominant perspective, a widow at Court is synonymous with a loose, scheming woman.[11]

Furthermore, the type of character just described is part of a cultural and literary tradition that associates women with the devil—in terms of cunning and manipulation and as a symbolic recreation of Eve, whose curiosity in the Garden of Eden leads her to taste the fruit of the tree of knowledge.[12] Melveena McKendrick notes that the identification of women with the devil was still very much a part of Spanish tradition up to the time of Luis de León's *La perfecta casada* [The perfect wife], written less than fifty years prior to *La dama duende*.[13]

Calderón's Angela fulfills this definition: she steals out of her house in disguise in order to flirt with the men of the Court. Only when her brother pursues her does she begin to recognize the dangerous implications of her game. Yet, Angela's curiosity about Don Manuel leads her to manipulate him by assuming the role of the *dama duende,* although those actions put her in even more danger. A young widow whose honor has been fiercely guarded by her two brothers, Angela acquires a new and unsavory reputation when, at the end of the play, her brothers describe her as a *traidora* [traitor] and *fiera* [wild animal or vixen]. These characterizations could lead to terrible consequences for the young woman: her life is literally at stake, since even the implication of her sexual misconduct could damage reputations, destroy honor, and lead her brothers to take Angela's life. Both through her own actions and discourse, then, and the comments of others, Angela is associated with a number of negative qualities, which link her metonymically to Eve and the forbidden apple of the Garden of Eden.

Still, Angela is also a martyr, buried alive (as she says) "entre dos paredes" [between two walls] (1.380). Her two over-protective brothers keep her locked up at home, dressed in mourning clothes, when, as a young, noble, and beautiful woman, she yearns for the freedom and excitement offered by the men outside the walls of her "prison":

> sin libertad he vivido,
> porque me enviudé de un marido,
> con dos hermanos casada.
>
> (1.390–92)

> [I have lived without freedom,
> since although I've been widowed,
> I'm married to two brothers.]

Angela has also suffered as the result of debts incurred by her late
husband; her economic martyrdom further underscores the sympathetic aspects of her character. Finally, and most obviously, Angela's very name suggests angelic associations. The signifier selected by Calderón to identify his protagonist could certainly not
have been chosen at random: the beautiful angel is given a name
designed to suggest her essence. Indeed, when Don Manuel first
sees his *dama duende,* he exclaims, "¡Un asombro de belleza, / un
ángel hermoso es!" [An astonishing beauty, / she's a beautiful
angel!] (2.2059–60). We see, then, that the language used to fix
Doña Angela's identity covers the entire spectrum of possible signifiers: positive and negative, sympathetic and accusatory, angelic
and diabolical.[14]

The other Angela, the mysterious woman who keeps appearing
to Don Manuel and his servant, Cosme, is, of course, the *dama
duende,* who also combines the opposing elements of angel and
devil. Cosme, the superstitious *gracioso,* perceives her devilish
qualities from the very beginning, describing her as a *demonio,* a
duende, or, at the very least, a *mujer-diablo:*

> Que es mujer-diablo;
> pues que novedad no es,
> pues la mujer es demonio
> todo el año, que una vez,
> por desquitarse de tantas,
> sea el demonio mujer.
>
> (2.2237–42)

> [She's a devil-woman;
> Of course, that's nothing new;
> since women are devils
> all year long, for once
> let the devil turn into a woman
> just to even the score.]

The *gracioso* consistently upholds the traditional link between
women and the devil. In the third act of the play, Cosme is led into
an "enchanted" room, and he tells the story of Lucifer dressing as a
woman in order to seduce a shepherd, concluding:

> aún horrible no es
> en traje de hembra,
> un demonio.
>
> (3.2661–62)

[even a demon
isn't so horrible
when he's dressed in women's clothes.]

This story, along with Cosme's description of the *dama duende* as a succuba, lends a note of sexual rebellion to the description of Doña Angela, pushing her even further beyond the limits of socially acceptable behavior. The *dama duende* embodies associations with the heavens and with hell, and both Cosme and Don Manuel are literally left in the dark as to her identity.[15]

In their explorations of the identity of the literary female, Sandra Gilbert and Susan Gubar describe the image of woman as angel and as monster in an analysis that offers many points of contact with this study of Calderón and *La dama duende*. These two critics posit that "the ideal woman that male writers dream of generating is always an angel;" they trace the image from the Middle Ages and the Virgin Mary through Dante, Milton, and Goethe to the nineteenth century's "angel in the house" of Victorian literature.[16] The ideal of the eternal feminine was, for these male writers, represented by pure, passive, and powerless female types, "for in the metaphysical emptiness their 'purity' signifies, they are, of course, *self-less,* with all the moral and psychological implications that word suggests" (21). For the Victorian woman—and, I would maintain, for the heroine of Golden Age texts—the surrender of her self was considered "the beautiful angel woman's key act" (25). Yet, numerous literary texts link the submissive angel to both ghosts and sprites; she is also capable of scheming and manipulation, refusing to stay in her ordained place: she displays a negative side that Gilbert and Gubar label monstrous—and Calderón would have described as diabolical—that functions in opposition to her angelic side.

Certainly, these views on the angel and monster that simultaneously exist in many of the female characters penned by male writers are directly applicable to our reading of *La dama duende*. Doña Angela, rebelling against the loss of self demanded by masculine perceptions of the eternal feminine, is both the angel and monster in her house. Even more significantly, although her assertiveness and manipulation, revealed in her role as the phantom lady, challenge the notion of the ideal woman, Calderón nonetheless leaves us with a woman who will again typify patriarchal definitions of the feminine at the conclusion of the play. The challenge to patriarchal authority that the phantom lady incarnates is subsumed at the end of the third act by the vision of Angela as adoring lover, as wife, as the "angel in the house."

Angela herself complicates the already-tangled plot, setting up barriers to confuse the male characters in the play. This Calderonian woman knows the most successful approaches for appealing to male vanity, seeking compassion based on her position as a weak and unhappy woman as, for example, when she asks Manuel for help:

> Si, como lo muestra
> el traje, sois caballero
> de obligaciones y prendas,
> amparad a una mujer.
>
> (1.101–4)

> [If, as your clothing suggests,
> you are a gentleman
> of honor and means,
> defend a woman.]

At other times, she presents herself as a foolish, empty-headed member of her gender:

> Yo fui necia en empeñarle así;
> mas una mujer turbada
> ¿qué mira o qué considera?
>
> (1.437–40)

> [I was silly to urge him on so;
> but a frightened woman,
> what does she see or consider?]

Yet, Calderón paints an even more detailed portrait of his protagonist. Doña Angela's actions are particularly revealing when she combines the conflictive elements of her character with the tricks that she plays on Don Manuel. Angela secretly leaves him gifts that include sweets and clothing, and she invites him to a banquet in which she creates the impression that she is a wealthy member of royalty. In each case, Doña Angela acts as the traditional "angel in the house," nurturing her man by giving him food and clean clothes. Nonetheless, each example of Angela's angelic role-playing is also tied to deception and manipulation.[17]

Indeed, Angela's characterization is so complex that sometimes even she can describe herself only in terms of absence: when Manuel uses conventionalized love vocabulary to describe her as "aurora, sol y alba" [dawn, sun, and daybreak], Angela replies:

> lo que soy ignoro;
> que sólo sé que no soy
> alba, aurora o sol.
>
> (3.2350–51)
>
> [I don't know what I am;
> I only know that I'm not
> the dawn, daybreak, or sun.]

Angela, who has been characterized throughout the play by a multitude of signifiers, ironically finds herself at a loss for words, particularly when those words operate within a semiotic system based on instant identification between the sign and its referent—here, between nature (the dawn and the sun) and the beautiful woman who serves as the subject of poetic inspiration.

Angela is a character marked by the opposition of presence and absence. Her mysterious appearances and disappearances through the hidden door covered by the *alacena* [cupboard] are emblematic of her role as both the present and absent object of desire for Don Manuel. This conflict is further repeated in the "flickers of incest" noted by Honig, which involves Don Luis's pursuit of his own disguised sister (117). Presence and absence surface in both situations when Angela, the widow lacking a male protector, begs Manuel to assume the roles of suitor and savior. The absence of a husband must be negated through substitutes who fulfill patriarchal definitions and serve as male providers and protectors. Finally, the opposition of presence and absence suggests yet another level of interpretation in the play, that of discourse, since signs always contain within themselves traces of their radical opposites. The presence of "angel" always signals the absence of "devil"; consequently, any definition of Doña Angela as ingenious or manipulative allows for that which is not ingenious or manipulative—in other words, that which is angelic in nature. Calderón both negates and synthesizes these metaphoric oppositions in Angela's *real* role, that of woman.

In a key confrontation scene at the end of act 2, Calderón has his characters bring together the central aspects of the phantom lady. Manuel surprises Angela in his room:

Angel, demonio, o mujer,
a fe que no has de librarte
de mis manos esta vez.

(2.2080–32)

[Angel, demon, or woman,
I swear you'll not slip
through my hands this time.]

Angela tries to defer revealing her true identity until the following
day, but Manuel replies:

Mujer, quien quiera que seas,
que no tengo de creer
que eras otra cosa nunca,
¡vive Dios, que he de saber
quién eres, cómo has entrado
aquí, con qué fin, y a qué!
Sin esperar a mañana
esta dicha gozaré;
si demonio, por demonio,
y si mujer, por mujer;

(2.2123–32)

[Woman, whoever you may be,
and I don't believe that you were ever anything else,
By God, I will find out
who you are, how you entered
here, for what end, and what you plan to do!
Without waiting until tomorrow
I intend to enjoy this delight,
if you're a devil, as a devil,
if you're a woman, as a woman.]

When Manuel threatens to kill her, Angela confesses that she is
only "una infelice mujer" [an unhappy woman] (2.2152), but after
she manages to slip away from him again, Manuel is left puzzled:

Como sombra se mostró;
fantástica su luz fue
pero como cosa humana,
se dejó tocar y ver;
como mortal se temió,
receló como mujer,
como ilusión se deshizo,
como fantasma se fue

Si doy la rienda al discurso,
no sé, ¡vive Dios! no sé
ni qué tengo de dudar,
ni qué tengo de creer.

(2.2225–2236)

[She appeared like a shadow;
gleaming fantastically
but as something human,
she let herself be touched and seen;
she was afraid as a mortal would be,
as an illusion she vanished,
as a ghost she left.
If I give rein to this idea,
I don't know—dear God, I don't know
what I should doubt,
and what I should believe.]

We find that throughout much of the play, Don Manuel is unable to verify the identity of his phantom lady. Calderón's demonic angel remains an enigma; even in act 3, she continues to cloud herself in mystery: "ni soy lo que parezco, / ni parezco lo que soy" [I'm not what I seem to be, / and I don't seem to be what I am.] (3.2375–76).

The *dama duende* finally identifies herself at the end of act 3 by uttering a simple statement that removes her from the realm of the supernatural and confirms her essence, that which both is and is not conveyed by the concept of angel or devil: "una mujer soy y fui" [I was and am a woman.] (3.2355). When she finally explains that she is the sister of Don Juan and Don Luis, Angela clarifies the identity question that has been plaguing Don Manuel. This, of course, only leads to further confusion in Doña Angela's complex characterization, since the flesh-and-blood sister also incarnates both angelic and devilish qualities. All of the linguistic signifiers used to characterize her (*fiera, torbellino, duende, mujer, ángel, diablo* [wild beast, whirlwind, spirit, woman, angel, devil]) join with the varying concepts that the male characters have of this woman, creating signs that can never completely and concretely define the referent, precisely because they indicate that she is—and is not—a composite of essences.

The idea that Angela is an amalgam of opposing concepts or images, as well as concomitantly opposing signifiers, is central to Calderón's treatment of his female character. For each of the male characters, Doña Angela is many things, including a beautiful woman, a widowed sister needing protection, a phantom lady, a veiled *dama* running from a man, the object of amorous desire, a giver of gifts, and the noble hostess of a fantastic banquet. These images of the woman are part of a constantly shifting mosaic and are underscored by a variety of signifiers that the male characters use in their attempts to attach a definition to her. The men in Doña Angela's life describe her in terms of malevolence and benevolence, as a weak woman and as an independent spirit, as the devil's helpmate and as an angelic essence. The varied linguistic markers that they use point, on a negative level, to a certain degree of ambiguity in Angela's characterization and, on a positive level, to a richly evolving character, representing not a stereotypical view of the seventeenth-century Spanish woman, but, rather, the image of a complex, well-rounded character who can be understood by modern audiences.

In that sense, we can appreciate the enigmatic quality of the ultimate definition of Doña Angela, one that she gives to herself: "soy / mucho más de lo que ves" [I'm / much more than you see] (2.2167–68). It is here, finally, that Calderón's protagonist moves beyond mere sexual stereotyping and expresses the complexity of her character. Angela is not solely angelic because of her beauty, nor devilish because of her ingenuity and manipulative actions. Although such stereotyping serves the creation of the kinds of baroque oppositions for which Calderón is famous, we should note that Angela is both (and neither) angel and devil—and that she truly *is* much more than she appears to be. This leads to the ending of the play and to its implications for Calderón's treatment of his female characters.

In many ways, Calderón's protagonist challenges the patriarchal notion that women cannot act as independent spirits, that they cannot play a major role in determining their own destinies. The dramatist foregrounds this concept by having his character act in a theatrically self-conscious manner; note again the self-conscious nature of Angela's use of the theatrical term, *tramoya*. In addition, Angela creates a play within the play, in which she not only stars as the phantom lady, but in which she casts Don Manuel as her lover and takes a firm hand in directing the course of the dramatic action. The play within the play consists of two main components: the scenes in which Doña Angela leaves notes and gifts for Manuel (prompting his subsequent responses) and the most clearly metadramatic scene, the one in which Angela adopts the role of noble hostess at a banquet to which Manuel is brought. In the scenes of the first type, Angela does not directly confront Manuel, but, rather, leads him to react in response to requests and presents left by her mysterious alter ego, the *dama duende*. Manuel responds by assuming a new role, as well. After reading her letters, he decides to imitate a literary character, becoming the "Cavallero de la Dama Duende," an avatar of Don Quixote. In this role, Don Manuel adopts a rhetorical style characteristic of the knights of the novels of chivalry; nevertheless, his actions are ultimately guided by the controlling hand of Doña Angela, who has given him a role in the play that she is directing.[18]

Such metatheatrical elements become even more obvious when Angela actually appears in person to Manuel as the hostess at a banquet, although it should be noted that she appears disguised as someone else, with her dialogue rehearsed, with a supporting cast of players, and with a stage clearly set to facilitate the dramatization of her interior play. These self-conscious theatrical gestures highlight the opposition of appearance and reality, as well as the entire notion of role playing, which lies at the heart of Calderón's multifaceted characterization of Doña Angela. In addition, they stress the idea that Angela can challenge societal limitations by acting in an autonomous manner.

Nevertheless, Calderón also shows that Angela's play carries within itself the potential for tragedy, and that the ending of this comedy reveals a type of social reintegration that undercuts the feminist gains made by his protagonist. Angela, the dramatist, director, and actress, is not quite able to pull off her production without problems. Her independence and ingenuity do lead to her goal of marriage, but marriage will in turn force her back into a more subservient role. Angela's price for theatrical success is a role that will allow her less freedom, independence, and control—at least as far as *comedia* tradition is concerned.

At the end of *La dama duende*, Angela discovered that her life is in peril and that her brother is engaged in a duel with her lover; she asks Don Manuel to help her, a parallel to her earlier request for masculine protection. In that sense, Doña Angela has come full circle—although perhaps in another sense she really has not changed at all. The witty woman who has controlled the actions of the males of the play now finds herself again in the position of pleading for help, based on her own self-definition as a helpless victim of love and her gender:

> Mi intento fue el quererte,
> mi fin amarte . . .
> mi deseo servirte,
> y mi llanto en efeto persuadirte

que mi daño repares,
que me valgas, me ayudes y ampares.

(3.2997–3004)

[My intention was to cherish you,
My goal to love you . . .
my desire to serve you,
and my plea, in effect, to persuade you
to come to my aid,
to defend me, help me, and protect me.]

One might speculate that Calderón's overall treatment of Doña Angela is as mutable as are her interior roles of angel and devil, *dama* and *duende*. The Angela of the beginning and end of the play differs markedly from the stronger character who controls the course of the dramatic action throughout most of *La dama duende*. This shifting characterization is highlighted by the nature of the ending of this comedy: the kind of societal reconciliation and reintegration represented in the denouement by the promised marriage of the central characters.

Yet, this type of ending is also part of a much larger picture: as K. K. Ruthven observes, "the device of ending stage comedies with a marriage is an economical way of tying up loose narrative ends; but as a device for bringing women legally under the control of men, its popularity as a dramaturgical device is not insignificant in a patriarchal society" (76). Within the world of the *comedia,* weddings acquire special meaning, as the sequel to the marriage of comedy is sometimes the death of the (often) innocent woman in the honor tragedy. One might well wonder about the future of a character like Doña Angela, who has tasted freedom, who has had great success in manipulating men, and who has proven herself clever and resourceful. As Matthew Stroud rightly observes:

Angela came out all right, but only by undergoing a role-name change from mischievous woman to wife. By the time she makes the change, she has, in effect, lost her former name and identity for the sake of society, a society which does not appreciate her as a clever individual intellect (she is almost killed as a result) but only as a sex object or a docile silent wife.[19]

Elaborating on Bruce Wardropper's seminal work on Golden Age comedy, Edward Friedman notes that comedy allows women to "exercise control over the male–dominated world in which they are forced to live," since the "inverted universe of comic drama allows women the opportunity to assume the role of aggressor. . . . The comic plays . . . reward daring, mettle, ingenuity—in short, active and anti-social behavior—with the desired object, a marriage pledge."[20] Yet, these "subversive aspects of drama" described by Friedman are also undermined as "the play progresses toward tragedy, and the playgoers renew their belief in institutions" (78). This is the "Catch-22" that marks Calderón's treatment of his title character: as a woman in a comedy, Doña Angela is allowed to manipulate, even to show herself as superior to the males in the play; still, the seeds of potential tragedy have ironically been sown at the moment of her greatest power and success. Doña Angela, a powerful, affirming figure in most of Calderón's comedy, also carries within her the threat of grave consequences in the future. These oppositions, present-future, comedy-tragedy, vitality-death, only serve to emphasize further the divisions within Doña Angela that mark her characterization in *La dama duende*. Angela, the *dama* and *duende,* the angel, the devil, and the woman, stands out as a character who both subverts and reaffirms the norms of the society of which she is a part, as well as those of her creator.[21] Since she, herself, evolves as the result of a constantly-shifting process of signification, Calderón's Doña Angela might well have understood the words of Adrienne Rich:

> A woman in the shape of a monster
> a monster in the shape of a woman
> the skies are full of them.[22]

(146)

Notes

1. Toril Moi, *Sexual/Textual Politics* (London: Methuen, 1985), 45.
2. Elaine Showalter, "Towards a feminist poetics," *Women Writing and Writing About Women,* ed. Mary Jacobus (London: Croom and Helm, 1979), 22–41.
3. Robert ter Horst, "The Ruling Temper of Calderón's *La dama duende,*" *Bulletin of the Comediantes* 27 (1975): 72.
4. Edwin Honig, *Calderón and the Seizures of Honor* (Cambridge: Harvard University Press, 1972), 110.
5. For a more detailed discussion of the androcentric oppositions that can occur in literary texts, see K. K. Ruthven's *Feminist Literary Studies* (40–42) and Toril Moi's *Sexual/Textual Politics* (102–126).
6. Adrienne Schizzano Mandel's stimulating analysis of the linguistic structure of *La dama duende* underlines a central point of this reading: "El lenguaje parece actuar a modo de disfraz que encubre y descubre una realidad" [Language seems to act as a disguise that conceals and reveals a reality] (42).

7. Frederick de Armas, *The Invisible Mistress* (Charlottesville: Biblioteca Siglo de Oro, 1976), 130.

8. Susan L. Fischer, "The Invisible Partner: A Jungian Approach to Calderón's *La dama duende*." *Revista canadiense de estudios hispánicos* 7 (1983): 231–33.

9. In *The Limits of Illusion,* Anthony Cascardi describes *La dama duende* as a "dialectic of positive and negative, inside and out, male and female, of reversible roles and values" (27). In spite of Cascardi's exuberant imagery ("Calderón's phantom lady flits across the stage like a bundle of veiled motion, a volatile packet of erotic energy, chameleon-like in her *duende*-like nature" [25]; "Like any shield . . . the house and its walls are vulnerable to penetration. . . . The house of males is itself a threat to Angela's honor, but it is Angela who penetrates the partition between her room and Manuel's [28–29]), his study complements the exploration of Angela as angel and demon that informs this study. It should be noted, however, that discussions (including my own) that emphasize binary oppositions also reinforce—at least to a certain degree—traditional patriarchal models of separation and disunion.

10. Richard Hornby's lucid study of metadrama describes role-playing within the role, suggesting that the theater is "an identity laboratory, in which social roles can be examined vicariously" (71).

11. See Merry Weisner's examination of women in the sixteenth and seventeenth centuries for a discussion of the increasing restrictions that widows faced in the Golden Age. Further, see Honig's analysis of the implications of such cultural realities in *La dama duende*.

12. See de Armas, *The Invisible Mistress,* for an analysis of the implications of Eve, the tree of knowledge, and curiosity in the creation of the Invisible Mistress plot of which *La dama duende* is representative (46).

13. Melveena McKendrick, *Woman and Society in the Spanish Drama of the Golden Age* (London: Cambridge University Press, 1974), 10–11.

14. In *The Development of Imagery in Calderón's* Comedias (York, S.C.: Spanish Literature Publications, 1983), William R. Blue carefully analyzes the problems that other characters encounter in pinning down Angela's identity.

15. Calderón includes Angela as part of an image of heaven and hell in act 2:

Don Manuel.	Imagen es
	de la más rara beldad,
	que el soberano pincel
	ha obrado.
Cosme.	Así es verdad;
	porque sólo la hizo él.
Don Manuel.	Más que la luz resplandecen
	sus ojos.
Cosme.	Lo cierto es,
	que son sus ojos luceros
	del cielo de Lucifer.
Don Manuel.	Cada cabello es un rayo
	del sol.
Cosme.	Hurtáronlos de él.
Don Manuel.	Sí será; porque también
	se las trujeron acá,
	o una parte de las tres.

(2.2041–2054)

[*DM:* She's the image of the rarest beauty that the hand of God has ever drawn.
C: That's true; because He alone did such a thing.
DM: Her eyes shine brighter than light.
C: True—her eyes are like Lucifer's lamps fallen from heaven.
DM: Each hair shines like the rays of the sun.
C: He must have stolen them from heaven.
DM: Her curls are like stars.
C: Of course, because they're also brought from there—or from Heaven, Purgatory, or Hell.]

16. Sandra Gilbert and Susan Gubar, *The Madwoman in the Attic* (New Haven: Yale University Press, 1984), 20. In Nina Auerbach's *Woman and the Demon,* a parallel study to that of Gilbert and Gubar, Auerbach states:

> It may not be surprising that female demons bear an eerie resemblance to their angelic counterparts, though characteristics that are suggestively implicit in the angel come to the fore in the demon. Their covert identification is motivated by their common cause: both are illicit invaders of traditional Anglican symbolism, announcing a new dispensation that is of pre-Christian antiquity. In the Socratic usage in the OED, "demon" need not designate an evil spirit alone but may incorporate divinity into its supernatural power: "thing of divine or demonic nature or character." The Soothsayer in Shakespeare's *Antony and Cleopatra* uses "demon" interchangeably with "angel": "Thy demon, that's thy spirit which keeps thee, is / Noble, courageous, high unmatchable, / Where Caesar's is not. But near him, thy angel / Becomes afeard" (II.iii.18–21). (75)

Auerbach's union of the angel and the demon, studied from the perspective of Victorian myth, is especially resonant of the union of these two elements in *La dama duende*.

17. Honig discusses the nature of Doña Angela's female role in courtship: "Her incursions into his apartment and his later induction into hers are all carried out . . . to test his fitness for the role she has chosen for him. If he is a true gentleman, and really prizes the mystery of courtship, he will be worthy of her love" (133–34). Angel Valbuena Briones underscores the social and cultural implications of Angela's actions when he observes, "La lucha vital, pero ingeniosa, de doña Angela en contra de las convenciones sociales para obtener el marido que anhela manifiesta una causa con la que las damas de la época se identificaron fácilmente" [Doña Angela's vital, but ingenious struggle against social conventions to get the husband she wants illustrates a cause with which the women of the epoch could readily identify] (41).

18. In *Calderón: The Secular Plays,* ter Horst explains the intertextual nature of Calderón's references to the romances of chivalry and, specifically, to *Don Quixote* (see especially 73–74).

19. Matthew D. Stroud, "Social-Comic *Anagnorisis* in *La dama duende,*" *Bulletin of the Comediantes* 29 (1977): 100.

20. Edward H. Friedman, " 'Girl Gets Boy': A Note on the Value of Exchange in the *Comedia.*" *Bulletin of the Comediantes* 39 (1987): 77–78.

21. This apparent ambiguity in Calderón's presentation of Doña Angela may be explained by the relationship between society and women in the seventeenth century: "If a society demands that its women both are and are not angelic, then its representations of them will be ambivalent" (Ruthven, *Feminist Literary Studies,* 75). Frederick de Armas interestingly uses similar language to describe this "basic ambiguity, this ambivalence in man's view of woman. . . . This essential ambiguity in the portrayal of women will become particularly striking in Golden Age versions of the Invisible Mistress plot" (17).

22. Adrienne Rich, "Planetarium," *Poems, Selected and New, 1950–74* (New York: Norton, 1975), 146.

Works Cited

Auerbach, Nina. *Woman and the Demon*. Cambridge: Harvard University Press, 1982.

Blue, William R. *The Development of Imagery in Calderón's* Comedias. York, S.C. Spanish Literature Publications, 1983.

Calderón de la Barca, Pedro. *La dama duende*. Edited by Angel Valbuena Briones. 6th ed. Madrid: Cátedra, 1984.

Cascardi, Anthony J. *The Limits of Illusion: A Study of Calderón*. Cambridge: Cambridge University Press, 1984.

De Armas, Frederick. *The Invisible Mistress: Aspects of Feminism and Fantasy in the Golden Age*. Charlottesville: Biblioteca Siglo de Oro, 1976.

Fischer, Susan L. "The Invisible Partner: A Jungian Approach to Calderón's *La dama duende*." *Revista canadiense de estudios hispánicos* 7 (1983): 231–47.

Friedman, Edward H. " 'Girl Gets Boy': A Note on the Value of Exchange in the *Comedia*." *Bulletin of the Comediantes* 39 (1987): 75–84.

Gilbert, Sandra, and Susan Gubar. *The Madwoman in the Attic*. New Haven: Yale University Press, 1984.

Honig, Edwin. *Calderón and the Seizures of Honor*. Cambridge: Harvard University Press, 1972.

Hornby, Richard. *Drama, Metadrama, and Perception*. Lewisburg, Pa.: Bucknell University Press, 1986.

McKendrick, Melveena. *Woman and Society in the Spanish Drama of the Golden Age: A Study of the Mujer Varonil*. Cambridge: Cambridge University Press, 1974.

Moi, Toril. *Sexual/Textual Politics*. London: Methuen, 1985.

Rich, Adrienne. "Planetarium." *Poems, Selected and New, 1950–1974*. New York: Norton, 1975.

Ruthven, K. K. *Feminist Literary Studies*. Cambridge: Cambridge University Press, 1984.

Schizzano Mandel, Adrienne. "La *dama* juega al *duende:* Pre-texto, geno-texto y feno-texto." *Bulletin of the Comediantes* 37 (1985): 41–54.

Showalter, Elaine. "Towards a feminist poetics." In *Women Writing and Writing About Women*, edited by Mary Jacobus. London: Croom Helm, 1979.

Stroud, Matthew D. "Social-Comic *Anagnorisis* in *La dama duende*." *Bulletin of the Comediantes* 29 (1977): 96–102.

ter Horst, Robert. *Calderón: The Secular Plays*. Lexington: University Press of Kentucky, 1982.

———. "The Ruling Temper of Calderón's *La dama duende*." *Bulletin of the Comediantes* 27 (1975): 68–72.

Weisner, Merry E. "Women's Defense of Their Public Role." In *Women and Society in the Middle Ages and Renaissance*, edited by Mary Beth Rose. Syracuse, N.Y.: Syracuse University Press, 1986.

La dama duende: Spatial and Hymeneal Dialectics

MARÍA MARTINO CROCETTI

> At times we think we know ourselves in time, when all we know
> is a sequence of fixations in the spaces of the being's sta-
> bility . . .
>
> —Gaston Bachelard[1]

The employment of scenic space as accentuated by Pedro Calderón de la Barca in his dramatic works provides us with an element of study that diversifies and extends itself to highly interesting dimensions. Calderón's *La dama duende* exemplifies this scenic use; a use that is uncommon in the theater of the Spanish Golden Age. In this play the author clearly privileges the scenographic aspect over its linguistic and dramatic elements. It is my objective to offer a possible evaluation of *La dama duende* through an interpretation of scenic space parallel to the poetic and dramatic texts. This third dimension presents characteristics that are similar to the function and form of the feminine body. I suggest that this dimension figures a conception of a hymeneal space through which the protagonist expresses her desire for liberation and self-definition in a universe/ house/prison that represents all Angela's longing and thirst for life. Furthermore, I suggest that this scenic map traces, in a schematic form, the diagram of the character's dreams and fantasies. Calderón charges the function and use of scenic space with a physical adaptation (or restriction) that is applied particularly to women.

In *The Poetics of Space,* Gaston Bachelard conceives the "space/ house" as "our first universe, a real cosmos . . . .," and he specifies that "space calls for action, and before action, the imagination is at work."[2] His insight can be satisfactorily applied in this scheme, as Angela moves within a geometry limited by the home.[3] From this center, she attacks the protective, limited aspect which the above enclosure offers, transforming it and attributing to it supernatural

51

powers. This "imagination at work" executed by the protagonist leads the other characters, specifically the masculine ones, to fluctuate between the real world and the world of the simulacrum and magic.[4] The spectator [el público], who is an accomplice to this game, does not participate in the confusion and error experienced, for example, by Don Manuel, but instead identifies the signs indicated by Angela and Isabel in order to interpret the manipulation of the scenic space. The spectator is—in this capacity—aware of the dramatic totality. Moreover, the protagonist finds in the audience a buttress of support and the nexus for the parody the viewers, as well as the two women, share.

Keeping in mind the scenographic distribution of the assigned spaces, the audience sees a clear stage divided into two areas and, at the same time, connected by a movable cupboard full of glass.[5] The Spanish word for "cupboard," *alacena,* is defined by the *Diccionario de Autoridades* as a "Hueco hecho en pared, con puertas y anaqueles, para guardar algunas cosas . . ." [a hole in the wall, with doors and shelves, for storage . . .] The "glass" is a transparent material that allows us to see what is behind it; at the same time, it is fragile and possesses the property of acquiring the color of the substance that fills it. The inscription of these same conditions on feminine geography is obvious. Women's hymeneal space is divided by an element as fragile and irreparable as the glass in and of the cupboard.[6] This is an internal space equal to Angela's room, invisible, untouchable, and officially incapable of being visited or known by strangers. The external space, Don Manuel's room, known and visited by everyone, finds again its equivalent in that space external to Woman that projects itself through an aperture (or a rupture) towards liberty and light. Feminine honor hinges on similarly vulnerable elements such as the glass(ware) placed in the false cupboard. The proverb "La mujer y el vidrio siempre están en peligro" [Woman and glass are always in danger] *(Diccionario de Autoridades),* corroborates this position.

In this same way, Don Luis defines the scenic hymeneal space in a few verses after finding out that his brother has placed a cupboard in front of the door to Angela's room:

> Don Luis. ¿Ves con lo que me aseguras?
> Pues con eso mismo intentas
> darme muerte, pues ya dices
> que no ha puesto por defensa
> de su honor más que unos vidrios,
> que al primer golpe se quiebran.[7]

[Do you see what you are reassuring me with?
With those very precautions
you try to give me death, for you tell me
that he has placed as a shield
of her honor mere glass
that will break at the first blow.][8]

Angela moves within this mimetic architecture. Her constant penetrations into the external space, one we can call masculine, as it belongs to men, graphically suggest her desire for liberation and her search for her own space. This intention takes place through the symbolic transgression represented by the pushing and opening of the cupboard to enter Don Manuel's room. Isabel's description of this space delineates the cupboard's placement:

> *Isabel.* Por cerrar y encubrir
> la puerta, que se tenía
> y que a este jardín salía,
> y poder volverla a abrir,
> hizo tu hermano poner,
> portátil, una alacena.
> Esta, aunque de vidrios llena,
> se puede muy bien mover.
>
> . . . .
>
> de suerte, que en falso agora
> la tal alacena está,
> y apartándose, podrá
> cualquiera pasar señora.

(45)

[Your brother has built a portable cupboard to shut off and conceal the door leading the way to the garden. The cupboard is movable so that it may be easily removed, and the door be replaced. And though made of glass, it may be moved at will. . . . so that the cupboard is falsely closed and anyone who would like to, madam, can go through it.]

That is, the man/brother is responsible for the protection of the space/body/woman; nevertheless, Isabel proposes the possibility of becoming owner of her own body through the maneuvering of the movable area where such glasses are kept. The terms "portable" and "false" are particularly accentuated. One could interpret that feminine honor may be falsified or "replaced" without men's knowledge of the manipulations through which woman can transform her body. It is relevant to recall in this context the Celestinesque profession of *coser virgos.* Hence, the context clearly suggests a rebellion on the part of the protagonist and her appropriation of the right of self-control.

This mockery and aggression takes place when passing into Don Manuel's room; that is, transgressing into the world of the "other." In contrast, man assumes that he is the possessor of "the key" to enter and to exit the intimate feminine space. There is an insistence in using the words *entrar* and *salir* by the masculine characters in their futile attempt to appropriate and control the house-body. Finally, this house will become a confused, unidentifiable structure through Angela's spatial manipulation.

Trying to secure his own hierarchy, Don Juan tells Don Manuel that

> *Don Juan.* Si quieres cerrar, ésta es del cuarto
> la llave; que aunque tengo
> llave maestra, por si acaso vengo
> tarde más que las dos, otra no tiene,
> ni otra puerta tampoco.
>
> (50)
>
> [If you want to close the door, this is the room's
> key. I have
> a master key in case I come home
> late. There are no other keys besides these two, however,
> and no other door to get in.]

The dominance of his house, as well as his sister's honor, is secured. For the established patriarchical canon, this dominance is the defined and acceptable position. Already Angela had corroborated it when she described herself as existing in a state of living death:

> *Doña Angela.* Vuélveme a dar Isabel
> esas tocas (¡Pena esquiva!)
> Vuelve a amortajarme viva,
>
> (37–38)
>
> . . . .
> entre dos paredes muera,
> donde apenas el sol sabe
> quién soy . . .
>
> . . . .
> Donde en efeto, encerrada
> sin libertad he vivido,
> porque enviudé de un marido
> con dos hermanos casada.
>
> (38)

[Here Isabel,
give me back
my widowhood, worse luck!
And wrap me alive in that black shroud again,

.   .   .
between these two walls I die
where the sun barely knows
who I am . . .

.   .   .
Where, in effect, locked
without freedom I have lived,
because I lost a husband
to find myself married to two brothers.]

Her body is a tomb. Her life, spent in a prison, is that of someone who has been innocently incarcerated. Nevertheless, these are recognizable and official practices of seventeenth-century Spain.

It is interesting to observe the significance that Gaston Bachelard has attributed to the concept of "door" in the aforementioned text:

> For the door is an entire cosmos of the Half-open. In fact, it is one of its primal images, the very origin of a daydream that accumulates desires and temptations: the desire to conquer all reticent beings. The door schematizes two strong possibilities. . . . At times, it is closed, bolted, padlocked. At other, it is open, that is to say wide open. . . . And how many doors were doors of hesitation! In *La romance du rétour* by Jean Pellerin, this tender, delicate poet wrote: La porte me flaire, elle hésite. (The door scents me, it hesitates.)[9]

The cupboard door serves a double signifying function. On the one hand, it equates the masculine figure on the level of dissimulation and deceit with the feminine one. In this case, the level/door/hymen is under the magical control and power of the protagonist and her maid. In her intent upon liberation, Angela executes by "opening" and "closing" the cupboard an act of self-aggression against her own womanhood, since her constant desire for escape incites her to go beyond the limits of her own body in an act of giving birth to her own self. From this structure originates the creative aspect of a character who is constantly inventing plots: the experience of escaping offers Angela the possibility of temptation and excitement, as Bachelard suggests. This process is summarized by Beatriz:

Beatriz.   Quedaste
            en que por el alacena
            hasta su cuarto pasaste,

que es tan difícil de verse
como fue de abrirse fácil;

(64)

[You were saying
that you entered his room
through the cupboard
which was as difficult to see
as it was easy to open;]

In following the second signifying function in this play—on the other hand—properties of the feminine sexual condition are attributed to the "door," but always under the control and dominance of men. In this case, such men may be Don Manuel or Doña Angela's brothers. *Abrir la puerta* is to possess and to make oneself present to the woman's body. *Tener la llave* is to exercise the right of possession, and, at the same time, to show the privilege of maintaining "that body/woman" under the exclusivity of the "other."[10] In this form, the masculine figure dominates and violates all possibility of feminine self-definition. Don Manuel, who has already been under Angela's control throughout the play, triumphs finally when he marries her and recuperates his lost power.

Woman, therefore, remains in the dark and in an alienated hemisphere of confusion, repudiating her proper characteristics. In *La dama duende,* Don Manuel, as well as Don Juan and Don Luis, has a particular interest in using "the key" to insure the inviolability of space; that is, the confinement and possession of the protagonist.

The terms *puerta, abrir, cerrar* and *llave* are charged with meaning in the following dialogues:

> *Don Luis.* . . . .
> —Rodrigo, una hermana bella,
> viuda y moza, y, como sabes,
> tan de secreto, que apenas
> sabe el sol que vive en casa:
>
> (36)
>
> [Rodrigo, my beautiful sister
> [is] a young widow, and as you know,
> it is such a secret that
> the sun barely knows that she lives at home.]
>
> . . . .
> *Rodrigo.*   Don Manuel no ha de saber
> que en casa, señor, se encierra
> tal mujer.
> . . . . .

y más habiendo tenido
tal recato y advertencia,
que para su cuarto, ha dado
por otra calle la puerta,
por desmentir la sospecha,
. . . o porque pudiera
con facilidad abrirse
otra vez, fabricó en ella
una alacena de vidrios,
labrada de tal manera,
que parece que jamás
en tal parte ha habido puerta.

(36–37)

[Don Manuel is not to know
that such a woman is locked in the house.
. . .
and having taken
such care and zeal
that her room door faces
another street
in order to dismiss any suspicion
. . . or because the door could
open easily
again, he built on the door
a glass cupboard
in such a manner
that there does not appear ever
to be a door anywhere.]

These dialogues exemplify the constant intention of the masculine character to rule over the spatial scenery in the same way as over woman's sexuality and honor. In listening to Don Manuel in his futile attempt to protect and dominate that space, the spectator becomes a knowledgeable witness to the impossibility of the success of such an attempt, and mockery and laughter are the results:

Don Manuel. Deja cerrado y la llave
          lleva; . . .

(85)

Don Manuel. . . . Mira si cerradas
          esas ventanas están
          [Leave the room locked, and take the key;
          See if those windows are closed]
Cosme.   Y con aldabas y rejas.

(61)

          [Yes, with locks and bars.]

In this last case, the term *ventana* could be substituted for *door*.

At the same time, by way of counterpoint, Angela's power of spatial metamorphosis causes others (D. Manuel and Cosme) to experience dissimulations and visual deceits. The masculine characters are not in control of their reality, since it is in constant movement, transforming and continually acquiring new dimensions determined by the protagonist. The spectator's enjoyment lies in watching Don Manuel and Cosme exposed to a double vision of what is real. The audience sees the dual possibility that is offered to both characters: to see what is apparent, and to discover what really is cannot be seen. This introduction of a *trompe d'oeil* keeps the public with a constant smile of expectation, and the male characters in constant confusion and disorder.

Angela and Isabel are the renewing elements of space. When they enter, the spatial dimensions become mutable and alive; the environment acquires an almost human, or more precisely a supernatural, character. The scenery becomes the texture where gesture, word and intention are all interwoven with the purpose of disorienting and ridiculing. Cosme describes Don Manuel's room after Angela and Isabel's first entrance with the following cry:

> Cosme. . . . .
> ¡Vive Cristo, que parece
> Plazuela de la Cebada
>
> (55)
>
> . . . .
>
> [Oh my God! This looks like
> a flea market]

Both women had taken care to scatter the guest's clothes on the floor. This is an obvious dimensional reorganization on the part of the protagonist. She becomes the owner of space and re-presents it with a touch of her own interpretation. Likewise, Angela neutralizes the masculine realm by guarding and controlling it. Notice how she watches Don Manuel's door:

> Doña Angela. . . . .
> porque tengo a sus umbrales
> un hombre yo, que me avisa
> de quién entra y de quién sale;
>
> (69)
>
> [. . . because I have at his threshold

> a man who informs me
> of who enters and exits;]

This threshold—before free and open to man—has become a spy-space. We find Don Manuel describing the vision of this macabre spy-space created by the psychological influence that the *dama duende* has over him:

> *Don Manuel.* . . . .
>   Y al fin a un portal de horror,
>   lleno de sombra y temor,
>   solo y a oscuras salí.
>
> (103)
>
>   [. . . And finally alone and in the dark,
>   I exit to a gateway of horror,
>   surrounded by shadows and fear.]

Again, Don Manuel sees the transformation that Angela carries out in and of her own chamber when he is introduced, blindfolded, to this private room by Isabel. The metamorphosis, charged with exoticism, is reiterated by Don Manuel:

> *Don Manuel.* (acecha por la cerradura)
>   ¡Qué casa tan alhajada!
>   ¡Qué mujeres tan lucidas!
>   ¡Qué sala tan adornada!
>   ¡Qué damas tan bien prendidas!
>   ¡Qué beldad tan extremada!
>
> (103)
>
>   [(who spies through the keyhole)
>   What an opulent house!
>   What elegant women!
>   What an ornate living room!
>   What well-dressed ladies!
>   What an extreme beauty!]

Again, Don Manuel's vision and intelligence are unable to see what reality is because the feminine character has already exercised her magic and has distorted the images.

The spatial distortion created by Angela, which Cosme and Don Manuel have to bear, is a symptom of the protagonist's purpose to re-present herself as a superficial, picaresque, and seductive woman. Nonetheless, her self is represented in ambivalent forms: as opposed to the already mentioned position, Angela is a critic of the feminine condition, who has decided to use strategies that will assure her the necessary mobility to affirm herself.[11] It is precisely the whimsical management of space that allows her such mobility. In the following verses terms that point to closed areas, thresholds, and clumsy *faux pas* are reiterated. Her discourse declares her marginalized position:

> *Doña Angela.* ¡Válgame el cielo! Que yo
> entre dos paredes muera,
> donde apenas el sol sabe
> quién soy, pues la pena mía
> en el término del día
> no se contiene ni cabe.
>
> (38)
>
> [God, help me! That I
> die between two walls
> where the sun barely knows
> who I am, that my sorrow
> does not fit or contain itself
> by the end of the day's journey.]

Later, she adds,

> *Doña Angela.* . . . .
> Aquí yerro, allí caigo, aquí tropiezo,
> y torpes mis sentidos,
> prisión hallan de seda en mis vestidos.
> Sola, triste y turbada,
> llego de mi discurso mal guiada
> al umbral de una esfera,
> que fue mi cárcel, cuando ser debiera
> mi puerto o mi sagrario.
> . . . .
> vio brillar los adornos de mi pecho,
> (no es la primera traición que nos han hecho.)
> y escucho de las ropas el ruido
> (no es la primera vez que nos han vendido.)
> . . . .
> "ven, dijo, hermana fiera,
> de nuestro antiguo honor mancha primera;
>
> (126–27)
>
> [Here I err, there I fall, here I trip,
> and my torpid senses
> find a silk prison in my dress.
> Alone, sad and perturbed,
> I reach, misguided by my own discourse,

the threshold of a sphere
which was my jail, when it should be
my port or my sanctuary.
. . .
He saw my chest's decor shine.
(It is not the first treason that they have done to us.)
And he heard the sound from the clothes.
(It is not the first time that they have given us away.)
. . .
"Come," he said, "untamed sister,
[you are] the first stain of our ancient honor";]

Add to those passages another one equally as significant:

Doña Angela. . . . .
No soy alba, pues la risa
me falta en contento tanto;
ni aurora, pues que mi llanto
de mi dolor no os avisa;
no soy sol, pues no divisa
mi luz la verdad que adoro,`
y así, lo que soy ignoro;
que sólo sé que no soy
alba, aurora o sol; pues hoy
no alumbro, río, ni lloro.

(106)

[. . .
I am not dusk because laughter
fails me in so much happiness;
I am not dawn because the tears
of my pain do not wake you.
I am not the sun because my insight does not see
the truth which I adore;
and so, what I am I ignore;
I only know that I am not
dusk, dawn, or sun because today
I do not shine, laugh, or cry.]

Her words are conjured up in a synthesis of disorientation and
oppression under which Woman lives her own existential disin-
tegration.[12] Space is limited by walls; walking through it is difficult
because she feels clumsy: she trips, falls, and errs. Angela perceives herself as *mal guiada* by her own discourse: not even she
understands it, for she is always being reminded of her inade-
quacies. She is called *hermana fiera* and *mancha primera* of the
family honor. It is interesting to question whether Calderón really

was aware of the subversive text he assigned to the protagonist. The monstrosity which is gratuitously attributed to woman by man (who in other occasions calls her *hidra*), disorients and confuses her, until even Angela herself claims: ". . . lo que soy ignoro; / que sólo sé que no soy . . ." (106). Hélène Cixous in "The Laugh of the Medusa" perspicaciously asserts those feelings of feminine impropriety:

> Who, surprised and horrified by the fantastic tumult of their drives (for she was made to believe that a well-adjusted normal woman has a . . . divine composure), hasn't accused herself of being a monster? Who, feeling a funny desire stirring inside her (to sing, to write, to dare, to speak, in short, to bring out something new), hasn't thought she was sick? Well, her shameful sickness is that she resists death, that she makes trouble.[13]

Does this not describe our *dama duende?* Her transgression, symbolized in spatial appropriation and manipulation, could be summarized as her refusal to die in silence. Angela writes, takes initiatives, authorizes herself, displaces herself, originates many problems and confusions, and dares to ignore all masculine authority. Angela describes and activates her subversive plans:

> *Salen Doña Angela y Isabel, por la puerta disimulada en la alacena.*
>
> *Doña Angela.* Por eso pude atreverme
> a hacer sola esta experiencia.
>
> . . . .
>
> que la puerta fácilmente
> se abre y se vuelve a cerrar,
> sin ser posible que se eche
> de ver.
>
> (51)

> [*Exit Doña Angela and Isabel through the concealed door in the cupboard.*
>
> That is why I dared
> go through this experience by myself.
> . . .
> the door easily
> opens and closes again,
> without it being possible
> to be noticed.]

To accomplish her objective, Angela depends on deceit and dissimulation pointing in a significant form to the trespass of the masculine space. Again, Angela affirms herself in her own authority, and plans, like a playwright, how to allow Don Manuel into her room:

> *Doña Angela.*   Escucha
> y sabrás la más notable
> traza, sin que yo al peligro
> de verme en su cuarto pase,
> y él venga, sin saber donde
>
>   (71)
>
> [Listen
> and you will know the most notable
> trick: without exposing myself to the danger
> of going into his room
> and he would come to mine not knowing
> where he might be]

She continues this behavior as she plots a spatial simulacrum to obtain what she wants. Don Manuel will come "sin saber donde" [without knowing where]. Finally, we can see a discourse in which Angela clearly expresses her disapproval of her imprisonment, and declares that the authority which disposes of her life is unjust. With extreme sarcasm, she dismantles the structure of the established canon, and affirms herself in her conviction that there is crime in the *jouissance* of certain liberties which are denied to women:

> *Doña Angela.* .   .   .   .
>   Y luego, delito sea,
> sin que toque en liviandad
> depuesta la autoridad
> ir donde tapada vea
> un teatro en quien la fama
>
>   (38)
>
>   .   .   .   .

[/. . ./ And then, the authorities will consider it a sin,
if I innocently go veiled to see a play at a theater where everyone else goes]

I perceive in her text some touches of judicial language raised in her own defense.

Finally, I would point out that all distribution and reorganization of space as designed by the protagonist and her maid lead the male characters to a constant state of blindness and misunderstanding. The men are not capable of discerning the truth from the simulacrum; likewise, their senses have lost the acuteness to identify the tricks which are being planned practically in their presence. In this dialectic of *lo abierto* and *lo cerrado,* of what is and what seems to be, of what enters and what exits, the men are almost somnambulant characters; they are in a distraught and peripatetic state. Conversely, the presence of the *dama duende* is affirmed in the context of a metatheatrical *Deus ex machina* who controls secret threads in darkness to imprison/misprison the "other," thus obtaining some freedom and access to knowledge. Space, light and shadow unite to offer a certain autonomy to the creative image of woman.

Notes

1. Gaston Bachelard, *The Poetics of Space* (New York: The Orion Press, 1964).

2. Bachelard, *Space,* 4 and 12.

3. See the "Prólogo" by Angel Valbuena Briones to the *Comedias de capa y espada of Pedro Calderón de la Barca* (Madrid: Espasa Calpe, 1962) in reference to the confining interior spaces that reflect the secluding social attitudes toward women, specifically widows.

4. The pseudo-supernatural events in *La dama duende* as well as the use of magic and fantasy as a symptom of desire for freedom by Angela are widely discussed by Frederick de Armas in chapter 4 of his book *The Invisible Mistress: Aspects of Feminism and Fantasy in the Golden Age,* (Charlottesville: Biblioteca Siglo de Oro, 1976).

5. For a study of the different possibilities of staging *La dama duende,* see J. M. Ruano de la Haza's article "The Staging of Calderon's *La vida es sueño* and *La dama duende,*" *Bulletin of Hispanic Studies* 64 (January 1987): 51–63. His work points directly to the *alacena* and its location on stage, separating masculine and feminine spaces in this *comedia.*

6. Adrienne Schizzano Mandel in "La dama juega al duende: pre-texto, geno-texto y feno-texto" *Bulletin of the Comediantes* 37, no. 1 (Summer 1985): 41–54) proposes a contextual semantic value in words like "poner" and "quebrar" which is directly related to sexual union and the hymen. Her article explores the realm of family honor in the metaphorical imagery of the glass' fragility as a traditional analogy of woman's physical geography.

7. *La dama duende* (Zaragoza: Editorial Ebro, S. L., 1977), 37. All references will be to this edition.

8. All passages were translated by Benigno Sifuentes-Jauregui with some

consultation of Edwin Honig's text, found on pages 217–306 of his *Calderón de la Barca: Four Plays* (New York: Hill and Wang, 1961).

9. Bachelard, *Space,* 222–23.

10. Edwin Honig has dedicated chapter 7 of his book *Calderón and the Seizures of Honor* (Cambridge: Harvard University Press, 1972) to the constant underlying threat of incest in *La dama duende.* Honig sums up his study stating that don Manuel restores a pastoral ethic in lieu of "the jaws of the honor-incest complex . . . the incest threat flickering across the anxious face of honor has been put down . . ." at the very end of the *comedia.* In this chapter he observes don Luis's hypocritical behavior towards don Manuel and his brother don Juan, both of whom he views as his "rivals for Angela's honor."

11. Alyce de Kuehne's article "Los planos de la realidad aparente y la realidad auténtica en *La dama duende* de Calderón" *Pacific Coast Philology* 2 (April 1967): 40–46) discusses the ambiguous behavior of the protagonist who "como 'duende' ella es más auténtica que como 'dama'" Kuehne offers us some insights on two planes of the human condition: she establishes *la vida convencional* as *la realidad aparente,* and *la vida auténtica* as *la realidad subjetiva del individuo.* Thus, Doña Angela creates a metaphoric world for her "authentic reality," allowing her to escape from her imprisonment.

12. See Bárbara Kaminar Mujica's article "Tragic Elements in Calderon's *La dama duende*" (*Kentucky Romance Quarterly* 16 no. 4 (1969): 303–28) in reference to Angela's lack of freedom and imprisonment as a result of a "rigorous social code." The tragic overtones of this imprisonment are clearly stated in her study: "*La dama duende* contains several tragic elements in a comic framework. Any of these elements—doña Angela's lack of liberty, don Luis's obsessions and frustrations tinged with overtones of incest, the struggle between paganism and faith—could contain the seed of an authentic tragedy" (303–28).

13. Helene Cixous, "The Laugh of the Medusa," in *Women, Gender and Scholarship: The Signs Reader* (Chicago: The University of Chicago Press, 1983), 280.

Works Cited

Armas, Frederick de. *The Invisible Mistress: Aspects of Feminism and Fantasy in the Golden Age.* Charlottesville: Biblioteca Siglo de Oro, 1976.

Bachelard, Gaston. *The Poetics of Space.* New York: The Orion Press, 1964.

Calderón de la Barca, Pedro. *Comedias de capa y espada.* Vol. 2 "Prólogo" by Angel Valbuena Briones. Madrid: Espasa-Calpe, S.A., 1962.

———. *La dama duende.* Zaragoza: Editorial Ebro, S.L., 1977.

———. *Calderon de la Barca: Four Plays.* Translated by Edwin Honig. New York: Hill and Wang, 1961.

Cixous, Hélène. "The Laugh of the Medusa." In *Women, Gender and Scholarship: The Signs Reader.* Chicago: The University of Chicago Press, 1983.

Diccionario de la Lengua Castellana de Autoridades. Pagés y Hervás, Barcelona.

Honig, Edwin. *Calderón and the Seizures of Honor.* Cambridge: Harvard University Press, 1972.

Kaminar Mujica, Bárbara. "Tragic Elements in Calderon's *La dama duende.*" *Kentucky Romance Quarterly* 16 no. 4 (1969): pp. 303–28.

Kuehne, Alyce de. "Los planos de la realidad aparente y la realidad auténtica en *La dama duende* de Calderón." *Pacific Coast Philology* 2 (April 1967): 40–46.

Ruano de la Haza, J. M. "The Staging of Calderón's *La vida es sueño* and *La dama duende.*" *Bulletin of Hispanic Studies* 64 (January 1987): 51–63.

Schizzano Mandel, Adrienne. "La dama juega al duende: pre-texto, geno-texto y feno-texto." *Bulletin of the Comediantes* 37, no.1 (Summer 1985): 41–54.

"¿Y sois hombre o sois mujer?": Sex and Gender in Tirso's *Don Gil de las calzas verdes*

MATTHEW STROUD

When Henry Sullivan opened the question of the insight that the writings of Jacques Lacan could bring to the *comedia,* he came somewhat early on to Tirso's magisterial *comedia de enredo* [comedy of intrigue and deception], *Don Gil de las calzas verdes.* As with most things Lacanian, his paper, "The Sexual Ambiguities of Tirso de Molina's *Don Gil de las calzas verdes,*" is not easily accessible, having been published in the *Proceedings of the Third Annual Golden Age Drama Symposium* in El Paso, Texas. It is an important contribution to Tirsian studies, however, and he identifies three themes that bring Lacan to bear on the text: "1) the fictionality of identity, 2) the role of desire in the subversion of convention, and 3) the arbitrariness of secondary gender distinctions between the sexes."[1] It is the first and third assertions that are of interest here, especially as they relate to Juana's identities and the reactions of other characters to her.

The primary motivation for the play comes from disturbances in the Imaginary registers of both Martín and Juana.[2] Martín fell in love with Juana and, in order to have sex with her, promised to marry her. Believing him, she said yes, but he was unwilling to submit his desire to the mediation of marriage (the Symbolic) by actually giving her the word he promised her. Her reaction to his egoistic treatment of her is to become his rival and seek revenge against him (*Don Gil* 1767).[3] By insisting on the satisfaction of her egoistic demands for Martín to honor his promise to her, she is partaking of the fundamental rivalry, the fight to the death, that constitutes the human world.[4] The fact that she does not end up killing him but marrying him does not alter the comic dénouement in the Imaginary. Both love and revenge are manifestations of *moi* [ego] illusions of unity and fulfillment (unlike Hesse and McCrary's

early assertion that they are in some way opposite motivations[5]).
Indeed, this rivalry is made manifest in that both become suitors of
Inés, rivals for her affection.

A close relationship exists between Juana's motivation in the
Imaginary (either destruction of her rival or fulfillment of her love)
and her goal in the Symbolic (marriage). Of course, the Imaginary
and the Symbolic are never completely separated, and sexuality, in
particular, takes place on both slopes. While the Symbolic appears
to totalize the system of the world, sexual relations always imply
the capture of the image of the other in the Imaginary.[6] At the same
time, one's sexuality is always tied to the Symbolic process: a
sexual position is achieved only through the symbolization of the
man or the woman.[7] For Ragland-Sullivan, there is an important
difference in the importance of each to the different sexes: "man
takes his sexual pleasure in woman principally on the Imaginary
slope, while she finds hers in him on the Symbolic plane,"[8] an
assertion that has particular relevance to Martín (who looks for
satisfaction in the *jouissance* [pleasure] offered by sex and money)
and Juana (who seeks hers in marriage).

Masculinity and femininity, then, are functions of the Symbolic;
they are one's response to the Law, the Name-of-the-Father. There
is, quite simply, no necessary link between one's anatomical sex
and one's object choice or sexual identification.[9] Sexuality is
strictly an ordering, a legislative contract that all human beings are
required to enter into if they are to become participating members
of human society. The choosing of the phallic function is not depen-
dent on anatomy—there are phallic women and feminine men, and
the secondary characteristics associated with each sex are completely arbitrary.[10] While it is a commonplace to say that men are
not always masculine and women are not always feminine, in the
comedia this disjunction between sex and gender produces an
amazing fluidity, especially in the identity of women. Without the
Symbolic one is amorphous, or rather, polymorphous, which recalls Juana's amazing ability to change who she is.

Juana has three personifications: Don Gil (dressed as a man as
we first see her in act 1); Doña Elvira (dressed as a woman—even in
the clothes of Doña Inés); and Doña Juana (also dressed as a
woman). She shifts among these identities with great ease (see, for
example, 1135–37). As testimony to the power of the Symbolic, the
only indication that the other characters seem to have regarding her
identity is her clothing. Except for Caramanchel and Martín, all
those around her accept at face value her apparent sexuality (Juana

or Gil) and her personal identity (Juana, Gil, or Elvira). On some level, she is not just Juana in disguise; she is Gil and Elvira as well (1930).

At first glance, it is surprising that the other characters, both men and women, seem not to know that Juana dressed up as Gil is a woman in disguise (see 254, 792–93, 911–12, 2015). Two reasons appear to obtain: the fluid nature of pre-Symbolic sexual identity in general, and the importance of *engaño a los ojos* [deception to the eyes]. Although much of the *enredo* [intrigue] of the play is the result of deliberate disguise on the parts of Juana, Martín, and others, it should also be noted that the very foundation of interpersonal discourse is misunderstanding.[11] The enormous fluidity of identity and sexuality demonstrated by Juana complements the others' inability to distinguish between appearance and reality. If reality itself is unstable, then what hope can one ever have of reaching a kind of totalized truth? It is no wonder that Inés calls this new suitor, "Don Gil el falso" [Don Gil the false] (2403); he is false in his not being the right Gil, in not being Gil at all, and in not even being a man, in addition to the further accusation that he is false in his inconstancy in love.

Caramanchel, as the *gracioso* who fits least easily within the boundaries of the Symbolic stage society that rules Juana, Inés, and Martín, has suspicions about his new master, but they are clearly not of the either-or type. Sullivan says that Caramanchel is never completely fooled by Juana, but that implies that he "knows" the truth.[12] I would rather characterize his reaction as one in which he is perfectly willing to accept that there is more than one kind of male or female. Because Juana doesn't have a beard (2224) and has a *voz tiplada* [soprano voice] (536), he makes a number of puns on *capón* (*¿capón y con cosquillas?* [a ticklish capon?] 743; also, 2868). When Juana-Gil says he/she is in love with Juana-Elvira, Caramanchel asks if (s)he has the teeth to eat her (1692–93). Unlike Martín, who at least created the surname "de Albornoz," Juana as Don Gil is castrated as to his/her name because (s)he has no patronym, no Name-of-the-Father, as Caramanchel links the two concepts:

> Capón sois hasta en el nombre;
> pues si en ello se repara
> las barbas son en la cara
> lo mismo que el sobrenombre.

> (519–22)

[You are a capon even in your name;
for if one looks into it
a beard on the face
is the same as a surname (name-of-the-father).]

Even when he finally sees Juana in feminine clothing, despite his previous suspicion, Caramanchel at first doesn't believe his eyes. Yet, he doesn't force her into either role ("¿De día Gil, de noche Gila?" [Gil by day, Gila by night?] 2689). Although Juana is unwilling to reveal to him just yet that she is also Gil, he calls her *hembrimacho* [a combination of *hembra,* female, and *macho,* male] (1699), *amo o ama* [master or mistress] (2701), *amo hermafrodita* [hermaphrodite master] (724, 2707), saying that it is forbidden to have fish and meat together (another eating metaphor, 2708–9). This Juana as Gil is a *capón,* a castrated man, but she is also a phallic woman. She is not yet enrolled in a fixed way in either category of the Symbolic (man or woman) because Martín has abandoned her, left her to suffer in the Imaginary without benefit of the mediation of the Symbolic. As a result, however, she possesses remarkable fluidity in her identity. She can be man, woman, not-man (but not woman), not-woman (but not man), or even not a person (but a soul, as we shall see).[13]

In a recent collection of essays, Everett Hesse includes the relationship between Juana and Inés under the heading, "El amor homosexual."[14] While he notes that Juana does not want a homosexual relationship with Inés, the fact that he would see homosexuality in this scene indicates that he is taking the situation on the level of the anatomical body: Juana is a woman, so any love interest between her and Inés is *de facto* homosexual.[15] In fact, if there is any homosexuality in this play, it is that of Inés or Clara.[16] Transvestism does not change one's sexual orientation; Juana never experiences passion for a woman. But Inés does, at least on one level:

Ya por el don Gil me muero;
que es un brinquillo el don Gil.

(862–63)

[Now I am dying for Don Gil;
Don Gil is a sweetie.]

Clara also falls for Juana-Gil (911–12), and the two women even have a half-hearted argument over which one gets to marry "him" (1000–7). Yet, this happens only when the woman (Juana) is dressed as a man. It is not the anatomy with which they fall in love; indeed, as Sullivan has pointed out,[17] biological sexual experience is simply not visible in the *comedia*—it takes place before or after the action or off-stage. Instead, they are captivated in the Imaginary by the trappings of masculinity which are defined as such in the Symbolic. Inés is not in love with Juana as a man or a body. She is not blind to Juana-Gil's lack of beard, but neither does it cause her concern; she calls it an *encanto* [enchantment] (2407), recognizing in the process the fictional nature of both Juana's identity and gender characteristics in general. Instead, Inés is in love with Juana's clothes. When confronted with Martín-Gil, she says that she is not in love with him, but with the one in the green breeches, to which Pedro responds, "Amor de calzas, ¿quién le ha visto?" [Who ever heard of being in love with breeches?] and Martín says he will start wearing green from then on (1011–14).

As a woman, Inés is both like Juana (seeking Imaginary satisfaction through the Symbolic mediation of marriage, although she does not have sex with her suitors out of wedlock) and quite different. She is extraordinarily fickle; at various times she declares her love for Juan (644–45) and for Juana as Gil (862–63), and she finally agrees to marry Martín (2531–34). In her own words, "quiero / ser mudable" [I want to be fickle] (1177–78). Her father's reaction is interesting:

> Mucho me espanto
> de que des palabra ya
> de casarte. ¿Tiempo tanto
> has que dilato el ponerte
> en estado?
>
> (653–58)
>
> [I am alarmed
> that you should give your word
> to marry. Have I tarried
> so long in placing you
> in a proper state?]

As her father, it is his responsibility to impose himself on her Imaginary desires, to lead her into the fold of human community, to mediate her desire. At the same time, money is not insignificant to this plot. Pedro wants to marry Inés to Martín-Gil because he believes that the young man is rich (538ff., 680–83). Likewise, Martín wants to marry Inés because of the promise of money. Inés, in a much more direct way than Juana, is depicted as woman-as-

exchange-object, interesting only for her use-value in increasing the
estate of the men who control her.

Early on, Juana, upon seeing Inés, remarks that she is quite
beautiful (with Caramanchel chiming in that Juana-Gil is more
beautiful, 774–75), stating, "por ella estoy perdido" [I am lost for
her] (776). There are at least three ways to take this sentence. The
first reading is Gil's, the superficial reading that he has "lost"
himself in love for Inés. Not only is this a well-worn topos of the
comedia, but it also reflects the Lacanian notion, already mentioned, that love involves the capture of one's Imaginary by the
other (thus losing even the appearance of self-control—which one
never had in any case). The second is from Juana's point of view. It
is because of Inés that Martín is now in Madrid rather than in
Valladolid doing his duty by marrying Juana. Juana is "lost" (as a
woman and as a man) as long as Martín does not provide her with
the empowering mediation she can get only from the Symbolic.

The third reading is ours, and it comes from the discrepancy
between the masculine *perdido* [lost] and the fact that Juana (and
the actress who played her) were female. The use of gender-specific
language is quintessentially Symbolic; this assignment of a masculine or feminine adjective ending is reminiscent of Lacan's example of the two doors, one marked "Ladies" and one marked "Gentlemen" to underscore the importance of language (the letter) for
identity and sex difference.[18] Whether a woman considers herself a
man or a woman, she is completely engaged in the question of her
Symbolic signification.[19] Of course, much of the humor of the play
comes from the fact that we know that Juana-Gil should not be
using the masculine form while the other characters are unaware.
Because this is fiction, because we *know* what is going on, we are
willing to allow the slip. Still, we must be cautious because we never
know what is going on at all, there is no necessary link between sex
and gender, and at some level the Symbolic of everyday life is as
fictional as the events in this play. As Mitchell points out, language
is itself indicative of the misunderstanding of human existence.[20] In
this play (and maybe in life?), Juana can be *perdido* or *perdida,* but
she is always and in every case "lost."

Martín is an important member of these doubled and redoubled
love triangles, and he is interesting for two primary reasons apart
from his jilting of Juana as the prime motivation of the plot. First is
his use of the disguise of Don Gil (although at first he does not wear
calzas verdes [green breeches]), an invention of his father, Andrés
de Guzmán (538ff.). It was his creation of false signification that was
usurped so easily by Juana. Second is Martín's suspicion about

Juana's identity. After all, the man had sex with her; we might expect him to be better able to identify her. Sometime between acts 1 and 2, Juana has learned that Martín suspects the truth, that the other Gil is she (1146–50). His doubts do not solve the mystery, but lead one instead to a consideration of the use of letters in the play.

Martín-Gil presents a letter to Pedro in order to begin his suit of Inés (and he receives another letter from home in act 2, 1621). When Juana suspects that Martín suspects that she as Gil is truly Juana, she has another false letter sent to him saying that she is pregnant in a convent in Valladolid (1146–66; 1444–61; 1625–28). While Martín gave Juana his word that he would marry her (1304), at least according to Juana-Elvira, Juana uses letters to make his word mean something. Just as we saw above with gender-specificity (perdido), language is again the tool of the Symbolic. By giving her his word he goes beyond the Imaginary (unsatisfied lust or love) to the promise of fulfillment through mediated desire.[21] Act 2 comes to a head when Juana uses the letters sent to Martín from Valladolid that Caramanchel found but did not return (1707–11). She uses these (purloined) letters to steal money promised to Martín and to convince Inés and her father that her story is true (1865–68), in the process giving Martín a new name, Miguel (1294ff., 1780ff., 1963ff.). So important is the possession of the letter that Pedro approves of Juana-Gil's story based on a lie supported by the purloined letter and gives his blessing to the marriage while accusing Martín, whom he now calls Miguel, of being the thief (1966–72). Curiously, Inés, in relating this to her father, changes "Miguel"'s last name from Ribera to Cisneros, thus underscoring the fluidity in his identity (as "Don Gil de Albornoz," as Martín de Guzmán, as Miguel de Ribera, as Miguel de Cisneros). Thus the man who promised Juana his name (and in the process of doing the same for Inés) is at once Gil, Martín, and Miguel—which name does he promise?

Juana-Gil writes another letter, this time to Elvira, saying that Inés disgusts "him," and declaring his love for Elvira (2270–79). Caramanchel shows the letter to Inés (for some strange reason), and Inés realizes her role as exchange object:

> ¡Válgame Dios! ¿Ya empalago?
> ¿Manjar soy que satisfago
> antes que me pruebe el gusto?
> ¿Tan bueno es el de su Elvira
> que su apetito provoca?
>
> (2285–89)

[May God help me! Am I boring him?
Am I something to eat that satisfies
before he even tastes me?
Is Elvira so good
that she whets his appetite?]

Not only does this continue the food and eating metaphors, but it
also brings up the question of satisfaction. The satisfaction of a
demand by an appetizer only increases the hunger for the fulfillment of one's desires.[22] Inés is quite right that she cannot satisfy Gil
(for many reasons), but she is wrong in thinking that Elvira can (for
even more reasons). Her reaction is to tell Juan to kill Gil for having
jilted her.

As the action is approaching its climax, Diego confronts Martín-
with Quintana's accusation (by means of another letter in Juana's
handwriting) that Martín killed Juana in Alcorcón. When Martín
protests, Diego reproaches him for defending himself:

> Diego. ¿Qué importa, tirano aleve,
>   que niegues lo que esta carta
>   afirma de tus traiciones?
> Martín. La letra es de doña Juana.
>
> (3131–34)

> [Diego. What does it matter, perfidious tyrant
>   that you deny what this letter
>   affirms about your treason?
> Martin. The letter (the handwriting) is Doña Juana's.].

When Martín asks how he could have killed her since she was in
San Quirce, Diego replies:

> Porque finges letras falsas
> del modo que el nombre finges.
>
> (3148–49)

> [Because you counterfeit false letters
> the same way you counterfeit your name.]

Here we have a concrete example of the power of the letter, the
signifier, over the signified, and the linking of the letter, the name,
and (false) identity. Don Martín is who he is only because he has
that name, carries that letter. Certainly that was the case with his
disguise as Gil early on. Juana was able to usurp his role with Inés
because she, too, could produce *letras falsas* [false letters] that

would result in a *nombre fingido* [counterfeit name]. Is she not, in this sense, somewhat like an analyst who substitutes one signifier for another in the chain of repetition (Martín-Juan, Martín-Inés), arriving finally at the cure?[23]

Elvira, too, participates in a love triangle with Juana and Inés is jealous of Elvira. Juana, as Elvira, explains that she purposefully imitated "Gil" (1391–92), even though no one seems to notice this resemblance, except perhaps Martín. The two ironies of this situation are, of course, that Elvira is Gil is Juana, and that Inés doesn't seem to care anyway. She is not in the least concerned by the physical similarities among the three. Elvira does not love Gil, she says, but she would have if she hadn't loved someone who loved badly (1399–1405). The interview with Inés ends with the egoistic gloating of Juana and her ability to fool these others:

> Ya esta boba está en la trampa.
> Ya soy hombre, ya mujer,
> ya don Gil, ya doña Elvira;
> mas si amo, ¿qué no seré?
>
> (1438–41)

> [Now the fool is in the trap.
> I am now a man, now a woman,
> now Don Gil, now Doña Elvira;
> but if I love, what will I not be?]

Juana (as Gil) tells Caramanchel that she is in love with Elvira:

> Yo he estado
> todo este tiempo escondido
> en una casa que ha sido
> mi cielo, porque he alcanzado
> la mejor mujer en ella
> de Madrid.
>
> (1686–91)

> [I have been
> hidden this entire time
> in a house that has been
> my heaven, because I have been with
> the best woman in Madrid
> in it.]

She obviously means herself, but it is quite curious that Juana-Gil should love Juana-Elvira but that Juana-Elvira does not love "him" back (2215–18). In trying to reconcile the Imaginary and the Symbolic, Juana has created concrete manifestations of the alienation within herself as subject. A final fiction adds to the complication by questioning whether she is dead or alive. Juana, so the first story goes, died from complications with her pregnancy. Her father, when he read (in a letter) about Martín's actions, swore revenge (2066–74). Martín's reaction is not to accept that Gil is someone else, but to believe that this other Gil is the *alma en pena* [soul in purgatory] of Juana (2098–2105). This is not merely the overactive imagination of a superstitious mind, but another indication of the function of placeholder that the woman can be. Her exchange value continues whether she is there alive and in person or not. In some ways, Juana-dead can be compared to Jakobson's "zero phoneme" in that she signifies even when she does not exist. On another level, the link between death and identity (and sexuality) is the result of the fact that one must always pass through the defiles of the signifer, make a choice, leave something behind. The more choices one makes, the more one leaves behind, resulting in a fading of the subject [*aphanisis*].[24] For Juana's original goal to be achieved, she will have to give up much of what she has become in its pursuit.

The reconciliation of the Imaginary and the Symbolic comes in the most complex and remarkable final scene. It is set up when, in order to forestall Inés's renewed interest in Martín, she tells her that she is Elvira (2554ff.). Of course, Inés doesn't believe her and won't until she puts on a dress:

> Ansí se ha de hacer:
> vestirte en tu traje puedes;
> que con él podremos ver
> como te entalla y te inclina.
> Ven y pondráste un vestido
> de los míos; que imagina
> mi amor en ése fingido
> que eres hombre y no vecina.
>
>   (2603–10)
>
> (Aparte.) ¡Qué varonil
> mujer! Por más que repara
> mi amor, dice que es don Gil
> en la voz, presencia y cara.
>
>   (2612–15)
>
> [Thus it must be:
> you can put on your dress;
> for with it we will see

how it fits you and shapes you.
Come and put on one
of my dresses; for my love
imagines that in that outfit
you are a man and not my neighbor.

(Aside) What a masculine
woman! However much my love
inspects him, it says that he is Don Gil
in voice, presence, and face.]

Even after she realizes that Juana is a woman, she still wishes she were Gil, "que yo adorara tu engaño" [that I might adore your deception] (2666). Isn't it, of course, the *engaño* [deception] with which one always falls in love?

Nearing the climax, Quintana tells Juana that she is "losing her name," her identity as Gil (3033), because Juan, Martín, and Clara also appear dressed as *Don Gil de las calzas verdes*. The timid Clara is empowered when she appears in men's clothes, threatening to take revenge on Gil (3031), but Martín is utterly confused because he believes that Juan (dressed as Gil), who is a live man, is a dead woman (Juana). Caramanchel, who thought his master was only a hermaphrodite, now believes he is lackey to an *alma en pena* [soul in purgatory] (2935–36), although Juana herself says that she appears not as an "alma sin cuerpo" [a soul without a body] but rather "en cuerpo y sin alma" [a body without a soul] (2950) as long as her mission is not yet accomplished. Just as Quintana accuses Martín of having stabbed his wife to death (the second version of Juana's death, 3120–26) and the authorities come to take him away, Juana enters, dressed once again as Gil (to which her own father asks, "¿Quién sois?" [Who are you?] 3206). The fathers (Diego and Pedro) are finally able to impose their names on the situation (Juana now has a paternal last name, not just the one she gave herself, *de las calzas verdes* [of the green breeches]). Caramanchel asks Juana the pivotal question of the play, "¿Y sois hombre o sois mujer?" [Are you a man or are you a woman?], to which Juana replies, "Mujer soy" [I am a woman] (3261–62), and the play ends in an apotheosis of marriage (Juana-Martín, Inés-Juan, Clara-Antonio). All are now assigned "proper" identities, and the play ends happily, or so we are led to believe.

Juana's adventure clearly allegorizes one's search for sexual identity. Because men and women in society are only signifiers and, as such, susceptible to shifting meanings,[25] she is able to alternate between them before the final fixing of her identity. For the play to end well, however, Juana must choose one role or the other, and by choosing that of wife, a position defined by the men to whom she subordinates herself, she must give up much of the independence and power she has shown.[26] In Irigaray's terminology, a woman "borrows the disguise which she is required to assume. She mimes the role imposed upon her."[27] Juana uses the masquerade that characterizes sexuality and femininity[28] in order to achieve her goal of bringing Martín under the rule of Law. Apparently, more important than love (or, ultimately, even revenge) is the order and tranquility promised by the Symbolic. Reichenberger's formula of "order disturbed to order restored," at least in this *comedia*, is the appearance of a successful working through of the passage from the Imaginary (love and revenge) into the Symbolic (of marriage and society). Of course, the happy ending is yet another Imaginary fiction given importance by the structure of the genre itself. We are, after all, dealing with literature here, not life. If Juana and Martín were people rather than characters, we would see that their problems do not evaporate, that marriage will not necessarily make him love her more or treat her better, that the Imaginary is never supplanted by the Symbolic, and that the Symbolic never completely delivers on its promise of harmony.

Notes

1. "The Sexual Ambiguities of Tirso de Molina's *Don Gil de las calzas verdes*." *Proceedings of the Third Annual Golden Age Spanish Drama Symposium. El Paso, 1983,* ed. Richard Ford (El Paso: University of Texas at El Paso, n.d.), 109.

2. This article cannot provide a comprehensive introduction to the work of Jacques Lacan. Moreover, the definition of Lacanian terms is a mercurial enterprise that can easily confuse more than it illuminates. Because of the importance of the Imaginary and the Symbolic to this study, however, the following definitions (incomplete and overly reductionistic as they are) may provide some aid to those unfamiliar with his highly nuanced use of language. The Imaginary and the Symbolic are idiosyncratic terms in the psychoanalytic writings of Lacan. Central to the Imaginary is the "mirror stage" occuring between six months and eighteen months of age. During this period the infant identifies with an image of integral individuality while at the same time coming to grips with the inevitable otherness of the image, the mother, the object of desire, and the like, with the resultant frustration of desire caused by the alterity of the object itself and the subject's necessary relationship with other subjects (intersubjectivity). The Imaginary is marked by the essentially narcissistic relation of subject to the ego, and by aggressivity and rivalry toward a counterpart. Indeed, the creation of the ego is a function of the Imaginary in the mirror stage. For Lacan, all Imaginary behavior and relations are always deceptive and will never fulfill their promise of satisfaction. The Symbolic is the external structure in which the subject must define himself or herself, and it includes language, social customs, and the law. Especially important here are the community's prescriptions for proper attire and behavior for

each gender. It should be noted, however, that the subject always functions in more than one register at a time. For further discussion of these terms, as well as brief definitions of such terms as desire, *jouissance,* and the Name-of-the-Father, see Alan Sheridan's translator's note to Lacan's *Écrits: A Selection* (New York: Norton, 1977), vii–xii; and J. Laplanche and J.-B. Pontalis, *The Language of Psycho-Analysis,* trans. Donald Nicholson-Smith (New York: Norton, 1973). For a more general and thorough discussion of Lacan's theories, see Ragland-Sullivan's impressive *Jacques Lacan and the Philosophy of Psychoanalysis* (Urbana: University of Illinois Press, 1987). For work on Lacan in relation to the comedia see Henry Sullivan, "The Problematic of Tragedy in Calderón's *El médico de su honra,*" *Revista Canadiense de Estudios Hispánicos* 5 (1981): 355–71; "Love, Matrimony and Desire in the Theatre of Tirso de Molina," *Bulletin of the Comediantes* 37 (1985): 93–95; and "Sexual" (109–11), with one correction—the locus of the unconscious is in the Other). I would like to thank Ellie Ragland-Sullivan, Henry Sullivan, and Alan Astro for their comments and suggestions during the preparation of this study.

3. All references are to Gabriel Téllez (Tirso de Molina), *Don Gil de las calzas verdes,* ed. E. W. Hesse and C. J. Moolick (Madrid: Anaya, 1971).

4. Jacques Lacan, *Le Séminaire. Livre III: Les Psychoses, 1954–1955,* ed. Jacques-Alain Miller (Paris: Seuil, 1981), 51.

5. Everett W. Hesse and William C. McCary. "La balanza sujetiva-objetiva en el teatro de Tirso: Ensayo sobre contenido y forma barrocos." *Hispanófila,* 1, no. 3 (1958): 3–4.

6. Lacan, *Séminaire* 3, 199.

7. Ibid., 200.

8. Ragland-Sullivan, *Lacan,* 293.

9. Lacan, *Feminine Sexuality,* ed. Juliet Mitchell and Jacqueline Rose, trans. Jacqueline Rose (New York: Norton, 1983), 119–20; Ragland-Sullivan, *Lacan* 268–70, 291; cf. Moustapha Safouan, *La Sexualité féminine dans la doctrine freudienne* (Paris: Seuil, 1976), 132.

10. Lacan, *Feminine,* 76, 109, 125, 143; *Le Séminaire. Livre II: Le Moi dans la théorie de Freud et dans la technique de la psychanalyse, 1954–1955* (Paris: Seuil, 1978), 68.

11. Lacan, *Séminaire 3,* 184.

12. Sullivan, "Sexual," 115.

13. The shifting nature of these beliefs brings to mind Freud's permutations through denial: I (man/woman) love/hate you (man/woman), although this time the terms living and dead can also be added to the mix; I (living man/dead man/living woman/dead woman) love/hate you (living man/dead man/living woman/dead woman). See Lacan, *Écrits,* 188; Eugen Bär, "Understanding Lacan," *Psychoanalysis and Contemporary Science* 3 (1974): 520.

14. Hesse, *La mujer como víctima en la comedia y otros ensayos* (Barcelona: Puvill, n.d.), 138–39.

15. That the alleged homosexuality serves primarily comic purposes is expressed by Sullivan, "Sexual," 118; Hesse, *La mujer,* 140–41. Sullivan adds that such "homosexuality" is considered more or less normal in the world of the play, unlike the real world. See "Tirso de Molina: Dramaturgo andrógino," *Actas del Quinto Congreso Internacional de Hispanistas,* ed. Maxime Chevalier et al (Bordeaux: Université de Bordeaux, Instituto de Estudios Ibéricos e Iberoamericanos, 1977), 814. It is important here to delineate the difference between the psychoanalysis of women and the implication of psychoanalytic concepts in these characters that are allegories of women. Dramatic characters are not human beings with concrete symptoms; rather they serve to represent or allegorize a concept that has

a certain resonance in psychoanalytic theory. As a result, the application of case studies of and theories about masculine women (as in Safouan 95–116, 129–39) is to reify these characterizations and thereby deny their power as emblems rather than real people. The same can be said about hysterical and obsessional neuroses even though the main questions that preoccupy them, "Am I a man or a woman?" and "Am I dead or alive?", respectively, are found in the confusions regarding Juana's identity.

16. Sullivan, "Tirso," 814.

17. Sullivan, "Love," 95.

18. Lacan, *Écrits*, 151.

19. Lacan, *Séminaire 2*, 315.

20. Juliet Mitchell, "Introduction—I" in Lacan, *Feminine*, 5, 29.

21. Lacan, *Séminaire 2*, 303.

22. Lacan, *Écrits*, 286–87.

23. Shoshana Felman, "On Reading Poetry: Reflections on the Limits and Possibilities of Psychoanalytical Approaches," in *The Literary Freud: Mechanisms of Defense and the Poetic Will*, ed. Joseph H. Smith (New Haven: Yale University Press, 1980), 138.

24. There is no subject without *aphanisis;* as soon as the subject "appears somewhere as meaning, he is manifest elsewhere as fading,' as disappearance" (Lacan, *The Four Fundamental Concepts of Psycho-Analysis*, ed. Jacques-Alain Miller, trans. Alan Sheridan [New York: Norton, 1978], 218; cf. 221. See also Régis Durand, "On *Aphanisis:* A Note on the Dramaturgy of the Subject in Narrative Analysis," in *Lacan and Narration: The Psychoanalytic Difference in Narrative Theory*, ed. Robert Con Davis (Baltimore: Johns Hopkins University Press, 1983), 863–64. The fading of the subject is related both to castration and (again) the basis of the Symbolic in language. "All that is language is lent from this otherness and this is why the subject is always a fading thing that runs under the chain of signifiers. For the definition of a signifier is that it represents a subject not for another subject but for another signifier" (Lacan, "Of Structure as an Inmixing of an Otherness Prerequisite to Any Subject Whatsoever," in *The Structuralist Controversy: The Languages of Criticism and the Sciences of Man*, ed. Richard Macksey and Eugenio Donato. [Baltimore: Johns Hopkins University Press, 1972], 194).

25. Lacan, *Le Séminaire. Livre XX: Encore, 1972–1973*, ed. Jacques-Alain Miller (Paris: Seuil, 1975), 34.

26. Because the Symbolic Order is androcentric in its initial function (Lacan, *Séminaire 2*, 303–5), Juana is subjected to what Ragland-Sullivan calls a "Second Castration" in which the Symbolic, in addition to the deferment of the Imaginary object, institutes in the Law the many myths of inferior women and self-sufficient men (277, 283, 287, 290, 298–301).

27. Luce Irigaray, "When the Goods Get Together," in *New French Feminisms*, ed. Elaine Marks and Isabelle de Courtivron (New York: Schocken Books, 1980), 108.

28. Safouan, *La Sexualité*, 110.

Works Cited

Bär, Eugen, "Understanding Lacan." *Psychoanalysis and Contemporary Science* 3 (1974): 473–544.

Durand, Régis. "On *Aphanisis:* A Note on the Dramaturgy of the Subject in Narrative Analysis." In *Lacan and Narration: The Psychoanalytic Difference in Narrative Theory,* edited by Robert Con Davis, 860–70. Baltimore: Johns Hopkins University Press, 1983.

Felman, Shoshana. "On Reading Poetry: Reflections on the Limits and Possibilities of Psychoanalytical Approaches." In *The Literary Freud: Mechanisms of Defense and the Poetic Will,* edited by Joseph H. Smith, 119–48. New Haven: Yale University Press, 1980.

Hesse, Everett W. *La mujer como víctima en la comedia y otros ensayos.* Barcelona: Puvill, n.d.

Hesse, Everett W. and William C. McCrary. "La balanza sujetiva-objetiva en el teatro de Tirso: Ensayo sobre contenido y forma barrocos." *Hispanófila* 1, no. 3 (1958): 1–11.

Irigaray, Luce. "When the Goods Get Together." In *New French Feminisms,* edited by Elaine Marks and Isabelle de Courtivron, 107–110. New York: Schocken Books, 1980.

Lacan, Jacques. *Écrits: A Selection.* Translated by Alan Sheridan. New York: Norton, 1977.

———. *Feminine Sexuality.* Edited by Juliet Mitchell and Jacqueline Rose. Translated by Jacqueline Rose. New York: Norton, 1983.

———. *The Four Fundamental Concepts of Psycho-Analysis.* Edited by Jacques-Alain Miller. Translated by Alan Sheridan. New York: Norton, 1978.

———. "Of Structure as an Inmixing of an Otherness Prerequisite to Any Subject Whatsoever." In *The Structuralist Controversy: The Languages of Criticism and the Sciences of Man,* edited by Richard Macksey and Eugenio Donato, 186–200. Baltimore: Johns Hopkins University Press, 1972.

———. *Le Séminaire. Livre II: Le Moi dans la théorie de Freud et dans la technique de la psychanalyse, 1954–1955.* Edited by Jacques-Alain Miller. Paris: Seuil, 1978.

———. *Le Séminaire. Livre III: Les Psychoses, 1955–1956.* Edited by Jacques-Alain Miller. Paris: Seuil, 1981.

———. *Le Séminaire. Livre XX: Encore, 1972–1973.* Edited by Jacques-Alain Miller. Paris: Seuil, 1975.

Laplanche, J., and J.-B. Pontalis. *The Language of Psycho-Analysis.* Translated by Donald Nicholson-Smith. New York: Norton, 1973.

Mitchell, Juliet. "Introduction—I." *Feminine Sexuality,* by Jacques Lacan. Edited by Juliet Mitchell and Jacqueline Rose, 1–26. New York: Norton, 1983.

Ragland-Sullivan, Ellie. *Jacques Lacan and the Philosophy of Psychoanalysis.* Urbana: University of Illinois, 1987.

Safouan, Moustapha. *La Sexualité féminine dans la doctrine freudienne.* Paris: Seuil, 1976.

Sullivan, Henry W. "Love, Matrimony and Desire in the Theatre of Tirso de Molina." *Bulletin of the Comediantes,* 37 (1985): 83–99.

———. "The Problematic of Tragedy in Calderón's *El médico de su honra.*" *Revista Canadiense de Estudios Hispánicos* 5 (1981): 355–71.

———. "The Sexual Ambiguities of Tirso de Molina's *Don Gil de las calzas verdes.*" *Proceedings of the Third Annual Golden Age Spanish Drama Symposium.* El Paso, 1983, edited by Richard Ford, 107–21. El Paso: University of Texas at El Paso, n.d.

———. "Tirso de Molina: Dramaturgo andrógino." In *Actas del Quinto Congreso Internacional de Hispanistas*. Edited by Maxime Chevalier *et al*, 811–18. Bordeaux: Université de Bordeaux Instituto de Estudios Ibéricos e Iberoamericanos, 1977.

Téllez, Gabriel (Tirso de Molina). *Don Gil de las calzas verdes*. Edited by E. W. Hesse and C. J. Moolick. Madrid: Anaya, 1971.

Part 2
Taking the Woman's Part

Ana Caro's Re-evaluation of the *Mujer varonil* and Her Theatrics in *Valor, agravio y mujer*

TERESA S. SOUFAS

During her lifetime the dramatist Ana Caro Mallén de Soto was listed in the work *Varones ilustres de Sevilla* [Illustrious Men of Seville] in which she is described as an "insigne poetisa que ha hecho muchas comedias, representadas en Sevilla y Madrid y otras partes" [distinguished poetess who has composed many plays, performed in Seville and Madrid and elsewhere].[1] This book's title reflects the contemporary practice of praising women by means of a term such as *varonil* (manly) that exposes the disconcerting options faced by a woman writer like Ana Caro in the intellectual atmosphere of seventeenth-century Spain. While promoting patriarchal values, it unabashedly proclaims the male standard against which she was most likely to be judged by her predominately male audiences and community of play-writing colleagues.[2] In her play *Valor, agravio y mujer* [Value/Valor, Offense And Woman], Caro gives evidence of both overt and subtle efforts to examine and question such evaluations of women as authors and characters.[3] In the process, the male-dominated dramatic conventions that also measure women's admirable characteristics and accomplishments against their capacity to seem *varoniles* are revised by Caro to the extent that she uses the theatrical devices of masculine disguise, love intrigues, and the honor code's double standard to present a female protagonist whose feigned masculine role is not a means to supersede her own sex but a way to offer to the males around her a better model for their own emulation.

The irony of including Caro as one of the *varones ilustres* is more enjoyable if *Valor, agravio y mujer* is read as a work that undermines the stereotypical linking of a woman's social, political, or emotional success to her imitation of men and their values or to her reliance upon them to resolve her dilemmas. In this play, Caro nevertheless follows at the structural level much of the typical

character and thematic development of other dramatized honor
dilemmas and does not represent a complete overturning of the
system of social roles that Golden Age drama depicts.[4] Rather, she
relies on role-playing techniques to represent a more just pattern for
men and women in the patriarchal society in which she herself must
live and write.

Scrutinizing the codified social and theatrical structures, Caro
insists on the worth of the abandoned woman as a desirable and
acceptable marriage partner. At the same time she takes into account alternative responses by the males and females in the community who must face questions of honor, the choice of marriage
partners, and the appropriate fulfillment of gender roles. Her challenge from within is thus similar to that made by other contemporary literary women whose confrontations with the injustice
inherent in the social realities and literary representations of their
day are undertaken at a moral level that does not displace the
accepted social balance.[5] In Caro's play, for example, she provides a
new model for thought and behavior, but she continues to promote
marriage as the goal toward which her women characters strive.[6]

In the male-authored Siglo de Oro dramas about love and honor,
it is easy to locate women characters who fulfill very traditionally
the unquestioned patriarchal expectations of their authors and contemporary audiences. These figures either fail because of their
attempts to behave in ways considered inappropriate or are denied
the opportunity to demonstrate their own independence. In a play
such as Lope de Vega's La moza de cántaro [The Pitcher Girl], for
example, María takes upon herself the defense of family honor in
order to avenge a wrong in her father's name. Lope portrays this
woman's efforts as misdirected because, in a disruption of theatrical
practice, she intends not to allow her brother to fulfill the role of
avenger. Lope upholds the convention, and María does not therefore triumph in her difficult task. Nor does Arminda in Mira de
Amescua's No hay burlas con las mujeres, o casarse o vengarse
[There are no deceptions with women, either get married or avenge
yourself], in which she behaves like many of the most unbalanced
Golden Age male characters in questions of honor—Calderón's
wife-murderers, for instance. Although Mira is considered by some
to have introduced a new type of pundonorosa [punctilious] female
character, he nonetheless should be credited with merely showing
how his protagonist uses male standards of retaliation to try to
overcome social injustice without being able to claim a moral
victory. Like the flawed model she emulates, Arminda commits a
bloody murder.[7]

Calderón's famous portrayal of the avenging woman in *La vida es sueño* [*Life is a dream*] shows Rosaura as a positive character in the drama, and her efforts, as in the case of each of the principals, are directed toward establishing herself within the proper context and role in the greater society. Dressed as a man, a woman, or a composite of the two, however, she is without a social identity until the last scene for she has no patrilineal name. Disguised as a man in the first act she is not shown to be powerful and self-protective because she is vulnerable to a death sentence for having unknowingly transgressed the injunction against communication with the imprisoned Segismundo. As a lady-in-waiting in the palace she is placed in a subservient role to Astolfo, who, until the last moment, considers her to be an unacceptable marriage partner because of her questionable lineage. As has been clearly demonstrated in earlier studies, Rosaura is indeed instrumental in the moral and political victory that Segismundo enjoys,[8] but she is always depicted as less than independent and in need of the sponsorship of a powerful male.

Efforts to explain the various manifestations of such characters now known as *mujeres varoniles* [manly women] in plays by men reveal that several modern scholars continue to offer readings based upon a critical endorsement of the patriarchal value system.[9] Melveena McKendrick, for example, observes that the Amazon-like María in *La moza de cántaro* "is forced to use all her positive masculine qualities to protect herself."[10] Holding Lope de Vega up as the male Siglo de Oro playwright most "intensely concerned with the question of woman's life and rights," McKendrick nevertheless concludes that Lope is essentially like the other male dramatists of the period for "again like them, only more emphatically, he was not prepared to emancipate [woman] from her dependence upon the male."[11] The best a female character can hope for in such a model is to triumph briefly over the restrictions placed on her femininity by imitating the behavior and attitudes of males before reaffirming publicly and permanently her female identity. McKendrick goes on to ponder what she posits as the effect of the typical final domestication of the *esquiva* [disdainful woman] figures upon the female members of the audience and even proposes that a sort of cathartic wish fulfillment was relished by these women:

> What, after all, is the *esquiva* but a more sophisticated version of Sleeping Beauty? Both are waiting to be awakened to love and life. The prince is a stylization of the man who wins the unattainable woman.

And the "prince" is probably the most common form of female wish-fulfillment. The woman of great strength or ability, one imagines, similarly appealed to the conqueror in man . . . Every man was the hero who transformed the masterful or powerful woman into an adoring consort, who made the scholar forget her books, and the career woman abandon her career, and who made the intrepid warrior dissolve into tears and start at the sight of a mouse.[12]

Matthew D. Stroud notes likewise that in the numerous studies of the *mujeres varoniles* (for instance, those by Matulka, McKendrick, Bravo-Villasante, de Armas, and his own examination of *La dama duende* [*The Phantom Lady*] the plays considered are by the canonical male playwrights and the exegetical conclusions typically reached declare that "a pesar de la grandeza de estas mujeres, las soluciones a los conflictos dramáticos restablecen la superioridad del hombre sobre la mujer" [in spite of the greatness of these women, the solutions to the dramatic conflicts reestablish the superiority of the men over the women].[13] These are female characters who parallel what Sandra M. Gilbert and Susan Gubar have argued is precisely the female author's dilemma as well. Building upon ideas put forth by Virginia Woolf and others, they suggest that a "literary woman . . . had to define her public presence in the world. If she did not suppress her work entirely or publish it pseudonymously or anonymously, she could modestly confess her female 'limitations' and concentrate on the 'lesser' subjects reserved for ladies as becoming to their inferior powers. If the latter alternative seemed an admission of failure, she could rebel, accepting the ostracism that must have seemed inevitable."[14] Woolf's focus upon the choice for these women authors delineates the two untenable extremes of their self-definition as "only a woman" or being "as good as a man."[15]

Also relying on such theoretical issues, Elizabeth Ordóñez considers the female characters and plots created by María de Zayas and Ana Caro to be "though . . . apparently safely within the bounds of convention . . . nevertheless at the same time outside it, inside another economy. They disclose the subversive straining of the woman author to find her own identity as she writes surrounded by, but not entirely lost in, largely alien textual territory."[16] In Golden Age male-authored plays, the female character frequently is portrayed as being "as good as a man" for a period when she must struggle against injustice so that she can settle back into the passive status of wife, usually of the very man who has mistreated her earlier. Caro suggests an alternative to this patriarchal evaluation because her female character disguised as a man does not conduct herself as do the typical males. She is a "better" (hu)man in the moral sense and enacts a more just and moral response to the question of male attitudes toward a woman deceived by an unfaithful man. Although at first glance Caro seems to be writing like her male colleagues, using what appears to be one of their favored plots, she actually conducts a subversion from within, "surrounded by, but not entirely lost in, largely alien textual territory"; Leonor openly validates the authority that she and her creator claim as they fashion a message about woman's worth and man's instruction:

> Semíramis, ¿no fué heroica?
> Cenobia, Drusila, Draznes,
> Camila, y otras cien mil,
> ¿No sirvieron de ejemplares
> A mil Varones famosos?[17]

> [Wasn't Semíramis heroic?
> Didn't Cenobia, Drusila, Draznes,
> Camila, and a thousand other women
> Serve as examples
> To a thousand famous men?]

Valor, agravio y mujer portrays a set of temporary inversions, the most obvious of which is Leonor's cross-gender dressing that is but the outer parallel of the more established and long term disorder upon which Caro focuses. Such a depicted subversion in literature often reveals the chaotic value system of a seemingly ordered society that, as in this instance, can allow a woman to be dishonored without proper legal and personal channels for redressing her grievance. Caro's inversion thus reiterates the underlying spirit of the popular sixteenth- and seventeenth-century literary interest in festive invocations of the "disorderly woman" which Leah S. Marcus describes with regard to Shakespeare's comedies in the following manner: "the overthrow and discarding of accepted gender roles helps to undo injustice, promote renewal and rebirth."[18]

Within the inverted order of her dramatic text Caro also acknowledges clearly her authorial crisis in terms of the conflict between her professional, social, and domestic roles—a conflict that in Medieval and Renaissance society is often exacerbated by uncertain access to formal education. What the sixteenth-century poet Catherine des Roches expresses in a sonnet to her spindle, for example, resounds as well in the works by other seventeenth-century women writers such as Sor Juana Inés de la Cruz, María de

Zayas y Sotomayor, and Anne Bradstreet. All these women respond
to external limitations imposed on them.[19] By means of inversive
patterns, such issues are articulated in *Valor, agravio y mujer* by
the male *graciosos* [clowns] Ribete and Tomillo at a point midway
through Act 2. Musing on the novelties of Madrid society, Ribete
explains to his companion:

> Sólo en esto de poetas
> Hay notable novedad
> Por innumerable, tanto,
> Que aun quieren poetizar
> Las mujeres, y se atreven
> A hacer comedias ya.

(193)

> [Only in the matter of poets
> Is there real novelty due to
> Their great number, so much so,
> In fact that even women
> Want to write poetry, and now dare to
> Compose plays.]

The scandalized Tomillo exclaims: "¡Válgame Dios! Pues ¿no fuera
/ Mejor coser y hilar? / ¿Mujeres poetas?" [Praise God! Well,
wouldn't it be better to sew and spin? Women poets?] (193). These
two men articulate, of course, the Renaissance resistance to women
as authors and active public figures, but it is nevertheless Ribete
who helps to establish his own author's legitimacy through recount-
ing the female precursors who, as Gilbert and Gubar argue, prove
"by example that a revolt against patriarchal literary authority is
possible."[20] His argument is:

> Mas no es nuevo, pues están
> Argentaria, Safo, Areta,
> Blesilla, y más de un millar
> De modernas, que hoy a Italia
> Lustre soberano dan,
> Discuplando la osadía
> De su nueva vanidad.[21]

(193)

> [But it is not new, since
> Argentaria, Sappho, Areta,
> Blesilla are there, and more than a thousand
> Modern women, who give supreme glory to Italy,

Excusing the boldness of
Their new vanity.]

This interchange is important not only because it is an affirmation
of the efforts of the female author to resist the categorization of
inferiority and/or oddity and to express her recognition of a *female*
tradition, but also because it expresses and enhances the unresolved quality of that struggle. Tomillo responds to Ribete's above
recitation with a demand for more information: "Y decidme . . ."
[And tell me . . .] only to be quieted by the other clown's impatient
refusal to continue discussing the topic: "¿Voto a Cristo, / Que eso
es mucho preguntar! [Christ, that is a lot of questioning!] (193).

This unresolved dispute is important as well because it is introduced by two figures whose type is marginalized socially but who
are able to practice a license for subversive dissent because of their
comic quality and association with the commentator fool. Numerous studies of the *gracioso* point out the value of such a figure as
the mouthpiece of truth and justice, and Caro's depiction of Ribete
foregrounds these very elements.[22] He is after all the only character
who knows the truth of Leonor's gender and identity until the final
scene of the play and the only one who knowingly aids her in
carrying out her charade. Caro's use of such an alliance is in
keeping with what Lee R. Edwards argues is an important one
between fools, simpletons, clowns, and women who function as
liminars, that is, "those who are typically powerless within society,
those who occupy its fringes and interstices [and who] are usually
ignored or degraded by the main legitimizing and power-conferring
social institutions."[23]

In act 1, moreover, Ribete directly challenges the stereotypical
portrayal of the servant as simpleton and coward:

> Estoy mal con enfadosos
> Que introducen los graciosos
> Muertos de hambre y gallinas.
> El que ha nacido alentado
> ¿No lo ha de ser si no es noble?
> Que ¿no podrá serlo al doble
> Del caballero el criado?
>
> (185)

> [I am sick of irksome
> Individuals who introduce the
> Clowns starving to death and
> Cowardly. He who has been

Born brave, isn't he so
Even if he isn't a noble?
Can't the servant be
Like the gentleman?]

His questions and assertion of worth are an indication of the self-
conscious quality of Caro's entire examination of theatrical and
social conventions, and her clown Ribete argues further for a
revised appreciation of his type's value in the following metatheatrical speech:

Ya me parece comedia,
Donde todo lo remedia
Un bufón medio alcahuete.
No hay fábula, no hay tramoya,
Adonde no venga al justo
Un lacayo de buen gusto,
Porque si no, ¡aquí fué Troya!

(186)

[Now it seems like a play
To me where the buffoon
Who is half go-between
Solves everything. There is
No story, no scheme in which
The clown of good taste doesn't
Bring about justice. And
If not, then there's
Nothing but ruins!]

Ribete thus serves as a promoter of the theatrical role reversal that
is typical with regard to the political identity of noble and lower
classes, but Caro uses him in *Valor, agravio y mujer* as the
mouthpiece of her own call for moral revision of gender com-
monplaces as well. That Ribete is a male character is significant
because his is at best a grudging acknowledgment of the tradition of
women's public rights, authorial or otherwise.[24] His position as a
licensed commentator and a clown, however, allows the playwright
to offer her challenge openly and safely while simultaneously using
a masculine character as another medium in her reworking of the
conventional gender representations.

The protagonist Leonor undertakes her performance as a man in
order to pursue and confront her lover Juan. As the play begins,
Juan arrives at court in Brussels and is befriended by Don Fernando de Ribera, Leonor's brother whom she has not seen since the

age of six. When Leonor arrives soon after, she is disguised in male attire. Answering to the name of Don Leonardo, she also is integrated into the court as a nobleman and thus is confident of not being recognized as a woman. Against Leonor's charade, the questionable ethics and inconstancy of the men and their support of the honor code's double standard is revealed. Juan, for example, attracts and woos the Countess Estela, whom Prince Ludovico also loves. She has not, however, reciprocated the latter's affection and behaves, in the Prince's view, as an *esquiva*. Estela's reticence is justifiable, as Caro makes clear, for it is based on her rejection of Prince Ludovico's ambition and arrogance, which the Countess finds disagreeable:

> No hay disgusto
> Para mí como su nombre.
> ¡Jesús! ¡Líbrenme los cielos
> De su ambición!

(190)

> [There is for me no greater
> Displeasure than his name.
> Jesus! May the heavens
> Save me from his
> Ambition!]

Estela likewise explains her sudden interest in Leonardo, saying to her cousin Lisarda: ". . . mas si mi elección / Jamás tuvo inclinación / Declarada, no fué exceso / Rendirme" [. . . but if I never dared a preference, then it was not an excess to yield] (190). Such sentiments invoke motivations very different from the vanity and arrogance frequently attributed by male playwrights to their *esquiva* figures, and, as McKendrick points out, both are sins whose "continued recurrence reveals the [male] dramatists' inability to conceive of any assertion of female independence other than that based on some reprehensible character trait."[25]

Now himself amorously attracted to Estela, Juan openly confesses to Fernando his deception of a noblewoman in Seville (as the audience knows, Leonor herself). He is nevertheless genuinely welcomed and admired by Fernando and the other courtiers. Fernando does, however, privately criticize Juan's fickleness ("Que aunque es muy hermosa Estela, / No hay, en mi opinión, disculpa / para una injusta mudanza" [Although Estela is very beautiful, there is not, in my opinion, any excuse for an unjust change of heart] [p. 188]), but he expresses none of this in public or to Juan directly.

Although he keeps silent about his disapproval and later behaves like a typical Siglo de Oro male character enraged over the suspected faithlessness of a sister, Fernando does suggest, though very subtly, that men too can challenge the premises of the double standard and its unfair consequences for women. This sort of male reaction, it must be admitted, is not entirely unique in Golden Age drama. In Guillén de Castro's *Progne y Filomena,* for instance, Teosindo also rejects the double standard and wants to marry Filomena after she has been raped.[26] Caro's presentation, however, does not allow the male figures to surpass the theatrical conventions so uncharacteristically. That is a privilege she accords Leonor alone.

Leonor/Leonardo proceeds to complicate the courtly value system by arranging mistaken identities, rendezvous in the dark, and a revelation to Estela of Juan's dishonorable treatment of the unnamed woman in Seville. Within this theatrical ambience that she organizes and promotes, her dramatization of an alternative approach to the usual reaction by male characters over the supposedly damaged reputation of a female relative or beloved is the most important factor. As Leonardo, she reveals to Fernando and all the assembled members of the court the truth about Juan's deception and, claiming to be Leonor's faithful suitor, she undertakes the role of her own champion and avenger and speaks as an ardent would-be husband:

> Mas yo, amante verdadero,
> La prometí de vengar
> Su agravio, y dando al silencio
> Con la muerte de don Juan
> La ley forzosa del duelo,
> Ser su esposo. . . .

(210)

> [But I, the authentic
> Lover, promised to avenge
> Her grievance, and to be her
> Husband upon silencing
> The affront with the death
> Of Don Juan through the
> Compulsory rules of the duel. . .]

Accepted as a male by the other characters, Leonardo raises a different voice in the matter of male reaction to female reputation, but still fulfills the part of superior masculine figure who must protect the inferior and weaker female. The audience in the theater, however, knows Leonor's true sex and must acknowledge that indeed not only is she actually defending herself but that also as a counterfeit male she shows the superiority of her own code of ethics, which no male on stage has as yet adopted.

In contradistinction to Leonardo's proclamation of faith and devotion, Juan decries Leonor's faithless behavior in having fallen in love with someone else and damaging *his* reputation by not remaining true in her original devotion to him—in clear adherence to the honor code's double standard. At this point, Fernando likewise displays the conventional reaction of the male relative: "¿Hay mayores confusiones? / ¡Hoy la vida y honor pierdo! / ¡Ah, hermana fácil!" [Are there any greater confusions? Today I lose my life and my honor! Ah, loose sister!] (210). A further typical reaction of male characters in a similar situation is expressed by Juan when he learns that the abandoned Leonor being spoken about in this scene is Fernando's sister. His remorse over his treatment of her still is not connected to guilt for a wrong committed against a woman. Jealousy is not remorse; on the contrary, he is concerned about having transgressed the laws of male friendship and the honor code's emphasis on defense of family reputation by brothers and other male relatives. To Fernando's declaration "Don Juan, / Mal pagaste de mi pecho / Las finezas" [Don Juan, you repaid badly my heartfelt courtesies] (210), Juan answers: "De corrido / A mirarle no me atrevo. / A saber que era tu hermana . . ." [I am so embarrassed that I don't dare look at you. If I had known she was your sister . . .] (210).

That the dishonorable man becomes trapped in the rules of the double standard is an irony that other playwrights also recognize. In Calderón's drama about rape, *No hay cosa como callar* [There is nothing like being silent], the reprehensibility of such immoral attitudes is given pronounced treatment when this play's Don Juan boasts to his friend Luis about having violated an unknown woman in the dark. The story, which reiterates the issue of women's bodies as male property, is told and received amid laughter and enjoyment, for both men are unaware that the woman in question is Luis's fiancée. In both cases, regret for such unjust treatment of women is felt by the males only when they realize that the impact of their behavior is also felt by her male family members. Tirso's Don Juan makes a game, of course, of just this very element.

The violence that informs the male code of honor is also at issue in *Valor, agravio y mujer*, as it is in so many Golden Age plays. Leonor claims to be ready to defend her honor in physical combat

with Juan ("Que he de morir ó vencer" [I have to die or conquer]
[189]), insisting that: "Salí á quitarle la vida, / Y lo hiciera, ¡vive el
cielo! / A no verle arrepentido" [I left in order to kill him, and I
would have done it, by heaven, if I hadn't seen him repentant] (211).
His repentance is certainly more likely attributable to those factors
such as jealousy and his ties to the involved brother than to a
change of heart over justice for women. Caro's play, however, has
been directed toward the intellectual trap that the protagonist pre-
pares instead of to violence which, on the other hand, is the only
solution the male characters seem to be able to envision. Juan's
willingness to fight Leonardo is matched by Fernando's acknowledgment that violence is unavoidable:

> ¡Qué laberinto tan ciego!
> Dice bien don Juan, bien dice,
> Pues si casarla pretendo
> Con Leonardo, ¿cómo pued[o],
> Vive don Juan? Esto es hecho:
> Todos hemos de matarnos,
> Yo no hallo otro remedio.

(210)

> [What a blind labyrinth!
> Don Juan is right, he is right,
> Since if I plan to marry
> Her to Leonardo, how
> Can I with Don Juan alive?
> This is a fact: we
> All have to kill each other,
> I see no other solution.]

Ludovico is immediately supportive of such thinking: "Ni yo le
miro, ¡por Dios! / Y ése es bárbaro y sangriento" [Nor do I, by God!
And that is a barbarous and bloody remedy] (210). Indeed, there is
a different option, and Leonor will soon explain and dramatize it.
    Leonardo and Juan confront each other as the principals in the
competition, each representing opposite poles in their response to
the worth of the woman over whom they are about to duel.
Leonardo professes "his" love for her, claiming only the desire to
eliminate his rival so as to be able to marry without the constraints
of any prior legal obligation on his wife's part. Such a stance also
reinforces the legitimacy of the private marriage contract which,
ironically, prompts Juan's jealousy but which he is unwilling to
observe. Indeed, until confronted with competition for Leonor's

affection, he does not acknowledge any commitment between them. Once jealous, however, Juan reasserts his love for Leonor and immediately abandons his ardent suit of Estela even though he makes it abundantly clear that he considers Leonor unfaithful and therefore unworthy as a marriage partner:

> Yo no me puedo casar
> Con doña Leonor, es cierto,
> Aunque muera Leonardo;
> Antes moriré primero.
> ¡Ah, si hubiera sido honrada!

(210)

> [I cannot marry
> Doña Leonor, it is certain,
> Even though Leonardo be dead;
> I will die first.
> Ah, if only she had been honorable!]

By the end of the play, the pairings of the characters have undergone some revisions, but it is only after Leonor reaffirms her identity as a woman that the confusion is dispelled, the truth is revealed, and satisfaction of the justice she has sought is attained. The confrontation between Leonardo and Juan evokes the latter's rigid adherence to the male pattern of rejection of a woman loved by another man, something that, unless overcome, prohibits the union of Leonor and Juan. The male identity that Leonor has adopted, therefore, proves to be the literal block to the desired marriage and a means to an end only in so far as it serves to trap Juan. Only as a woman can Leonor bring about a righting of the wrong done unto her, and so the masculine disguise is not the instrument of resolution.

Leonor's transformation into Leonardo is, on the one hand, an adherence to the social tenets that deny independence and a public voice to women and, on the other, a way of showing men how to better their role in that same social system. Stepping back into her true identity as Leonor, she effects the undoing of the model in which only a man can take on the responsibility for defending or avenging the family honor. Having elicited Juan's public acknowledgement of his belated wish to honor his commitment to her (though if only there were no Leonardo), she then fulfills the conditions he demands and leaves him no graceful or safe way to renege. Leonor thereby gains a victory by an intellectual outmaneuvering rather than by bloodshed. The play's outcome, nevertheless, does

not overcome the conventional system, for Leonor is vindicated in
her faithful devotion of Juan, and thus *his* rejection of an adjudged
unfaithful woman is never reversed.

That Juan could again shirk his responsibilities is a possibility
suggested by the textual evidence of his questionable integrity; his
devotion to both Leonor and Estela has proven to be alterable very
quickly. Leonor is, on the other hand, the only character who has
not wavered or changed in her allegiance to her original partner.
Though the other principal female, Estela, has consistently favored
Leonardo, she of necessity must eventually shift her affections
elsewhere because a union with "him" is impossible and illusory
from the very start. Estela ends by forgiving the deceit
("Quedemos / Hermanas, Leonor hermosa" [Let's remain sisters,
beautiful Leonor] [211]) as she parallels Leonor's decisiveness and
proposes marriage to Fernando. The one-dimensional and ambitious Ludovico unchivalrously, though characteristically, then
asks for Lisarda's hand: "Ganar quiero tu belleza, / Lisarda hermosa; pues pierdo / A Estela, dame tu mano" [I want to win your
beauty, lovely Lisarda; since I lose Estela, give me your hand] (211).
Up to this point as the ardent but unrequited suitor of the Countess,
Ludovico has been unaware of Lisarda's romantic interest in him,
briefly stated in secret to Estela in act 1. Lisarda's acceptance of his
proposal expresses an attitude consistent with the more passive
personality she herself exhibits throughout the play: "La mano y el
alma ofrezco" [My hand and my soul I offer] (211). What is revealed
in these pairings is a whole range of possible responses to the social
and literary norms examined. Caro acknowledges the superficial
status quo: in society's opinion, a woman's honor and reputation are
vulnerable to damage by an unfaithful man, and marital partnership
is the desired goal for her principals. She suggests, however, a
different set of appropriate responses, and her suggestions come
without any indication of hope or confidence in the permanence of
such a new value system.

Of the united couples, for example, Estela and Fernando constitute a pair whose firm emotional commitment is suspect. He has
been from the beginning the most uncommunicative of the three
men who want to win the Countess for a wife. He has even agreed
to serve as Ludovico's advocate before Estela ("Por vos / La
hablaré" [I will speak to her in your behalf] [186]). In even this
undertaking, he is ambivalent, however, for in representing
Ludovico he feels disloyal to Juan:

> Ludovico, hermosa Estela,
> Me pide que os venga á hablar.

> Don Juan es mi amigo, y sé
> Que os rinde el alma don Juan;
> Y yo, humilde, á vuestras plantas . . .
> ¿Por dónde he de comenzar?
> Que, ¡por Dios que no me atrevo!
> A pediros . . . .

(190)

> [Beautiful Estela, Ludovico
> Requests that I come to
> Talk to you. Don Juan is my
> Friend, and I know that
> He surrenders his soul to
> You; and I, humble at your feet . . .
> Where do I begin? Why, by God
> I don't dare to ask of you . . . .]

Then when Estela refuses to choose between these two rivals (". . . tan lejos está / Mi voluntad de elegir" [. . . my will is so far from choosing] [190]), Fernando reveals in an aside his own romantic interest: "¡Qué dichoso desdeñar! (Aparte) / Pues me deja acción de Amante" [What blessed scorn! (Aside) Well she leaves the lover's plot to me] (190). Until he accepts her marriage proposal in the last scene, this sentiment is never openly declared or acted upon.

In the end, it is Estela who proposes marriage and Fernando accepts, further attributing his newfound happiness to his sister's machinations: "Estas dichas / Causó Leonor; yo soy vuestro" [Leonor caused these happy events; I am yours] (211), a point Caro articulates through this male figure. Lisarda then quickly accepts Ludovico as husband (she is a minor character who is portrayed as the most acquiescent to the social system and its demands on women.) This is the man whose personality and values are repugnant to her cousin and confidant, the more actively discerning Countess Estela. Both women represent variations within the social and dramatic possibilities that Leonor confronts in her own struggle to obtain justice and an assurance that all individuals fulfill their roles properly. On the one hand, Lisarda's silence and passivity lead to a marriage with the man she prefers, but only through happenstance and then as his second choice. On the other, Estela's decision is more thoughtful and purposeful and is made because she rejects unsatisfactory options—Ludovico and his arrogant ambition; Juan after all belongs to another; and Leonardo does not even exist—in favor of the more practical alternative of marrying Fernando.

Caro thus fashions an alternative paradigm for the theatrical conventions associated with the *mujer varonil* by means of her protagonist's double performance both before the audience of players on stage and before the threater-going public. As Ordóñez explains in her helpful interpretation, Leonor is as well "an analogue for the woman writer's relationship to the patriarchal texts," since she exercises a certain control over numerous other figures in the play by means of her role-playing and theatrical manipulation (11). Through her, Caro is able to "offer revealing insights into how a woman playwright may weave into conventional plot boundaries a self-consciousness of woman as maker of dramatic texts" (10). This is a convincing argument, but Ordóñez also contends that Caro's male characters change, indeed repent, and that the seemingly conventional end of the play thus "may be based on firmer bedrock than those in male-inscribed plots, plots in which more passive females accommodate to a hollow conformity more central and insistent than justice and love" (12). My present reading diverges from Ordónez's with regard to her latter affirmation and is based instead on the textual evidence of Caro's deeper pessimism over the accepted abuses of justice for women. She moves toward an open-ended structure that affirms a more profound questioning of the portrayed society in which the female author herself inevitably will continue to struggle with the issue of professional identity and in which the debate over woman's worth and her right to a public voice and social justice can be addressed effectively only by the woman herself.

Leonor's desire to marry and regain her place of propriety and respect—her role—in the larger society reveals her underlying willingness to work within the norms of the system. However, she proposes to improve the system by holding the men accountable for the dishonor they attribute to women alone. Leonor intends to punish the offending man himself and does so without assistance from the politically powerful males with whom she interacts. This strategem differs, for example, from Calderon's portrayal of the wife-murderers who kill their wives whether or not their male rivals can be punished. It also differs from the *alcalde* [mayor] of Zalamea's solution, which demands that a daughter who is wronged by a disreputable man must abandon her previous life by retiring to a convent at her father's insistence. Caro's Leonor likewise makes clear her contention that Juan is her husband, evident in her refusal to let him abandon her and in her words in the final scene when, as a woman, she addresses the assembled men as "Hermano, Príncipe, esposo" [Brother, Prince, husband] (211). The three male titles are significant indicators of power, but these partiarchal authorities are for a time controlled by and compelled to listen to her in what is but another moment imbued with a carnivalesque subversion of the norm.

Leonor's goal is public and private recognition of her married status and this she wins, but, as the play ends, many questions remain unanswered. Nothing in the words or deeds of the three male principals indicates that Leonor's enactment of a new exemplary role model has been taken to heart. None renounces his belief in the double standard, and Leonor's transformation back to her rightful feminine identity brings about the disappearance of a supposed male character, Leonardo, from that society. Indeed, Caro insures the impermanence of the new social value system she envisions by having Leonor engineer the whole charade in order to marry her deceiver. Caro's depiction of the social reality is pessimistic, and the positive model enacted by Leonor will not be a lasting part of the society represented in *Valor, agravio y mujer*. The play thus depicts what the title announces. The issues communicated by the word *valor* include an estimation of quality (both as a person and as property) which is inherent in the struggles that both Caro and her protagonist must confront. *Valor* likewise means courage and stamina, and so the playwright's insistence on this additional implication is enhanced by its association in the title with the concepts of *agravio* [offense] and *mujer* [woman]: together they proclaim the ongoing nature of the debate over society's opinion of woman's worth and point to the offenses she must endure and/or repudiate. *Valor, agravio y mujer* therefore posits the continued need for reconsideration of the values that promote conventional male behavior as a positive human and theatrical standard and suggests a very different connotation for a term like *varonil*.

Notes

My thanks to Professor Stacey Schlau for suggestions offered after reading a late draft of this article.

1. Rodrigo Caro de Torres, *Varones ilustres de Sevilla*. Cited in Cayetano Alberto de la Barrera y Leirado, *Catálogo bibliográfico y biográfico del teatro antiguo español desde sus orígenes hasta mediados del siglo xviii* (Madrid: Gredos, 1969), 71. All English translations in this paper are my own.

2. Melveena McKendrick and Dawn Smith comment upon the use of the word *varonil* as a compliment for a woman in seventeenth-century Spain. See their respective studies *Woman and Society in the Spanish Drama of the Golden Age: A Study of the "Mujer varonil"* (Cambridge: Cambridge University Press, 1974), 62,

and "Women and Men in a World-Turned-Upside-Down: An Approach to Three Plays by Tirso de Molina," in *Proceedings of the Fifth Annual Golden Age Spanish Drama Symposium,* ed. Jean F. Chittenden (El Paso: University of Texas at El Paso Press, 1985), 62.

3. The difficulty of translating the term *valor* of Caro's title is indicated by my inclusion of the two words *value* and *valor*. As defined in the *Diccionario de Autoridades* (Madrid: Gredos, 1979), 3 vols, *valor* means: "Ia calidad, que constituye una cosa digna de estimación, u aprecio . . . ; Se toma también por el precio, que se regula correspondiente, e igual a la estimación de alguna cosa . . . . Se toma assimismo por ánimo, y aliento, que desprecia el miedo, y temor en las empressas, o resoluciones . . . . Significa assimismo subsistencia, y firmeza de algún acto . . . . Significa también fuerza, actividad, eficacia, o virtud de las cosas, para producir sus efectos" [the quality that constitutes a thing worthy of esteem or appreciation . . . . It is also taken to mean price that is regulated respective and equal to the value of something . . . . It is understood as well by spirit and courage that scorns fear or dread in undertakings or resolutions . . . . It likewise means endurance and firmness of an act . . . . It also means strength, activity, effectiveness or virtue of things, in order to produce their effects] (3.417–18).

4. In "Women's Defense of Their Public Role," in *Women in the Middle Ages and the Renaissance: Literary and Historical Perspectives,* ed. Mary Beth Rose (Syracuse: Syracuse University Press, 1986), Merry E. Wiesner considers women writers' stress upon spiritual equality with men but also asserts the following: "This recognition of spiritual equality did not lead women to demand political or social equality; there were no calls for woman's suffrage in the Renaissance. In this divided awareness they followed the thinking of most Catholic and main-line Protestant leaders, for whom spiritual equality was a private, internal matter and so was no justification for upsetting or opposing the established social order. The reaction against those who took the spiritual message to be a social, political, or economic one was sharp and swift . . ." (20–21).

5. Recent studies of women like Madeleine and Catherine des Roches, Louise Labé, Pernette du Guillet, Tullia d'Argona, Margaret Cavendish, and the Countess of Pembroke examine the textual strategies of these women. See, for example: Ann Rosalind Jones, "Surprising Fame: Renaissance Gender Ideologies and Women's Lyric," in *The Poetics of Gender,* ed. Nancy K. Miller (New York: Columbia University Press, 1986, 74–95); Mary Ellen Lamb, "The Countess of Pembroke and the Art of Dying," in *Women in the Middle Ages and the Renaissance,* 207–26; Ann R. Larsen, "Louise Labé's *Debat de Folie et d'Amour,*" *Tulsa Studies in Women's Literature* 2 (1983), 43–55; Jacqueline Pearson, " 'Women may discourse . . . as well as men': Speaking and Silent Women in the Plays of Margaret Cavendish, Duchess of Newcastle," *Tulsa Studies in Women's Literature* 4 (1985), 33–45; Tilde Sankovitch, "Inventing Authority of Origin: The Difficult Enterprise," in *Women in the Middle Ages and the Renaissance,* 227–43; Merry E. Wiesner, "Women's Defense of Their Public Role," in *Women in the Middle,* 1–27.

6. That a real-life woman or a female character enters a convent need not, of course, be considered a defeat or an unsatisfactory choice for her. The positive elements of convent life for a woman include its provision of a community in which she can find support, be educated, and exercise her creative talents in artistic and literary ways not available to her in the outside world. Numerous studies consider the importance of this option for historical figures such as Sor Juana Inés de la Cruz, Madre Isabel de Jesús, and Sor Marcela de San Félix as well as female

characters in Golden Age drama and in the prose of María de Zayas y Sotomayor, whose narrator proclaims at the end of *Desengaños amorosos* that to enter the convent "no es trágico fin, sino el más felice que se pudo dar" [is not a tragic end, but rather the happiest that could come about] (*Desengaños amorosos: parte segunda del sarao y entretenimiento honesto*, ed. Agustín G. de Amezúa [Madrid: Biblioteca Selecta de Clásicos Españoles, 1950], 461). See for example: Electa Arenal, "The Convent as Catalyst for Autonomy: Two Hispanic Nuns of the Seventeenth Century," in *Women in Hispanic Literature: Icons and Fallen Idols*, ed. Beth Miller (Berkeley: University of California Press, 1983), 147–83; Electa Arenal and Stacey Schlau, *Untold Sisters: Hispanic Nuns in Their Own Works* (Albuquerque: University of New Mexico Press, 1989; Sandra M. Foa, *Feminismo y forma narrativa: Estudio del tema y las técnicas de María de Zayas y Sotomayor* (Valencia: Albatros, 1979), 89–90; Lucía Fox-Lockert, *Women Novelists in Spain and Spanish America* (Metuchen, N.J.: Scarecrow, 1979), 25; and Teresa S. Soufas, " 'Happy Ending' as Irresolution in Calderón's *No hay cosa como callar*," *Forum for Modern Language Studies* 26 (1988): 163–74.

7. See McKendrick, *Woman and Society*, 264, for a different interpretation.

8. See, for example: A. E. Sloman, "The Structure of Calderón's *La vida es sueño*," in *Critical Essays on the Theatre of Calderón*, ed. Bruce W. Wardropper (New York: New York University Press, 1965), 90–100, and William M. Whitby, "Rosaura's Role in the Structure of *La vida es sueño*," in *Critical Essays on the Theatre of Calderón*, 101–13.

9. See McKendrick's preface to *Woman and Society* in which she discusses the difficulty of translating the term *mujer varonil*, ix–xiii. Rejecting the expressions "masculine women" or "manly women" because they "have too strong a flavour of sexual deviation," she suggests that "by *mujer varonil* is meant . . . the woman who departs in any significant way from the feminine norm of the sixteenth and seventeenth centuries" (xi).

10. McKendrick, "Women Against Wedlock: The Reluctant Brides of Golden Age Drama," in *Women in Hispanic Literature*, 127.

11. McKendrick, *Woman and Society*, p. 330. For a different approach to such issues, see Mary Beth Rose, "Women in Men's Clothing: Apparel and Social Stability in *The Roaring Girl*," *English Literary Renaissance* 14 (1984): 367–91.

12. McKendrick, *Woman and Society*, 322.

13. Matthew D. Stroud, "La literatura y la mujer en el Barroco: *Valor, agravio y mujer* de Ana Caro," in *Actas del Octavo Congreso de la Asociación Internacional de Hispanistas 2*, ed. A. David Kossoff, José Amor y Vázquez, Ruth H. Kossoff, and Geoffrey W. Ribbans (Madrid: Ediciones Istmo, 1986), 605. Stroud's interpretive conclusions about *Valor, agravio y mujer* are different from my own.

14. Sandra M. Gilbert and Susan Gubar, *The Madwoman in the Attic: The Woman Writer and the Nineteenth-Century Literary Imagination* (New Haven: Yale University Press, 1980), 64. See also Sankovitch, "Inventing Authority of Origin," in *Women in the Middle Ages*, 227–29.

15. Virginia Woolf, *A Room of One's Own* (New York: Harcourt Brace, 1929), 77. See also Wiesner, "Women's Defense," in *Women in the Middle Ages*, 1–13; Hilda Smith, *Reason's Disciples: Seventeenth-Century English Feminists* (Urbana: University of Illinois Press, 1982), 7; and Nancy K. Miller, "Emphasis Added: Plots and Plausibilities in Women's Fiction," *PMLA*, 96 (1981), 36–48.

16. Elizabeth Ordóñez, "Woman and Her Text in The Works of María de Zayas and Ana Caro," *Revista de Estudios Hispánicos* 19 (1985): 9.

17. "Valor, agravio y mujer," in *Apuntes para una biblioteca de escritoras españolas,* ed. Manuel Serrano y Sanz (Madrid: Biblioteca de Autores Españoles, 1975), 194–195. All quotations from the play will be taken from this edition.

18. Leah S. Marcus, "Shakespeare's Comic Heroines, Elizabeth I, and the Political Uses of Adrogyny," in *Women in the Middle Ages,* 148.

19. The tercets of Catherine des Roches's poem (quoted and translated in full in Sankovitch, "Inventing Authority of Origin," in *Women in the Middle Ages and the Renaissance,* [239–40]) record the ambivalence over the dichotomous demands of traditional household activities like spinning and the woman's urge to write:

> Mais quenoille m'amie, il ne faut pas pourtant
> Que pour vous estimer, et pour vous aimer tant
> Je delaisse du tout cest'honneste coustume.
>
> D'escrire quelque fois; en escrivant ainsi
> J'escri de voz valeurs, quenoille mon souci,
> Aryant dedans la main le fuzeau et la plume.

(239–240)

> [But, spindle, my dearest, I do not believe
> That, much as I love you, I will come to grief
> If I do not quite let that good practice dwindle
>
> Of writing sometimes, if I give you fair share,
> If I write of your merit, my friend and my care,
> And hold in my hand both my pen and my spindle.]

20. Gilbert and Gubar, *Madwoman,* 49.

21. With regard to the crisis of authorship and questions of intertextuality, see also Harold Bloom, *The Anxiety of Influence* (New York: Oxford University Press, 1973), 11, 26; Terence Cave, *The Cornucopian Text. Problems of Writing in the French Renaissance* (Oxford: Clarendon, 1979), 325; Gilbert and Gubar, *Madwoman,* 51; and Sankovitch, "Inventing Authority of Origin," in *Women in the Middle Ages and the Renaissance,* 227–32.

22. Concerning the comic or foolish figure as an agent of the truth in Golden Age literature, see, for example: Anthony Close, "Sancho Panza: Wise Fool," *MLN,* 68 (1973), 344–57 and Teresa S. Soufas, "Carnival, Spectacle, and the *Gracioso*'s Theatrics of Dissent," forthcoming in *Revista Canadiense de Estudios Hispánicos.* See also Walter Kaiser's study of the fool's wisdom in a broader European context, *Praisers of Folly* (Cambridge: Harvard University Press, 1963) as well as Enid Welsford, *The Fool: His Social and Literary History* (London: Faber and Faber, 1968).

23. Lee R. Edwards, "The Labors of Psyche: Toward a Theory of Female Heroism," *Critical Inquiry* 6 (1979): 47.

24. His disapproval of Leonor's activites are frequently expressed in misogynistic terms, as evinced in the following passage:

> ¿Qué intenta Leonor, qué es esto?
> Mas es mujer; ¿qué no hará?
> Que la más compuesta tiene
> Mil pelos de Satanás.

(192)

[What does Leonor plan, what is this?
But she is a woman; what will she not do?
For the most composed woman
Is diabolical.]

25. McKendrick, *Woman and Society,* 145. As McKendrick likewise notes
(*Women and Society,* 74), Cervantes's sympathetic portrayal of Marcela in *Don
Quijote* (part 1, chapters 13–14) is a notable literary exception not matched in the
drama of his male colleagues.

26. See McKendrick for further discussion of these issues in Castro's play,
Women and Society, 96–98.

Works Cited

Arenal, Electa. "The Convent as Catalyst for Autonomy: Two Hispanic Nuns of
the Seventeenth Century." In *Women in Hispanic Literature: Icons and Fallen
Idols,* edited by Beth Miller, 147–83. Berkeley: University of California Press,
1983.

Arenal, Electa, and Stacey Schlau, *Untold Sisters: Hispanic Nuns in Their Own
Works.* Albuquerque: University of New Mexico, 1988.

Bloom, Harold. *The Anxiety of Influence.* New York: Oxford University Press,
1973.

Caro Mallén de Soto, Ana. "Valor, agravio y mujer." In *Apuntes para una
biblioteca de escritoras españolas,* edited by Manuel Serrano y Sanz, 179–212.
4 vols. Madrid: Biblioteca de autores españoles, 1975).

Cave, Terence. *The Cornucopian Text. Problems of Writing in the French Renaissance.* Oxford: Clarendon, 1979.

Close, Anthony. "Sancho Panza: Wise Fool" *MLN* 68 (1973): 344–57.

Diccionario de Autoridades. 3 vols. Madrid: Gredos, 1979.

de la Barrera y Leirado, Cayetano Alberto. *Catálogo bibliográfico del teatro
antiguo español desde sus orígenes hasta mediados del siglo xviii.* Madrid:
Gredos, 1969.

Edwards, Lee R. "The Labors of Psyche: Toward a Theory of Female Heroism,"
Critical Inquiry 6 (1979): 33–49.

Foa, Sandra M. *Feminismo y forma narrativa: Estudio del tema y las técnicas de
María de Zayas y Sotomayor.* Valencia: Albatros, 1979.

Fox-Lockert, Lucía. *Women Novelists in Spain and Spanish America.* Metuchen,
N.J.: Scarecrow, 1979.

Gilbert, Sandra, and Susan Gubar. *The Madwoman in the Attic: The Woman
Writer and the Nineteenth-Century Literary Imagination.* New Haven: Yale
University Press, 1980.

Jones, Ann Rosalind. "Surprising Fame: Renaissance Gender Ideologies and
Women's Lyric." In *The Poetics of Gender,* edited by Nancy K. Miller, 74–95.
New York: Columbia University Press, 1986.

Kaiser, Walter. *Praisers of Folly.* Cambridge: Harvard University Press, 1963.

Lamb, Mary Ellen. "The Countess of Pembroke and the Art of Dying." In *Women
in the Middle Ages and the Renaissance,* edited by Mary Beth Rose, 207–26.
Syracus, N.Y.: Syracuse University Press, 1986.

Larsen, Anne R. "Louise Labé's *Débat de Folie et d'Amour:* Feminism and the Defense of Learning." *Tulsa Studies in Women's Literature* 2 (1983): 43–55.

McKendrick, Melveena. "Women Against Wedlock: The Reluctant Brides of Golden Age Drama." In *Women in Hispanic Literature: Icons and Fallen Idols,* edited by Beth Miller, 115–46. Berkeley: University of California Press, 1983.

———. *Women and Society in the Spanish Drama of the Golden Age: A Study of the "Mujer varonil"*. Cambridge: Cambridge University Press, 1974.

Miller, Nancy K. "Emphasis Added: Plots and Plausibilities in Women's Fiction," *PMLA* 96 (1981): 36–48.

———, ed. *The Poetics of Gender.* New York: Columbia University Press.

Ordóñez, Elizabeth. "Woman and Her Text in The Works of María de Zayas and Ana Caro," *Revista de Estudios Hispánicos* 19 (1985): 3–15.

Pearson, Jacqueline. " 'Women may discourse . . . as well as men': Speaking and Silent Women in the Plays of Margaret Cavendish, Duchess of Newcastle." *Tulsa Studies in Women's Literature* 4 (1985): 33–45.

Rose, Mary Beth. "Women in Men's Clothing: Apparel and Social Stability in *The Roaring Girl,*" *English Literary Renaissance* 14 (1984): 367–91.

———, ed. *Women in the Middle Ages and the Renaissance: Literary and Historical Perspectives.* Syracuse, N.Y.: Syracuse University Press, 1986.

Sankovitch, Tilde. "Inventing Authority of Origin: The Difficult Enterprise." In *Women in the Middle Ages and the Renaissance,* edited by Mary Beth Rose. Syracuse, N.Y.: Syracuse University Press, 1986, 227–43.

Smith, Dawn. "Women and Men in a World-Turned-Upside-Down: An Approach to Three Plays by Tirso de Molina." In *Proceedings of the Fifth Annual Golden Age Spanish Drama Symposium,* edited by Jean S. Chrittenden, 56–66. El Paso: University of Texas at El Paso Press, 1985.

Smith, Hilde. *Reason's Disciples: Seventeenth-Century English Feminists.* Urbana: University of Illinois Press, 1982.

Soufas, Teresa S. "Carnival, Spectacle, and the *Gracioso*'s Theatrics of Dissent." *Revista Canadiense de Estudios Hispánicos,* forthcoming.

———. " 'Happy Ending' as Irresolution in Calderón's *No hay cosa como callar,*" *Forum for Modern Language Studies* 26 (1988): 163–74.

Stroud, Matthew D. "La literatura y la mujer en el Barrocco: *Valor, agravio y mujer* de Ana Caro." In *Actas del Octavo Congreso de la Asociación Internacional de Hispanistas 2,* edited by A. David Kossoff, José Amor y Vázquez, Ruth H. Kossoff, and Geoffrey W. Ribbans, 605–12. Madrid: Ediciones: Istmo, 1986.

Welsford, Enid. *The Fool: His Social and Literary History.* London: Faber and Faber, 1969.

Wiesner, Merry E. "Women's Defense of Their Public Role." In *Women in the Middle Ages and the Renaissance: Literary and Historical Perspectives,* edited by Mary Beth Rose. 1–27. Syracuse, N.Y.: Syracuse University Press, 1986.

Woolf, Virginia. *A Room of One's Own.* New York: Harcourt Brace, 1929.

Zayas y Sotomayor, María de. *Desengaños amorosos: parte segunda del sarao y entretenimiento honesto.* Edited by Agustín G. de Amezua. Madrid: Biblioteca de Clásicos Españoles, 1950.

Subversion through Comedy?: Two Plays by Sor Juana Inés de la Cruz and María de Zayas

CONSTANCE WILKINS

Among the many hundreds of plays written in Spanish during the seventeenth century, very few are by women writers. Two surviving texts, Sor Juana's *Los empeños de una casa* [The obligations of a house] and *Traición en la amistad* [Betrayal in friendship] by María de Zayas, make it possible to approach an understanding of the feminine from its own point of view and thus provide the opportunity to make visible something that is invisible in male-authored works. Although these two plays have not been widely studied, their richness admits a variety of approaches and interpretations. While each text stands alone, they share certain structures and intentions which are produced by a combination of historical and literary contexts plus the authors' personal situations and experiences. My approach to the plays begins with the assumption that literary works are governed by, or reveal, a male or female perspective depending on the gender of the author.[1] I intend to examine the possibility that these two authors, writing from a female perspective, used the comedic form both to subvert the literary standards of the genre and to call into question the social and political status quo. The status quo of their times is a hierarchical arrangement of society in which men are privileged over women.

Commenting on the world of Spain in the sixteenth and seventeenth centuries, Ruth El Saffar refers to the kinds of characters found in *Lazarillo de Tormes* and in *Don Quijote* who are "at odds with their contexts, isolated, abandoned and abandoning, outside the order of patriarchy, and homeless."[2] She sees in the drama of this period a literary reaction to these characters. El Saffar apparently is referring to male-authored plays, written for the tastes and values of the dominant society, which sustain the patriarchal structure. In these female-authored dramas, however, a sense of marginality also surfaces which in some ways is similar to the marginalization observed in *Lazarillo* and *Don Quijote*. Sor Juana and María de Zayas simultaneously are within their culture and, because of their sex, outside of it. As a result of this position, a critical stance toward the hierarchical society of the epoch is manifestly evident in the prose and poetic works by these two hispanic authors. Sor Juana's defense of intellectual activity by women, her reinterpretation of biblical passages that seemed to silence women, her sense of loss and isolation in not being able to communicate with other intellectuals, and her challenge to male standards in *Hombres necios* [Foolish men] are all well known. In recent years a number of studies have explored Zayas's feminist statements in her novels. Her observation in *La esclava de su amante* [The slave of her lover] that "ni comedia se representa, ni libro se imprime que no sea todo en ofensa de las mujeres" [no play is performed, nor book printed that is not completely against women] provides a clear example of her position on oppression of women.[3] A subversive or critical intention in their *comedias* then should not be unexpected. The Zayas play in particular contains a great deal of social criticism, most of it in some way related to female-male relationships. Although it is neither possible nor desirable to separate the authors' political and aesthetic aims, some sections of my study may tend to emphasize one aspect or the other.

Some critics see these plays totally within the seventeenth-century dramatic tradition of amorous intrigue and love triangles. Matthew Stroud examines the ways that female and male characters deal with the problems of love in Zayas's play and relates this work to her novels. Although Stroud makes sound observations about the play, his article privileges the male characters and inadvertently expresses many culturally embedded negative judgments of women. For example, he describes the women as reacting with: "shock and horror *rather than rise to the challenge as men do*." Stroud's acknowledgment of the active role of the women in the play is put in predominantly negative terms such as "they are *not* helpless," "Liseo is *caught* by means of a *deceptive trick*," the women "*coerce* from him a signed pledge," and "use *tricks* as a *defensive* mechanism."[4] He also finds the ending unsatisfactory because of what he calls the weak moral of the final scene. In an article comparing Sor Juana's play with Calderón's similarly titled comedy *Los empeños de un acaso* [The obligations of an accident], James Castañeda comments on the difference in focus of the two works. For Castañeda, the accidents of Calderón's title serve solely as "adequate pretexts in order to set up another illustration of the

Calderonian formula of honor."[5] In contrast, he criticizes Sor Juana for parodying the serious treatment of an important theme by means of a change in focus and tone, with a resultant substitution of playful intrigue instead of what he considers a more weighty theme in Calderón's play.

It is not surprising that when Sor Juana and María de Zayas decided to write dramas, they chose a comedic rather than tragic form and that superficially the works appear to be contained in the usual theatrical mold. The difficulty for a seventeenth-century woman in writing plays at all is staggering when one considers the nature of the genre. Walter Ong observes the seeming paradox that drama, although intended for oral presentation, is a genre completely integrated into a written culture.[6] As such, in Spain and Mexico playwriting affirmed the patriarchal order to an extent not superseded by any other contemporary or prior genre. In addition, the fact that plays are the most public form of literature makes them especially subject to influence by internal or external censorship. Susan Lanser points out that "the sanctions against women's writing have taken the form not of prohibitions to write at all but of prohibitions to write for a public audience."[7] One way the split between the public or male world and the private or female world is imaged in these plays by being within the house or outside the house. Sor Juana situates nearly all the action of her play indoors and emphasizes this by changing the last words of Calderón's title *un acaso* [an accident] to *una casa* [a house], a one-letter switch from masculine to feminine. In Zayas's play, women are seen primarily within the house except for Fenisa, who breaks into the male world in many ways. In contrast to many male-authored plays that focus on matters of honor and on swordplay, Leonor in Sor Juana's play says she will not talk about the usual details of courtship such as "duels and dangers." Jonathon Dollimore points out that the two basic characteristics of masculine honor are sexual prowess and violence, which, as he observes: "are inextricably related, as indicated for example by the conventional but still revealingly obsessive association of sword and phallus . . ."[8] Leonor specifically rejects this, preferring to focus on matters of character and values, her own and those of her lover. Both plays contain very clear value statements. Sor Juana's major theme deals with the nature of love and Zayas's with the importance of women's friendship, which she considers more valuable than sexual desire.

The problem, or lesson, in these plays deals in one case with women's role in society, the valuing of that role, and the woman's right to choose her own love object and, in the other case, with

relationships between women and the disruption caused by their
love interests. Each play offers a different model from that current
in their day: they bring to the foreground the concerns of women
and feature the female characters as they control the dramatic
process and, in doing so, win out in some way. Linda Bamber, in
*Comic Women, Tragic Men, A Study of Gender and Genre in
Shakespeare,* says that Shakespearean comedy is a decentralized
form.[9] Zayas's and Sor Juana's choice of this form and the use of
multiple protagonists or shared protagonist roles leads to a sense of
fluidity between characters reminiscent of Luce Irigaray's images of
women as multiple, decentered, and undefinable.[10] Mary Jacobus
views plurality as a contrast "to the unified 'I' which falls as a
dominating phallic shadow across the male page."[11] María de Zayas
centers what is usually marginal by giving all the important roles to
women. Marcia begins the play speaking to her friend Fenisa about
Liseo with whom she has just fallen in love. Marcia has the more
prominent role, but she and Fenisa control most of the action.
Marcia's motives are born from her relationship to women in general. She immediately gives up her interest in Liseo when she
discovers how he deceived Laura. The emphasis here is on Marcia's
compassion for Laura, not on her anger at Liseo. Marcia consistently acts in groups, avoiding the phallic "I"; she even takes on the
identity of another woman, as does Laura. Although the faulty text
causes some confusion about who is speaking, the fluidity between
characters seems deliberate. Another character, Belisa, does things
that we expected Marcia or Laura to do. The women are passionate
in love, verbally and physically expressive, while the men lack
much interest at all, being simply adequate to their function in the
play, acceptable as sex objects, love objects, or marriage objects.
Even Liseo, who is loved by three women, is not an admirable
figure and does not control anything in the play. His meeting with
Marcia is an accident; Fenisa pursues him and arranges their meetings; and he is tricked by Marcia, Belisa, and Laura and openly
criticized by the *gracioso,* or fool.

Sor Juana blurs the focus by using two ambisexual couples in
opposition to each other. Leonor and Carlos support the importance of human relations and stress the unitive nature of love, while
the brother-sister team of Ana and Pedro are motivated by their
own selfish interests. Control over the action of the play is multiple
also, passing from Ana in the first act, to the maid Celia in the
second, and finally to the *gracioso,* Castaño, who, disguised as
Leonor, determines Pedro's actions in act 3. Nonetheless, because
of their unswerving devotion, Leonor and Carlos ultimately deter-

mine the outcome and may represent a utopian dream of female-male integration. Ana and Pedro try to be subjects with Leonor and Carlos as objects. But the intended objects rebel, refusing to conform to the usual standards and expectations demanded by the male honor code. The multiple nature of the protagonist in both works expresses an alternative construction of literature and of reality which is not "I" centered. It is a structure of discourse which mirrors the message—love is unity or betrayal in friendship. The knowledge of the usual structure of the seventeenth century drama makes it possible to see a difference here and to draw from that difference an implicit critique of the dominant culture.

Both authors also deal to some extent with the nature of human desire and the cultural construction of gender in their times. In Sor Juana's play, Leonor openly rebels against her father, leaving his house with her chosen lover and later deciding that she will go to the convent rather than marry another man. Leonor refuses to be silent about her deeds, explaining to Ana:

> Señora, aunque la vergüenza
> me pudiera ser mordaza
> para callar mis sucesos,
> la que como yo se halla
> en tan infeliz estado,
> no tiene por qué callarlos."[12]

> [My Lady, although shame
> could be a gag
> to silence me about my deeds,
> one who finds herself as I do
> in such an unhappy state
> has no reason to keep them silent.]

She locates the main cause of her problem in her intelligence and expresses resentment at being placed on a pedestal to be worshipped. The intellectual work she has done is not valued but instead looked upon as a divine gift.[13]

In Zayas's play, Fenisa's expression of her sexuality approaches or enters male terrain and does not conform to the approved concept of women in her time. She delights in having the attention of many men at once and insists that she loves them all. With her unrestrained sexuality Fenisa represents a threat to difference and maintenance of hierarchy, thus provoking turmoil in her world. Both plays reveal the tendency of men to either idealize or degrade women. Liseo's devotion to Marcia contrasts with his condemnation and rejection of Laura and Fenisa. In *Los empeños,* Leonor complains of being idealized and worshipped, but a short time later her father violently condemns her and calls her a hypocrite. He then expands his comments into a diatribe against all women who, wise or ignorant, cannot be trusted and act with equally wild abandon.

Dramatic closure is achieved in both plays through conventional means. The marriages reflect the usual heterosexual model of human desire, regulate sexuality, and restore order at the end of the plays. Nevertheless, the works contain intriguing suggestions of either androgyny or same-sex attraction between both men and women. In the second act of *Traición,* both Marcia and Belisa are impressed by Laura's beauty. Marcia says to her: "Descubríos, que los ojos / me tienen enamorada. . . . Hermosa sois" [Take off your hood, for the sight of you / has enamored me . . . You are beautiful.] Belisa also comments: "No hay más bien / que ver cuando viendo estoy / tal belleza; el cielo os dé / la ventura cual la cara; / si hombre fuera, yo empleara / en vuestra afición mi fe."[14] [There is nothing better/ than seeing when I am seeing/ such beauty; may heaven give you/ fortune befitting your face; / if I were a man, I would use/ my efforts on your behalf.] In Sor Juana's play, the only case of mistaken identity which changes the course of events is when Pedro accepts as Leonor the fool dressed in Leonor's clothes. The fool in drag preens before the audience, commenting on his appearance and charms, and makes fun of young men who love not beauty but what they think beauty is. The boundary between female and male identity is most blurred, however, when Leonor describes Carlos in her first-act monologue. The description brings to mind Irigaray's words commenting on woman and her language: "Contradictory words seem a little crazy to the logic of reason, and inaudible for him who listens with ready-made grids, a code prepared in advance."[15] Leonor is attracted by some mysterious or incomprehensible quality in Carlos. She describes him in these words:

> Era su rostro un enigma
> compuesto de dos contrarios
> que eran valor y hermosura,
> tan felizmente hermanados,
> que faltándole a lo hermoso
> la parte de afeminado,
> hallaba lo más perfecto
> en lo que estaba más falto.

(1. 404–14)

[His face was an enigma
composed of two opposites
which were valor and beauty,
so happily joined,
that, while effeminacy was lacking in his beauty,
the greatest perfection was found
in what was most lacking.]

Leonor's words can be understood as an expression of androgyny which for Carolyn Heilbrun is an "unbounded and hence fundamentally undefinable nature."[16] or as Jacobus interprets Woolf's remarks on androgyny: "a harmonising gesture, a simultaneous enactment of desire and repression by which the split is closed with an essentially Utopian vision of undivided consciousness."[17] In both plays, voices are heard questioning dominant notions of gender difference.

As indicated, these two authors provide a difference of view in many ways. It seems natural that a woman writer would attribute the privileges of the subject to the female characters. But how does changing the role of women from spectators and objects to the position of actors and subjects affect reader/spectator identification with the characters and the interpretation of the authors' purposes? In the case of comedies, it is often tempting to have more interest in those who disrupt an orderly situation and therefore make the action occur. Nevertheless, the forces that re-establish order win explicit approval from the authors as certain characters are rewarded while others are punished. The topic of identification is also related to the question of the target audience. In both plays, servants turn and direct themselves to *señoras* in the audience. If Zayas and Sor Juana were writing for women, or were perceived to be writing for a female audience, their plays would be more acceptable within the partriarchal order, as then they would form part of a private rather than public world. In any case, if the plays were looked on as less than serious drama (for example, Castañeda's negative idea of parody or Stroud's reference to amorous triangles), they would have been acceptable for any audience, not simply a female one. Yet another possibility exists—that these authors may have included other meanings beneath the *fermosa cobertura* [attractive exterior].

In *Los empeños de una casa,* the author clearly wants the audience to identify with the pair Leonor/Carlos. It is Leonor who both causes disruption and, with Carlos, brings about resolution. She disturbs the established order by her resistance to her father's

control and her rejection of Pedro's attempts to manipulate her. The
idea of sharing or mutuality between Leonor and Carlos is so
omnipresent that their marriage cannot be viewed as a simple
validation of *his* love and a return to the status quo of male decision
making. A clear opposition between Leonor and Ana facilitates
identification with Leonor. Since they are both women, Leonor
looks to Ana as a natural ally and because of this, Ana is able to
conceal her true motives from Leonor. Although Leonor believes
that Ana is helping her, the audience always is aware that Ana is
deceiving everyone (that is, Leonor, Pedro, Carlos and Juan). Ana
may attract interest at first because she begins the play and seems
to dominate the action in act 1. Actually, in terms of proportion of
dialogue, even in this act Leonor has nearly seventy more lines than
Ana. If Ana were to win out, it would have the effect of supporting
male hegemony, just as would Leonor's acquiescence in her father's
plan for her marriage to Pedro. Of course, order is restored by the
end of the play, but only the Leonor/Carlos marriage is satisfactory.
Ana must settle for marriage to Juan, pretending that this is what
she wanted all along. Juan has to overlook Ana's rejection of him in
favor of another man and he must ignore his own angry plan to rape
her as an act of vengeance. Leonor is successful in challenging the
usual sources of power and, by achieving her desired outcome, she
has a voice in shaping her world.

In contrast, the question of identification and author's purpose in
Traición en la amistad is ambiguous for several reasons. First, there
is no clear opposition between the two main characters, Marcia and
Fenisa. Fenisa causes social instability because she refuses to follow the prescribed role for women in patriarchy. She zestfully
engages in adventures with every man in the play and views her
sexuality as natural and desirable. In a twist on a well-known line
from the *Burlador* [*The Trickster*] which also occurs in its original
form several times in this play, Fenisa proclaims: "Mal haya la que
sólo un hombre quiere" [Woe to the woman who loves only one
man] (605). It is tempting to identify with Fenisa in the validity of
her bursting the constraints on women's freedom of sexual expression. Such identification is hampered, though, because self-
expression brings with it betrayal of her women friends. Identification with Marcia is also problematic if we only observe her relations with men. Marcia is very similar to Fenisa in that she also
readily switches lovers at the beginning of the play, saying that she
had responded to Liseo "más de lo justo" [more than was right]
(590). She is headstrong and willful; referring to her independence,
she asserts: "No digas, / que á nadie estoy obligada / sino a mi

gusto" [Don't say / that I am obliged to anyone / except to my own pleasure.] (591). The real distinction between the two women is that they choose different courses of action regarding their friends. Marcia's decision to stop her relationship with Liseo is based not on a belief that it is wrong, but rather on her desire to help the woman whom Liseo had used and then rejected.

Another reason for ambivalence in identifying with one or the other of these women is found in the conclusion of the play. Although all the right couples are formed, none of the relationships is satisfactory. Whereas order is restored for idealistic reasons in *Los empeños de una casa*, pragmatism rules in the Zayas play. Fenisa is apparently punished by not being paired off with any of the men, but, one after another, the women in the play make it clear in very strong language and actions that Fenisa's real punishment is rejection by the women. She is cast out of the circle of friendship because of her disloyalty to them, not for deceiving the men. As the title makes clear, her isolation results from her betrayal of female friendship. The women's actions in support of each other and in condemnation of Fenisa constitute a forceful affirmation of female community. On the other hand, Fenisa is not totally condemned for her dealings with the men, as would normally happen in a male-authored *comedia*. The fool's final words inviting the men in the audience to contact Fenisa seem on one level a condemnation of her loose ways. But since her sexuality is not the focus of the women's words, it is alluring to fill in the silence about the end of Fenisa's story and to see her continuing in her free-flowing sexuality, uncontrolled by cultural or societal constraints. She is left without a husband, but she never wanted to settle for just one anyway. León's joking invitation may imply a continuation of Fenisa's endless desire that will keep her in motion and continue to disturb society.[18]

Condemnation of societal norms and values is a probable purpose in both of these works. The portrayal of the extremes of the hierarchy—the father and the fool—reveal additional suggestions of a critical stance. The mysogynist statements of Leonor's father epitomize society's views against which she struggles. Leonor specifically complains about her father's lack of attention to her; a servant suggests that the father is responsible for the problems; and, at the end, the father and the father's choice of a husband for her are both made to look ridiculous. Perhaps Leonor's choice of a foreigner for a mate also suggests rejection of the father's world. While Sor Juana's play provides a clear example of a flawed patriarch, there is no father present and only a single mention of one in *Traición,* when Marcia comments that she will take advantage of her father's absence to pursue her love for Liseo. The women in this play make all their decisions. At the other end of the spectrum from the fathers, the two fools are the most prominent males in terms of number of lines as well as in comedic function. *Graciosos,* like their *picaro* cousins, are often characters without a place in the structure of society. This seems particularly true in these plays, as León identifies himself as the bastard son of a priest, and Castaño in *Los empeños* attracts attention for his transvestism. Castaño's cross-dressing provides the opportunity for the funniest lines and visual effects of the play, all of which make fun of men in general and of Pedro in particular. León provides what Bamber refers to as an "example of love reduced to its lowest common denominator, without any sentiment at all."[19] León's jokes are really critical of male behavior. Moreover, Liseo's association with him, especially as an audience for his crude sexual stories, reflects and reinforces the negative impression we form of Liseo. Humor serves to undermine the male world and its values. As in the case of León, it is also possible to consider Fenisa an example of a subculture, a marginalized woman, who imitates the dominant culture from below, revealing that the original source and full extent of corruption is within the dominant itself. While it is true that love is the positive theme of Sor Juana's play, she may also be imitating Calderón's treatment of honor precisely to show its defects. Throughout the play, Ana uses the rules of the conventional code of honor to deceive and manipulate others. She adopts her brother's plan for her own purposes. Only the actions and ideals of Leonor and Carlos are not governed by the dominant standards of honor, showing that the source of true dishonor lies in those very standards which make possible a willing sacrifice of home, family, and friendship.

The worlds of the drama created by Sor Juana and María de Zayas are not the same as the dramatic worlds created by their male contemporaries. In their references to intellectual pursuits of women, female friendships, sexual expression by both sexes, and rejection of the restrictive forces of the honor code and of public opinion, these women interrogate the dominant notions of gender difference and of societal standards for behavior. Structural and thematic aspects such as location of action, choice of theme, foregrounding of women characters and their concerns, use of a diffuse focus, and direct address to women in the audience suggest a reformation of current practices of the genre and creation of alternate literary standards. Virginia Woolf's meditations on George

Eliot can be as aptly applied to María de Zayas, to Sor Juana, and perhaps to most writing women, when she comments that "the burden and the complexity of womanhood was not enough; she must reach beyond the sanctuary and pluck for herself the strange bright fruits of art and knowledge. Clasping them as few women have ever clasped them, she would not renounce her own inheritance—the difference of view, the difference of standard . . . ."[20]

Appendix: Relationship Charts

Los empeños de una casa

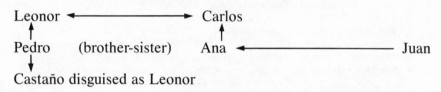

Leonor ⬌ Carlos

Pedro   (brother-sister)   Ana ⬌ Juan

Castaño disguised as Leonor

Traición en la amistad

Marcia ⬌ Gerardo

Liseo ———— Fenisa ———— Juan

Laura   Lauro   Belisa

Notes

1. In "The Spanish Priest and the Mexican Nun: Two Views of Love and Honor" *Calderón de la Barca at the Tercentenary: Comparative Views* (Lubbock: Texas Tech Press, 1982) Patricia Kenworthy examines Sor Juana's play in comparison with three works by Calderón. She indicates a number of points of contrast between the plays of Calderón and Sor Juana and achieves a very valid insight into the Mexican playwright's treatment of love. Nonetheless, Kenworthy is reluctant to conclude that the differences she observes are the result of one play being written by a man and the other by a woman. In previous papers presented at the Asociación Internacional de Hispanistas in Berlin, 1986 and at the Golden Age Drama Symposium in El Paso, 1987, I used psychological studies that observe and compare female and male development to support the idea that *Los empeños de una casa* provides evidence of a particularly female way of thinking about relationships. Most useful was Carol Gilligan's book *In a Different Voice* (Cambridge: Harvard University Press, 1982), in which she reports her research on the way females and males speak about moral problems and how they describe relationships. She concludes that different ways of thinking about relationships can be

associated with male and female voices. Gilligan finds that the female voices reveal sensitivity to the needs of others, assumption of responsibility for taking care, reluctance to judge others, and an overriding concern with relationships and responsibilities. She also reports that morality is inseparable from concern with caring and maintaining relationships. In contrast, the male voices affirm the primacy of the individual, along with the necessary concomitant of autonomy, separation, and natural rights.

2. Ruth El Saffar, "Way Stations in the Errancy of the Word: A Study of Calderón's *La vida es sueño.*" *Renaissance Drama* 17 (1986): 85.

3. María de Zayas, *Novelas ejemplares y amorosas,* primera y segunda parte (Paris: Baudry, 1847), 186. All translations are mine.

4. Matthew D. Stroud, "Love, Friendship, and Deceit in *La traición en la amistad,* by María de Zayas," *Neophilologus* 69 (1985): 541; italics added.

5. James Castañeda, "*Los empeños de un acaso* y *Los empeños de una casa:* Calderón y Sor Juana—la diferencia de un fonema," *Revista de Estudios Hispánicos* 1 (1967): 113.

6. Walter Ong, "Media Transformation: The Talked Book," in *Interfaces of the Word* (Ithaca and London: Cornell University Press, 1977).

7. "Toward a Feminist Narratology," *Style* 3 (1986): 352.

8. Jonathan Dollimore, "Subjectivity, Sexuality and Transgression: The Jacobean Connection," *Renaissance Drama.* 17 (1986): 74.

9. Linda Bamber, *Comic Women, Tragic Men, A Study of Gender and Genre in Shakespeare* (Stanford, Calif.: Stanford University Press, 1986).

10. Luce Irigaray, "This sex which is not one," in *New French Feminisms,* trans. Claudia Reeder, ed. Elaine Marks and Isabelle de Courtivron (Amherst: University of Massachusetts Press, 1980), 99–106.

11. Mary Jacobus, "The Difference of View," in *Women Writing and Writing About Women,* ed. Mary Jacobus (London: Crown Helm; Totowa, N.J.: Barnes & Noble, 1979), 19.

12. Juana Inés de la Cruz, *Obras completas 4 Comedias, sainetes y prosa* (México: Fondo de Cultura Económica, 1957), 35 (1.243–48). Subsequent references are to act and line.

13. This part of the speech in which Leonor describes her devotion to intellectual activities is frequently quoted in order to suggest an autobiographical element in the play. See, for example, the following studies: José Juan Arrom, "Cambiantes imágenes de la mujer en el teatro de la América virreinal," *Latin American Theatre Review* 12, no. 1 (1978): 9–11; James A. Castañeda, "*Los empeños de un acaso* y *Los empeños de una casa:* Calderón y Sor Juana—la diferencia de un fonema," *Revista de Estudios Hispánicos.* 1 (1967): 115; Ezequiel A. Chávez, *Sor Juana Inés de la Cruz: su vida y su obra* (Barcelona: Araluce, 1931): 165–71; Lee Alton Daniel, "A 'Terra Incognita': Sor Juana's Theatre" (Unpubl. Diss. Texas Tech University, Lubbock, 1979), 90–91; Frank Dauster, "De los recursos cómicos en el teatro de Sor Juana," *Caribe* 2, no. 2 (1977): 51; Julio Jiménez Rueda, *Estampas de los Siglos de Oro* (México, 1957), 140; and Enrique Laguerre, "Las comedias de Sor Juana," *Anales de literatura hispanoamericana* 6, no.7 (1978): 185. In addition, Margaret Sayers Peden analyzes autobiographical traits in "*Amor es más laberinto:* Sor Juana Inés de la Cruz: The Fourth Labyrinth," *Bulletin of the Comediantes* 27, no. 1 (1975): 44–47.

14. María de Zayas, *La traición en la amistad,* in Serrano y Sanz, Manuel (*Apuntes para una biblioteca de escritoras españolas,* vol. 2, 2d pt. Madrid:

Sucesores de Rivadeneyra. Reprint in *Biblioteca de autores españoles* 1903), 599. Subsequent references are to page numbers.

15. Irigaray, "This sex which is not one," 101.
16. Carolyn Heilbrun, *Toward a Recognition of Androgyny* (New York: Alfred A. Knopf, 1973), xi.
17. Jacobus, "The Difference of View," 20.
18. I would like to express my appreciation to Professor Dale M. Bauer, department of English, Miami University, for sharing with me the typescript of her work in progress titled "A Theory of Identificatory Reading."
19. Bamber, *Comic Women,* 39.
20. Virginia Woolf, *Collected Essays,* vol. 1. (first American ed.) (New York: Harcourt, Brace & World, 1966), 204.

Works Cited

Arrom, José Juan. "Cambiantes imágenes de la mujer en el teatro de la América virreinal." *Latin American Theater Review* 12, no. 1 (1978): 5–15.

Bamber, Linda. *Comic Women, Tragic Men A Study of Gender and Genre in Shakespeare.* Stanford, Calif.: Stanford University Press, 1982.

Castañeda, James A. "*Los empeños de un acaso* y *Los empeños de una casa:* Calderón y Sor Juana—la diferencia de un fonema." *Revista de Estudios Hispánicos* 1 (1967): 107–16.

Chávez, Ezequiel A. *Sor Juana Inés de la Cruz: su vida y su obra.* Barcelona: Araluce, 1931.

Daniel, Lee Alton. "A 'Terra Incognita': Sor Juana's Theatre." Unpubl. Diss. Texas Tech University, Lubbock, 1979.

Dauster, Frank. "De los recursos cómicos en el teatro de Sor Juana." *Caribe* 2, no. 2 (1977): 41–54.

Dollimore, Jonathan. "Subjectivity, Sexuality and Transgression: The Jacobean Connection." *Renaissance Drama* 17 (1986): 53–81.

El Saffar, Ruth. "Way Stations in the Errancy of the Word: A Study of Calderón's *La vida es sueño.*" *Renaissance Drama* 17 (1986): 83–100.

Gilligan, Carol. *In a Different Voice.* Cambridge, Mass. and London: Harvard University Press, 1982.

Heilbrun, Carolyn G. *Toward a Recognition of Androgyny.* New York: Alfred A. Knopf, 1973.

Irigaray, Luce. "This sex which is not one." Translated by Claudia Reeder. In *New French Feminisms,* edited by Elaine Marks and Isabelle de Courtivron, 99–106. Amherst: University of Massachusetts Press, 1980.

Jacobus, Mary. "The Difference of View." In *Women Writing and Writing About Women,* edited by Mary Jacobus, 10–21. London: Crown Helm; Totowa, N.J.: Barnes & Noble, 1979.

Jiménez Rueda, Julio. *Estampas de los Siglos de Oro.* México, 1957.

Juana Inés de la Cruz. *Obras completas, IV: Comedias, sainetes y prosa.* Edited by Alberto G. Salceda. Mexico and Buenos Aires: Fondo de Cultura Económica, 1957.

Kenworthy, Patricia. "The Spanish Priest and the Mexican Nun: Two Views of

Love and Honor." In *Calderón de la Barca at the Tercentenary: Comparative Views*, edited by Wendell N. Aycock and Sydney P. Cravens, 103–17. Lubbock: Texas Tech University Press, 1982.

Laguerre, Enrique. "Las comedias de Sor Juana." *Anales de literatura hispanoamericana* 6, no. 7 (1978): 183–90.

Lanser, Susan S. "Toward a Feminist Narratology." *Style* 3 (1986): 341–63.

Peden, Margaret Sayers. "Sor Juana Inés de la Cruz: The Fourth Labyrinth." *Bulletin of the Comediantes* 27, no. 1 (1975): 41–48.

Stroud, Matthew. "Love, Friendship, and Deceit in *La traición en la amistad*, by María de Zayas." *Neophilologus* 69 (1985): 539–47.

Woolf, Virginia. *Collected Essays*. Vol. 1. (First American ed.) New York: Harcourt, Brace & World, 1967.

Zayas, María de. *Novelas ejemplares y amorosas,* primera y segunda parte. Paris: Baudry, 1847.

———. *La traición en la amistad*. In Manuel Serrano y Sanz, *Apuntes para una biblioteca de escritoras españolas*. Vol. 2, 2d pt. Madrid: Sucesores de Rivadeneyra, 1903. Rpt. *Bibilioteca de Autores Españoles* 271: 590–620.

Profeminist Reactions to Huarte's Misogyny in Lope de Vega's *La prueba de los ingenios* and María de Zayas's *Novelas amorosas y ejemplares*

DANIEL HEIPLE

Although traditional critical opinion viewed Lope de Vega and María de Zayas as strong proponents of feminism,[1] several critics recently have called into doubt the feminist positions of the two authors, mainly by placing emphasis on those passages in which the female character is integrated into society through marriage and accepts a secondary position at the side of the more important male.[2] Even Díez Borque, who finds María de Zayas to have stated a strong and original case for feminism,[3] considers Lope to be a sexist writer.[4] While it is obvious these two writers do not fit the pattern of twentieth-century feminist thought, they do show, when studied within the context of the feminist debate in sixteenth- and seventeenth-century Spain, undeniable profeminist stances. They both clearly maintain that women are not per se inferior to men, and María de Zayas even maintains that with proper education, women would be superior. While neither writer holds views about woman's place in society that coincides with modern feminist ideas, both, in attacking Huarte de San Juan's misogynist postulates, definitely reject the concept of an inherent inferiority of women and argue specifically that there exists an intellectual equality between women and men, an argument that, because of its technical nature, leaves no room for doubt where they stood in the feminist debate.

Juan Huarte de San Juan's very popular *Examen de ingenios* [Test of wits] produced a devastating attack on the intellectual capacities of women. Using a brilliant style whose clarity of exposition must have sufficed for many as convincing proof of his thesis, he attempted to establish as fact the intellectual inferiority of women based on humoral, that is, in modern terms, biological and

121

chemical, observations. A convinced biological determinist, he proposed to demonstrate that the individual's unique mental aptitudes and capacities are chemically based in the humoral composition of the body. For Huarte, all human characteristics—including sex, physique, personality traits, and mental abilities—were part and parcel of the same chemical imbalance of the bodily humors. His main purpose in writing the book was to propose that for the general public good, mental aptitude tests be given to insure that each male citizen find a career suitable to his talents. He states in Proemio to the king that the government should establish

> examinadores para saber si el que quiere estudiar dialéctica, filosofía, medicina, teología o leyes tiene el ingenio que cada una de estas ciencias ha menester. Porque si no, fuera del daño que este tal hará después en la república usando su arte mal sabida, es lástima ver a un hombre trabajar y quebrarse la cabeza en cosa que es imposible salir con ella.[5] (19)

> [examiners to determine if he who wants to study dialectics, philosophy, medicine, theology or law has the genius that each one of these sciences needs. Because, if not, besides the harm that this person will do later in the republic using his poorly learned art, it is a shame to see a man struggle and break his head in a subject in which is impossible for him to be successful.]

The extremity of his biological determinism and the ambitious scope of his undertaking are seen in a hypothetical example intended to demonstrate the validity of his arguments that personality depends on the chemical composition of the body. He argues that confession and penitence have their greatest effect when they reform the imbalance of humors in the body. Passing quickly over the efficacy of moral advice, he gives an example of the effect of penitence on a lustful sinner:

> Tras esto le aconsejaría el ayuno, el rezar y meditar, el poco dormir, el acostarse en el suelo y vestido, la disciplina, el apartarse de mujeres y ocuparse en obras pías. . . . Con estos remedios, perseverando muchos días en ellos, se porná el hombre flaco y amarillo y tan diferente del que solía ser, que el que antes se perdía por mujeres y por comer y beber, ahora le da pena y dolor oíllo mentar. (86)

> [After this I would recommend to him fasting, prayer and meditation, little sleep, sleeping on the floor dressed, self flagellation, distancing himself from women and occupying himself in pious works. . . . With these remedies, persevering many days in them, the man will become

skinny and yellow and so different from that which he used to be that he
who before threw himself after women and eating and drinking, now is
pained and grieved to hear them mentioned.]

He explains the medical effects of each part of this penitence and
concludes that all virtue and vice are somatically determined:

> Todo esto que hemos dicho y probado de la lujuria y castidad, se ha de
> entender de las demás virtudes y vicios. Porque cada uno tiene su
> particular temperamento de calor y frialdad, ya en el modo de sustancia
> que cada miembro adquiere, ya por la intensión o remisión destas dos
> calidades. (90)

> [All this that we have said and proved about lust and chastity, must be
> understood about the other virtues and vices. Because each one has his
> particular temperament of heat and coldness, either in the manner of
> sustenance which each member acquires, or because of the intensifying
> or remission of these two qualities.]

Within the context of his blind conviction and closely-argued
biological determinism, he presents arguments for the innate inferiority of women. He maintains the biological differences between
man and woman also are based on humoral temperament, men
being naturally hot and dry and women naturally cold and humid.
He believes women and men differ only in that the sex organs are
internal in the female and external in the male. These differences
are so slight that a radical change of bodily humors could cause a
man or woman to change to the opposite sex. A rapid influx of heat
and dryness in a woman could make her organs descend and she
would become a man, and vice versa. Huarte cites a number of
cases in which such sex changes have taken place. He adduced as
further proof of these observations the hybrid and borderline cases
of the effeminate male and the masculine female which he maintained were produced by a combination of humors (370–71).

Although Huarte considered the physical differences between
women and men to be inconsequential, he judged the mental differences to be major indeed.[6] Using the traditional medical, rather
than theological, division of the mind into faculties, he claimed that
human mental ability or *ingenio* excelled in three categories: imagination, judgment, and memory. An excess of any one humor would
produce an exceptional ability in one of these areas. A superabun-
dance of heat (choler) would create a strong imagination capable of
producing poets, artists, inventors, and such, depending on the
degree of excess. An excess of dryness (melancholy) would create a

strong intelligence or judging faculty, making for good phi-
losophers, judges, and mayors, for example. An excess of coldness
created a strong memory, making good Latin students. A thinker of
the post-Gutenberg age, Huarte's low estimation of the memory is
strikingly modern. This last type of genius served for little, for the
real geniuses were those of strong imagination and reasoning
powers. The fourth quality of humidity (phlegm) did not create a
distinctive personality. Included in his system were possibilities of
combinations. As it is not possible for something to be hot and cold
at the same time, then it was impossible for a person with a good
imagination (hot) to have strong memory (cold), although a person
with reasoning power (dry) could have good memory (cold). The
well-tempered person will be strong in all three areas of wit (ingenio) but will not be outstanding in any one of them, for real
geniuses are caused by a distempered excess of one humor (137–
47). It is noteworthy that the separation of the creative temperament from that of the intellectual is unusual for the Renaissance,
and foreshadows the Romantic exaltation of artistic genius.

Within this carefully worked out scheme, Huarte concluded that
the humoral imbalances produced major differences of intelligence
between men and women: ". . . la compostura natural que la mujer
tiene en el celebro, no es capaz de mucho ingenio ni de mucha
sabiduría" [the natural composition which woman has in her brain
is not capable of much genius or of much wisdom] (25). Since males
were determined by an abundance of heat and dryness, they enjoyed the highest mental faculties of imagination and reason,
whereas, women because of their humidity could have only a strong
memory, which Huarte thought to be of little use anyway: ". . . nos
acordamos que la frialdad y humidad son las calidades que echan a
perder la parte racional, y sus contrarios, calor y sequedad, la
perfeccionan y aumentan . . ." [we remember that coldness and
humidity are the qualities that ruin the rational part, and their
contraries, heat and dryness, perfect and increase them] (374).
These differences were so linked with sex characteristics that there
could be no crossover, for a further excess or deficiency of humors
would result in a change of sex:

> Porque pensar que la mujer puede ser caliente y seca, ni tener el ingenio
> y habilidad que sigue a estas dos calidades, es muy grande error;
> porque si la simiente de que se formó fuera caliente y seca a pre-
> dominio, saliera varón y no hembra; y por ser fría y húmeda, nació
> hembra y no varón. (374)

[Because to think that woman can be hot and dry and have the genius and ability that come from these two qualities is a great error; because if the seed from which she was formed was predominantly hot and dry, a boy, and not a girl, would result; and because of the coldness and humidity, a girl was born and not a boy.]

Huarte states clearly that an intelligent woman with the highest degree of heat and dryness could never be as intelligent as the dumbest of men. He repeats several times that women are incapable of learning because of their cold and damp temperament:

> Pero quedando la mujer en su disposición natural, todo género de letras y sabiduría es repugnante a su ingenio. Por donde la Iglesia católica con gran razón tiene prohibido que ninguna mujer pueda predicar ni confesar ni enseñar; porque su sexo no admite prudencia ni disciplina. (375)

> Los padres que quisieren gozar de hijos sabios y que tengan habilidad para letras, han de procurar que nazcan varones; porque las hembras, por razón de la frialdad y humidad de su sexo, no pueden alcanzar ingenio profundo. Sólo vemos que hablan con alguna apariencia de habilidad en materias livianas y fáciles, con términos comunes y muy estudiados; pero metidas en letras, no pueden aprender más que un poco latín, y esto por ser obra de la memoria. De la cual rudeza no tienen ellas la culpa; sino que la frialdad y humidad que las hizo hembras, esas mesmas calidades hemos probado atrás que contradicen al ingenio y habilidad. (388)

[But when woman remains in her natural disposition, all types of learning and wisdom are repugnant to her genius. For which reason the Catholic Church rightfully prohibits any woman to preach and hear confession and teach, because her sex does not admit prudence or discipline.

Parents who wish to enjoy bright children who have abilities for learning have to assure that they are born boys, for girls, because of the coldness and humidity of their sex, cannot attain profound genius. We see that they speak only with some appearance of ability in frivolous and easy materials, with common and very studied words, but engaged in learning, they cannot learn more than a bit of Latin, and that because it is a function of the memory. They are not to be held to blame for this primitiveness, but for the coldness and humidity which made them girls, we have proved previously that these very qualities contradict genius and ability.]

This condemnation of the intellectual powers of woman is probably one of the most devastating attacks on women in Spanish Golden

Age letters. Quite distinct from other misogynist works whose impassioned discourse made evident the lack of rational foundations, this scientific treatise produces its misogyny as a byproduct of a carefully reasoned thesis, and makes its point with scientific-sounding arguments. Huarte's method must have seemed to many to have a rational basis in nature which would make it very difficult to counter and combat.

Reactions to Huarte's misogynist attacks are easy to identify, because they must deal with his so-called proofs of the natural inferiority of women.[7] Both rebuttals studied in this paper follow the same format. They maintain that women do possess humoral temperaments capable of producing mental abilities for learning and they conclude their arguments with a list of women who had been successful in war, government, and letters.[8]

Although Lope does not mention Huarte by name, the title of his play, *La prueba de los ingenios*, [The trial of wits], recalls both Huarte's title *Examen de ingenios* and his proposed aptitude tests. The play dramatizes the motif of the test of the suitor, but in this case, instead of a test of arms, Laura and Florela decide on a competition of letters to test the intelligence of the suitors. The tests consist of enigmas, a debate, and a labyrinth, and the third act of the play is in effect the test of the ability of man to measure up to the wit of woman. As often in Lope's plays, the theme of the play is reduplicated in a separate incident or dialogue. In this case, Florela announces the topic of the debate as:

> Sustento que las mujeres
> son aptas y son perfectas
> para el gobierno y las armas,
> lo mismo para las ciencias.[9]

(318)

> [I maintain that women
> are suited and are perfect
> for ruling and for arms,
> as well as for study.]

Using an old Aristotelian and scholastic argument, the suitors claim that woman is imperfect, created by a lack of effort on the part of nature, and therefore not capable of high enterprise.

> digo, famosa Diana,
> que es la mujer imperfecta
> criatura, y que jamás

quiso la naturaleza
producirla ni engendrarla;
. . . solamente aumentan
número al mundo, ¿quién duda
que no la dio para ciencias
aptitud ni habilidad . . . ?

(318b)

[I say, famous Diana,
that woman is an imperfect
creature, and nature
never intended
to produce her or engender her;
. . . they only serve to increase
the number in the world. Who could believe
that aptitute or ability
were given to her . . .?]

Florela wins the first round of the argument for the feminists by asserting that woman is the completion of God's plan for nature:

Mas en orden a la causa,
que a nuestra naturaleza
común es universal,
la mujer no es imperfecta
criatura, ni ocasionada,
mas perfectísima y bella.

(319b)

[But regarding the cause
which for our common
nature is universal,
woman is not an imperfect
creature, nor created by chance,
but is most perfect and beautiful.]

Another suitor, the Infante de Aragón, then takes up Huarte's argument that women are inherently inferior to man:

La mujer
es más que el hombre imperfecta;
el hombre más imperfecto
no es hábil para las ciencias;
luego menos la mujer.

(320a)

[Woman
is more imperfect than man;
the most imperfect of man
is not suited for studies;
therefore, even less so woman.]

Huarte's arguments of woman's inferiority to man seem to lie behind this discourse. Like Zayas, Lope's Florela counters by
maintaining that there must be equality because of the equality of
souls: ". . . y queda / probado con que las almas / son iguales" [and
it stands proved because souls are equal] (320a). The Infante reasserts his position by assuming a posture contrary to Huarte's central arguments. He maintains that the correspondence of body and
soul and balanced temperaments (rather than the excess of one or
two humors) produce excellence of intelligence:

> . . . hay almas cuyos cuerpos
> tienen partes más dispuestas,
> más igual temperamento;
> luego serán más perfectas.
> Que fuese el alma de Adán
> más noble que la de Eva,
> y perfecta, porque tuvo
> proporción, correspondencia
> e igualdad a más perfecto
> cuerpo, el gran Doctor lo enseña.

(320a)

> [. . . there are souls whose bodies
> have better disposed parts,
> more equal temperaments;
> there they will be more perfect.
> That the soul of Adam was
> more noble and more perfect
> than that of Eve, because it had
> proportion, correspondence
> and equality with a most perfect
> body, the great Doctor teaches.]

Another suitor concludes the promasculine case by asserting that
women do not have the temperament nor the ability for learning:

> luego la mujer que no tiene
> temperamento a las ciencias
> dispuesto, no puede ser
> que ella hábil sea para ellas.

(321)

[since woman does not have
a temperament disposed
for knowledge, it cannot be
that she has ability in it.]

Florela returns to Huarte's arguments that an excess of one or two
humors (rather than a balance of all humors) creates a superior
intelligence. Using Huarte's own presuppositions, she produces the
final destruction of his arguments concerning the intellectual inferiority of women. She argues that women do have the proper
temperament to possess great ability in learning.

> Sequedad, melancolía,
> acompañan la grandeza
> del ingenio, aunque Galeno
> estas partes diferencia:
> melancolía, con cólera
> y sangre pura, gobiernan
> los ingenios altamente;
> y estas dos vemos que reinan
> en millones de mujeres;
> pero Aristóteles cierra
> mi réplica, con decir
> que quien tiene carnes tiernas,
> y dulce la complexión,
> ése es natural que tenga
> ingenio más superior;
> pues siendo cierta sentencia,
> el temperamento tierno
> de las mujeres os muestra
> que las más hábiles son
> para las divinas ciencias.

                                                              (322a)

> [Dryness and melancholy
> accompany the greatness
> of genius, although Galen
> distinguishes these parts:
> melancholy with choler
> and pure blood produces
> the highest geniuses;
> and we see that these two reign
> in millions of women;
> but Aristotle closes
> my reply by saying
> that whoever has tender flesh

and sweet complexion,
it is natural that he have
a superior genius;
since it is a certain truth
the tender temperament
of the women shows you
that they are the most capable
for divine knowledge.]

The *gracioso* declares Florela winner and finishes her argument by citing a list of great women in letters and arms as proof of woman's innate ability of excellence in intelligence and learning. The references to classical authorities in Florela's arguments should not mislead concerning the sources of her ideas. The arguments have their bases in Huarte's biological determinism. The names of Galen and Aristotle are more authoritative for this type of debate; moreover, the usual method of authorial citation for Lope and other Renaissance writers is to take the names from the footnotes rather than the book at hand.[10] The direct references to Huarte's sources and the essence of the debate show Lope's dependence on Huarte in these arguments. The fact that the women debaters win their case would argue for Lope's dissatisfaction with Huarte's conclusions. The explicit refutation of Huarte's arguments gives us a standard by which to judge Lope's position on the feminist question.

María de Zaya's unflinching feminist stance meets Huarte's arguments head on. In the preface to her *Novelas amorosas y ejemplares* [Amorous and exemplary novels] she boldly denies the thesis that women are inferior. She first argues that because woman and man are made of the same material, there should be no difference in intellectual capacity:

porque si esta materia de que nos componemos los hombres y las mujeres, ya sea una trabazón de fuego y barro, o ya una masa de espíritus y terrones, no tiene más nobleza en ellos que en nosotras, si es una misma la sangre, los sentidos, las potencias y los órganos por donde se obran sus efectos son unos mismos, la misma alma que ellos, porque las almas ni son hombres ni mujeres; ¿qué razón hay para que ellos sean sabios y presuman que nosotras no podemos serlo?[11](21)

[because if this material of which we men and women are composed, either is an artifice of fire and mud, or is a mass of spirits and clods, it does not have greater nobility in them than it does in us, if our blood is the same, if our senses, ours powers and our organs through which things are produced are the same, if the soul is the same, for souls are neither man nor woman; what reason is there by which they should be intelligent and presume that we cannot be?]

As a second argument, she maintains that the apparent differences of intellect are due to education and training rather than an innate physical difference, a theme she develops throughout her works:[12]

> Esto no tiene a mi parecer más respuesta que su impiedad o tiranía en encerrarnos, y no darnos maestros; y así, la verdadera causa de no ser las mujeres doctas no es defecto del caudal, sino falta de la aplicación, porque si en nuestra crianza como nos ponen el cambray, en las almohadillas y los dibuxos en el bastidor, nos dieran libros y preceptores, fuéramos tan aptas para los puestos y para las cátedras como los hombres, y quizá más agudas. . . .(21–22)

> [This does not need in my opinion more reply than their impiety or tyranny in locking us up and not giving us teachers; and thus, the real cause of women not being learned is not a defect of potency, but the lack of application, because if in our childhood instead of putting fine linen on the pillows and drawings on the embroidery frame, they gave us books and tutors, we would be as suited for high positions and for professorships as men, and perhaps sharper. . . .]

Almost as an afterthought, she discusses temperament, rebutting Huarte's humoral demonstration of the inferiority of women. She does not deny that women are cold and humid by nature, but she contradicts Huarte's conclusion and argues that coldness can produce the greatest of intellects, saying women are

> más agudas por ser de natural más frío, por consistir en humedad el entendimiento, como se ve en las respuestas de repente y en los engaños de pensado, que todo lo que se hace con maña, aunque no sea virtud, es ingenio; y cuando no valga esta razón para nuestro crédito, valga la experiencia de las historias. . . .(22)

> [Sharper for having a colder nature, since understanding consists of humidity, as seen in impromptu rejoinders and in plotted deceptions, for all that which is done with trickery, even though it is not virtue, is genius; and when this reason is not to our credit; then let the experience of history prove. . . .]

As in Lope's play, these arguments are followed by a list of learned women, proving through a myriad of examples that women can excel in all fields of endeavor.

Even though succinctly stated, María de Zaya's arguments are

neither superficial nor easily dismissed. She meets Huarte's
pseudoscience head on and rebutts the weak point in his biological
determinism—namely the fact that he completely ignores the education and training of the individual. Her most important argument
deftly counters Huarte's convictions of biological determinism: she
alleges that women only seem inferior because of their education
and formation. As a biological determinist Huarte formulated his
central premise, that the differences between people are a result of
body chemistry, purposefully to exclude any possibility on the part
of individuals to form themselves contrary to the disposition of
their *ingenio*. Zayas maintains that upbringing and education are
the important components in the formation of the individual.

Huarte's misogyny attacked the intellectual abilities of women,
and the profeminist arguments of Lope and Zayas clearly address
and refute his position. The two writers, however, may not seem
liberal on other feminist issues, especially on the important questions of the social status of the female and domestic relations. In
these areas both writers, especially Lope, are more conventional,
although Zayas in her fiction consciously explores the disturbed
relations between women and men with the result that she seems
uncomfortable with domestic relations in her time. On the other
hand, the question addressed in their response to Huarte reveals a
strong defense of the intellectual powers of women, especially in
regard to their ability for greatness and learning. Zayas realizes
women's lack of equal social status lies with the established social
norms, such as the question of honor, the double standard for
sexual conduct, and the guarding of women from free social interchange. Lope is less ready to address these issues, but even so, is
eager to understand the complaint of women and to defend their
intellectual capacities. While neither writer comes to defend a full-
fledged feminist position, each is willing to defend the intellectual
equality of women. Within the context of the feminist debate in the
seventeenth century, both writers assume a profeminist stance on a
key issue. Huarte's cruel attack on women's inherent intellectual
powers allows us to define with more precision the actual position
of Golden Age writers.

Notes

1. For Lope: "Con razón ha escrito Vossler que Lope nunca fué misógino;
lejos de eso, toda su producción dramática y buena parte de su lírica y novelística
son como una constante defensa y exaltación de la mujer" [With reason Vossler

has written that Lope never was a misogynist; far from it, all his dramatic production and a good part of his lyric and novels are like a constant defense and exaltation of woman], Agustín G. de Amezúa y Mayo, *Lope de Vega en sus cartas: Introducción al epistolario de Lope de Vega Carpio,* vol. 2 (Madrid: Escelicer, 1940), 547–48. Matulka and Foa present more balanced evaluations: Barbara Matulka, "The Feminist Theme in the Drama of the Siglo de Oro," *Romanic Review* 26 (1935): 191–231; and Sandra M. Foa, *Femenismo y forma narrativa. Estudio del tema y las técnicas de María de Zaya y Sotomayor* (Valencia: Albatross, 1979), 40–54. For Zayas: ". . .había en doña María un sentimiento dominante que preside a sus libros, como verdadero origen y fautor de ellos: su arraigado e intrasigente feminismo," [there was in María a dominant sentiment that presides over her books, like a real cause and stimulus of them: her deeply rooted and intransigent feminism], Agustín G. de Amezúa y Mayo, "Doña María de Zayas: Notas Críticas," *Opúsculos histórico-literarios,* vol. 2 (Madrid: Consejo Superior de Investigaciones Científicas, 1951), 12. See also Lena E. V. Sylvania, *Doña María de Zayas y Sotomayor. A Contribution to the Study of her Works* (New York: Columbia University, 1922), 7–17, and Irma V. Vasileski, *María de Zayas y Sotomayor: Su época y su obra* (Madrid: Editorial Playor, 1973), 52–55.

2. Melveena McKendrick, "The 'mujer esquiva'—A Measure of the Feminist Sympathies of Seventeenth-Century Dramatists," *Hispanic Review* 40 (1972): 162–97; and Susan C. Griswold, "Topoi and Rhetorical Distance: The 'Feminism' of María de Zayas," *Revista de Estudios Hispánicos,* 14 (1980): 97–116.

3. José María Díez Borque, "El feminismo de Doña María de Zayas," in *La mujer en el teatro y la novela del siglo XVII.* Actas del IIº coloquio del grupo de estudios sobre teatro español, Toulouse, 16–17 Noviembre 1978 (Toulouse: Université de Toulouse-Le Mirail, 1979), 61–88.

4. Ibid., 67.

5. All quotations come from Juan Huarte de San Juan, *Examen de ingenios para las ciencias,* ed. Rodrigo Sanz (Madrid: Imprenta la Rafa, 1930).

6. Mauricio de Iriarte, (*El doctor Huarte de San Juan y su examen de ingenios* [Madrid: Consejo Superior de Investigaciones Científicas, 1948]), apologist for Huarte, agrees wholeheartedly with this point of view: "La inferioridad de la mujer para las obras del ingenio es indiscutible" [The inferiority of woman for works of genius is undeniable] (271).

7. Ian Maclean (*Woman Triumphant. Feminism in French Literature 1610–1652* [Oxford: Oxford University Press, 1977], 47–48) discusses the topic of humors among the French writers.

8. Simon Vosters has studied the lists of *damas doctas* in Lope's prologues: "Lope de Vega y las damas doctas," in *Actas del Tercer Congreso Internacional de Hispanistas* (México: El Colegio de México, 1970), 909–21.

9. All quotations come from Felix Lope de Vega Carpio, *Obras,* vol. 30, ed. Marcelino Menéndez Pelayo, Biblioteca de Autores Españoles, vol. 246 (Madrid: Ediciones Atlas, 1971).

10. Edwin S. Morby, "Levinus Lemnius and Leo Suabius in *La Dorotea,*" *Hispanic Review* 20 (1952): 108–22.

11. All quotations come from María de Zayas y Sotomayor, *Novelas amorosas y ejemplares,* ed. Agustín G. de Amezúa (Madrid: Real Academia Española, 1948).

12. Sandra M. Foa, "María de Zayas y Sotomayor: Sibyl of Madrid (1590?–1661?)," in J. R. Brink, ed., *Female Scholars: A Tradition of Learned Women Before 1800* (Montreal: Eden Press Women's Publications, 1980), 54–67.

Works Cited

Amezúa y Mayo, Agustín G. de. "Doña María de Zayas: Notas Críticas." *Opúsculos histórico-literarios.* Vol 2, 1–47. (Madrid: Consejo Superior de Investigaciones Científicas, 1951).

————. *Lope de Vega en sus cartas: Introducción al epistolario de Lope de Vega Carpio.* Vol. 2, 547–66, 664–67. (Madrid: Escelicer, 1940).

Díez Borque, José María. "El feminismo de Doña María de Zayas." In *La mujer en el teatro y la novela del siglo XVII.* Actas del IIº coloquio del grupo de estudios sobre teatro español, Toulouse, 16–17 Noviembre 1978. Toulouse: Université de Toulouse-Le Mirail, 1979, 61–88.

Foa, Sandra M. *Femenismo y forma narrativa. Estudio del tema y las técnicas de María de Zayas y Sotomayor.* Valencia: Albatross, 1979.

————. "María de Zayas y Sotomayor: Sibyl of Madrid (1590?–1661?)." In *Female Scholars: A Tradition of Learned Women Before 1800,* edited by J. R. Brink, 54–67. Montreal: Eden Press Women's Publications, 1980.

Griswold, Susan C. "Topoi and Rhetorical Distance: The 'Feminism' of María de Zayas." *Revista de Estudios Hispánicos* 14 (1980): 97–116.

Huarte de San Juan, Juan. *Examen de ingenios para las ciencias.* Edited by Rodrigo Sanz. Madrid: Imprenta la Rafa, 1930.

Iriarte, Mauricio de. *El doctor Huarte de San Juan y su examen de ingenios.* Madrid: Consejo Superior de Investigaciones Científicas, 1948.

Maclean, Ian. *Woman Triumphant. Feminism in French Literature 1610–1652.* Oxford: Oxford University Press, 1977.

Matulka, Barbara. "The Feminist Theme in the Drama of the Siglo de Oro." *Romanic Review* 26 (1935): 191–231.

McKendrick, Melveena. "The 'mujer esquiva'—A Measure of the Feminist Sympathies of Seventeenth-Century Dramatists." *Hispanic Review* 40 (1972): 162–97.

Morby, Edwin S. "Levinus Lemnius and Leo Suabius in *La Dorotea.*" *Hispanic Review* 20 (1952): 108–22.

Sylvania, Lena E. V. *Doña María de Zayas y Sotomayor. A Contribution to the Study of her Works.* New York: Columbia University, 1922.

Vasileski, Irma V. *María de Zayas y Sotomayor: Su época y su obra.* Madrid: Editorial Playor, 1973.

Vega Carpio, Felix Lope de. *La prueba de los ingenios,* in *Obras.* Vol. 30. Edited by Marcelino Menéndez Pelayo, 275–338. Biblioteca de Autores Españoles. Vol. 246. Madrid: Ediciones Atlas, 1971.

Vosters, Simon. "Lope de Vega y las damas doctas." In *Actas del Tercer Congreso Internacional de Hispanistas.* México: El Colegio de México, 1970, 909–21.

Zayas y Sotomayor, María de. *Novelas amorosas y ejemplares.* Edited by Agustín G. de Amezúa. Madrid: Real Academia Española, 1948.

Lope's Other *dama boba:* The Strategy · of Incompetence

MARGARET R. HICKS

La boba para los otros y discreta para sí [The counterfeit simpleton] is yet another of Lope de Vega's plays in which the linguistic strategies employed by the principal characters virtually constitute the dramatic action. While self-conscious displays of linguistic virtuosity are a characteristic feature of Golden Age drama, the foregrounding of the creative and manipulative function of language in this play is in certain ways distinctive. Of particular interest is the way in which social conventions and conventions of language use are exploited by the protagonist in the furtherance of her cause. A shepherdess who suddenly finds herself heir to a dukedom, Diana must face and overcome the formidable opposition represented by her astute and well-educated cousin, Teodora, and the courtiers who support her. During the course of the play, Diana perfects her manipulation of linguistic and social conventions so as to misrepresent herself to her enemies, to convey hidden meanings to her allies and to entertain the reader-spectator with these adroit maneuvers.

At variance with the protagonist's seemingly brilliant performance, however, are the antifeminist sentiments expressed by various characters throughout the play. For example, a number of explicit statements concern the deficiency of woman's intelligence, abilities, and talents. These opinions are offered by the very rational adviser, Fabio, by the scheming suitors and by Diana herself. But aside from an outburst of jealous anger and an exhibition of vanity, Diana is the controlling figure in this play. Aided by the prudent Fabio, she conceives and stages her bid for the throne of Urbino; therefore, what she actually accomplishes onstage seems to belie the assumption of limitation ascribed to feminine judgment. It is she who plans and then directs the course of the play, completely overshadowing the rational adviser, loyal lover, intellectual cousin, and scheming suitors.

In the dual role of director and leading lady in her own production, Diana is successful precisely because she exploits the expectations of other characters and of the reader / spectator regarding linguistic, social, and even dramatic conventions. She takes advantage of the language of *bobería* [nonsense], or more precisely, of the dramatic convention of *bobería,* in order to achieve her ends. Making use of the courtiers' assumption that she, a shepherdess, is necessarily a country bumpkin, she creates the illusion of ignorance and stupidity. While playing the *boba,* she is also exploiting certain negative assumptions about woman's intellectual capacity, convincing others in the process that she is an unlikely contender for a ducal throne.

But Diana's fictional role as *boba* is only one aspect of her strategy for gaining control of the kingdom. She also conceives and orchestrates an elaborate plot in acts 2 and 3 to introduce loyal troops into Urbino without arousing suspicions or allowing hostilities to erupt into civil war. Having created an effective smoke screen, she trades on her fiction of *bobería* and on the expectations of other characters inspired by this ruse.

The play itself inspires some interesting questions regarding Lope's intentions in creating just such a heroine only to place her in a context of explicit misogynist rhetoric. In this regard, it may be useful to consider the play and its heroine in the light of similar plays or of female protagonists depicted in similar situations. Certainly the feminine norm portrayed in Lope's theater is a somewhat flexible one, for he has created numerous heroines who, in addition to the more conventional attributes of beauty, modesty, and virtue, also possess some exceptional but traditionally unfeminine quality, such as remarkable intelligence. But as Melveena McKendrick has pointed out, this particular quality is portrayed as "acceptable, perhaps even desirable, as long as it is not assertive and as long as it does not give a woman wrong ideas about her role in life."[1] In this play, the heroine's intellectual gifts are made to serve ends that are acceptable becasue they are conventional. In order to carry out her assigned role as Duchess of Urbino, Diana must outwit those who wish to usurp the throne; she must likewise employ intelligence and judgment in choosing a suitable husband so as to secure her position as ruler.

The inevitable love intrigue is developed within a context of political plots and schemes in which Diana herself makes all the important decisions. Yet she is unlike the numerous female protagonists who adopt masculine disguise or who usurp male prerogatives in some way. She bears little resemblance to Laurencia in *Fuenteovejuna* [*The Sheepwell*], to doña María in *La moza de cántaro* [The girl with the pitcher], or to the host of male impersonators in Lope's theater. In fact, Diana more closely resembles some of Lope's male protagonists who find themselves facing an antagonist of higher rank and who consequently adopt a strategy of subterfuge or indirect attack. These figures frequently adopt fictional roles; and in such plays as *El príncipe melancólico* [The melancholy prince] and *La batalla del honor* [The battle of honor], they feign melancholy or madness. Such protagonists typically appear in honor plays and it is they who create the fictions and direct the action.

Like her male counterparts, who are themselves bound by social and dramatic conventions within which they must operate, Diana attempts to circumvent the constraints imposed by similar conventions. Outwardly, at least, she accepts the rules of the game. She never questions the assertions of male superiority, for instance, and she follows the advice of Fabio, meekly accepting his judgments of her behavior. But just as the desperate maneuvers of a *caballero* caught in the toils of a conflict of honor may serve to expose the inhumanity of the honor code itself, so Diana's demonstration of her own ingenuity tends to undercut the conventional notions of feminine weakness and limitation expressed in this play. Without openly challenging the assumption of woman's inferiority and without stepping outside the bounds of acceptable feminine behavior, Diana executes a performance that dramatically contradicts this negative valuation of women. Moreover, the contradiction itself forms an ironic comment on the validity of such anti-feminist sentiments.

Diana actually represents a type not uncommon in the *comedia;* she is that familiar pastoral figure, the natural daughter of a duke, reared by shepherds, and very conscious of her superiority in the arcadian setting that is both home and prison. In the introductory scene in act 1, she expresses both affection for her village and its rustic inhabitants and a restless dissatisfaction because it offers no scope for her exceptional talents. Diana's particular talent, her characteristic *ingenio,* is her ability to use language effectively. This special aptitude is illustrated by her first speech in the opening scene and then explicitly acknowledged by the shepherd, Riselo, in the second. Addressing the emissary from Urbino who has come to escort Diana to the court, Riselo boasts of her cleverness with words:

¡Qué mal la conocéis! Porque podría
venderos más retórica, si hablase,
que cuantos la profesan en Bolonia.[2]

(475)

[You certainly do not know her well.
She could offer you more rhetoric
than those who teach it in Bologna.]

This linguistic ability is put to good use once Diana is translated
from the *aldea* [village] to the world of the court. Having been
designated heir to her father's dukedom, much to everyone's sur-
prise, she is suddenly confronted by smiling enemies whose own
expectations have been dashed. Her chief antagonist is her intellectual cousin, Teodora. Over against the two suitors, who scheme and
plot with Teodora, is the faithful servant of the late Duke who
becomes Diana's guide and confidant. It is he who suggests that she
play the role of country bumpkin while secretly enlisting support
for the eventual confrontation with Teodora and her party. It is
important to note that Fabio has chosen to ally himself to her cause,
not because he judges her more intelligent or capable than her
cousin, but simply because she is the Duke's heir and because, like
the Duke, Fabio objects to Teodora's choice of husband. Insisting
that her suitor, Julio, would be an inadequate ruler of Urbino,
Fabio's argument underscores his primary concern for the welfare
of the state. In this regard, he urges Diana to consider carefully
when choosing her own husband and subsequently offers his help
and guidance in the search for an appropriate candidate.

Diana is duly warned of the dangers confronting her in the person
of her clever cousin and the scheming suitors. Fabio does not mince
words when he counsels the shepherdess to make use of her *entendimiento y prudencia* [understanding and prudence], assuring her
that Teodora and Julio will stop at nothing to insure her downfall.
(474). It is presumably Diana's special application of intelligence
and prudence that allows her to control the course of events in the
second and third acts.

Once at court, her strategy is one of calculated misinterpretation.
By registering inappropriate responses to almost every aspect of life
at court, she conveys the impression of extreme ignorance and of
virtual linguistic incompetence. She stubbornly clings to country
customs and interprets new experiences in terms of her former life
among the shepherds. Upon her arrival in Urbino, for example,
Diana identifies the welcoming volley of artillery as thunder and
proceeds to reminisce about life in her native village (477). Her

surprising verbal responses to new sights and experiences and her consistent failure to respond appropriately to social cues set her apart as a misfit.

Diana pretends ignorance of word meanings, thereby seeming to misunderstand the literal thrust of statements. Attempting to establish herself as an ignorant country girl, she perfects this technique early in the first act. When the emissary from Urbino first addresses her as *duquesa generosa,* Diana makes a nonsense of his respectful greeting, responding with a ludicrous question: "¿Qué duquesa decís o calabaza?" [Duchess, did you say? or calabash?] (475).

In like manner, she accepts literally those statements whose figurative or implied meanings are obvious to the other dramatic interlocutors and to the reader / audience. This ridiculous distortion of literal and implied meanings is typical of the *bobo* figure in the *comedia.* As Ronald Surtz has pointed out, an essential characteristic of the *bobo* is "his failure to grasp symbolic language."[3] In fact, the *bobo* consistently fails to grasp implied meanings and, therefore, interprets all speech literally. Characteristic of the rustic clown's language is not his inability to generate or convey meanings effectively, for he is usually very adept at this; it is rather the failure to comprehend because of an inability to make inferences and to calculate implicatures. One explanation of this incapacity is, of course, the limited frame of reference associated with these figures. Their presumed ignorance of the world precludes their comprehension of utterances that require a listener-supplied context. These characters tend to interpret or to assign meanings without reference to the relevant features of context such as appropriate social conventions, without reference to conventions of language use and apparently without recourse to inference making processes. They simply focus on the literal meaning of words spoken—or at least they seem to do so.

In effect, Diana consistently fails, or seems to fail, to calculate implicatures. This strategy is also introduced early in the play. Camilo, the emissary mentioned above, apparently assumes that she knows of her parentage or that, at the very least, she has the social competence to respond courteously to the news that he brings. After his solemn announcement that the Duke is dead, he expresses shock at Diana's inappropriate response:

> Pues, ¿qué se me da a mí? Pero, si es cierto,
> enterralde, señores,
> que yo no soy el cura.
>
> (475)

[Well, what's that to do with me? But, if it's true,
bury him, gentlemen;
for I'm not the priest.]

In the course of the first and second acts, Diana perfects her
ability to manipulate other characters' attitudes and actions by
means of her own imaginative misreadings. In the second act, for
instance, Teodora becomes suspicious of the attentions given the
country cousin by her own suitors, Camilo and Julio, and warns
Diana to shun the company and the deceptions of men. Pretending
not to grasp the implications of Teodora's warnings, Diana counters
with a very literal interpretation of the commandment to "love thy
neighbor."

> Que huyese de los hombres me dijistes;
> pero, como yo sé los Mandamientos,
> que es más obligación que vuestros cuentos,
> "y amarás a tu prójimo—decían—
> como a ti mismo," vi que no tenían
> vuestras lecciones buenos fundamentos.

(486–87)

[You told me to avoid men;
but since I know the Commandments,
which carry more weight than your warnings, and they say,
"Love your neighbor as yourself,"
I saw that your lessons
were not based on a sound foundation.]

Teodora's rejoinder that Diana could comply with the commandment by loving her cousin instead is quickly countered by the latter
with another quibble involving literal word meanings:

> No debéis de sabellos.
> No veis que dice "prójimo"?; y si fuera
> para mujer, que "prójima" dijera.
> Veis coma vais, Teodora,
> contra los mandamientos?

(487)

[You must not know them.
Don't you see that it says "male neighbor"? If it meant
a woman, it would say "female neighbor."
Do you see, Teodora,
how you are going against the Commandments?]

An important feature of Diana's misinterpretations throughout the second and third acts is her apparent ignorance of the relevant social conventions. In one scene, for instance, the comic effect of her verbal blunders derives from her distortion of both the literal meaning of the verb *casar* and of its social context. When the fickle suitors Camilo and Julio have finally grasped that they are, in fact, rivals for Diana's affections, a quarrel breaks out and swords are drawn. Learning the reason for the quarrel, Diana surprises everyone with the announcement that she is already married. Attempting to explain, she reminds her cousin of her earlier advice to avoid the company of men, concluding that she and Teodora might as well marry each other. Diana's suggestion for the resolution of the quarrel is a second marriage between Camilo and Julio. With these ludicrous proposals, she creates a diversion that effectively terminates the fight and reinforces the fiction of her own stupidity.

In other scenes it is rather the violation of social conventions that produces comic results. Since oral exchanges are never just conversational but are governed by social as well as conversational rules, the violation of such rules inevitably "calls attention to itself and invites inference as to why it occurs."[4] For Diana's audience, her obtuseness regarding social customs simply confirms their opinion of her simplicity. The pretended ignorance of both social and linguistic conventions gives rise to the comic effects in one of the most amusing scenes of the play that occurs near the end of act 3 and represents the culmination of Diana's attempts to deceive her adversaries. Having devised a scheme by which she may safely bring loyal troops into the city, Diana makes her first public move by pretending to receive the Turkish ambassador, who is actually Fabio in disguise. Her plan is to pretend to challenge the Sultan through the "ambassador," threatening to send an army against him. This imaginary crusade thus provides an excuse for the assembling of soldiers within sight of her court. In her reception of the fake ambassador, she creates a farcical situation comprised of feigned misunderstandings and pretended linguistic misfires. The interview begins with Diana's literal misinterpretations, all of which are based on a feigned ignorance both of the protocol appropriate to such an occasion and of the most commonplace expressions of courtesy. The effect is that of a comedy routine:

> *Fabio.* Alá guarde a vuestra Alteza.
> *Diana.* Venga vuestra turquería
> con salud.
> *Fabio.* Deme las plantas.

> Diana. Están a los pies asidas.
> Fabio. Las manos.
> Diana.   Si se las doy,
>   ¿con qué quiere que me vista?
> Laura. Dele silla vuestra Alteza.
> Diana. ¿Por qué no se la traía
>   de su tierra?

(500)

> [Fabio. May Allah bless your highness.
> Diana. May your Turkishness enjoy
>   good health.
> Fabio. Give me your feet.
> Diana. I cannot; they are attached to me.
> Fabio. Your hands.
> Diana. If I give them to you, how will I dress myself?
> Laura. Give him a chair, your highness.
> Diana. Why didn't he bring one from his own country?]

At the end of the comic interview, Diana once again displays an amazing disregard for social and linguistic conventions:

> Diana.   Dime:
>   sería descortesía
>   matar este embajador
>   por las que me tiene dichas,
>   o darle algunas valonas
>   para el camino?
> Marcelo.   Sería
>   contra su salvaconducto.
> Diana. ¿Luto este moro traía?

(502)

> [Diana. Tell me:
>   would it be discourtesy
>   to have this ambassador
>   killed for the things
>   he has said to me?
>   Or should I send him on his way
>   with a gift of lace collars?
> Marcelo. It would be against his safe conduct.
> Diana. Was this moor dressed in mourning?]

Diana's adversaries have recognized Fabio and assume that he is deceiving her for purposes of his own. It is they, of course, who are

deceived and the efficacy of the ruse is revealed in Julio's comments
to Teodora:

> Ya no es duda su ignorancia;
> que sola esta acción confirma
> la simplicidad mayor
> que ha sido vista ni escrita.

(501)

> [There is no longer any doubt about her ignorance.
> She has shown herself to be the greatest simpleton
> ever seen or recorded.]

The inventiveness exhibited by Diana and Fabio in the burlesque
described above recalls the extemporaneous acting skills displayed
in an earlier scene at the end of act 2. Highlighted here is Diana's
ability to conceive and, at the same time, direct the performance,
supplying her confederates with the necessary cues without alert-
ing her adversaries to the fact that she is playacting. She has
arranged a private meeting with Fabio and Alejandro, whom she
has secretly agreed to marry; as they discuss their plans, Fabio
emphasizes the need to bring armed supporters into Urbino without arousing the suspicions of Teodora's followers. Alejandro
agrees to enlist loyal men from his native Florence and Diana
assures them that she can invent a suitable cover story. When the
three allies suddenly become aware that Teodora and the two
suitors are spying on them, Diana initiates her hastily conceived
stratagem. Addressing Teodora, she reveals her desire to imitate
the actions of the *mujeres valerosas* [valiant women] whose stories
she has been reading. To accomplish this ambition, she announces
her intention to mount a crusade against the Sultan of Turkey.
Attempting to draw Alejandro into the act and to produce an
explanation for his presence, Diana insists that he has foolishly
tried to dissuade her from carrying out her plan. Taking his cue,
Alejandro pretends to advise her against such an ambitious project.
Diana's response to his counsel is an ambiguous exclamation, "¡qué
donosa resistencia!" [What a fine objection!], followed by her exit
from the stage. To her astonished enemies, who infer an ironic use
of *donosa*, these words convey her annoyance at being thwarted;
whereas to Alejandro, they imply praise for his convincing performance.

Diana's strategy is successful precisely because she does understand both the literal and implied meanings of other characters'

speech and is clearly aware of the ways in which language can be used to conceal and to misrepresent. Early in act 1, for instance, she confides to Fabio that she will speak openly and without subterfuge only when she has accomplished her ends and can do so in safety:

> Y advierte que esta ignorancia
> tengo de usar, entre tanto
> que aseguro Estado y vida;
> que después hablaré claro,
> y tan claro, que se admiren
> que pueda un inculto campo
> producir tan raro ingenio.

(479)

> [Be advised that I am assuming this pose of ignorance
> only while I attempt to secure my life and my estate.
> Afterwards, I shall speak clearly,
> so clearly that everyone will be amazed
> that an uncouth countryside
> could produce such rare wit.]

Throughout the play, she displays a kind of perverse linguistic virtuosity, skillfully calculating her misinterpretations so as to elicit the desired responses from her two different audiences. Her enemies are convinced of her stupidity and, therefore, of her powerlessness. Her allies, like the reader / spectator, know to read between the lines of the apparently nonsensical speech and are both amused by her cleverness and impressed by her ability thus to deceive and disarm her adversaries.

The strategy fails at crucial points in the play, however, and these failures are attributed by the protagonist herself to the traditional feminine weaknesses of vanity and emotional instability. Near the beginning of act 2, Diana allows her vanity to overcome her discretion and she skillfully outmaneuvers the clever *bachillera*, Teodora, displaying her own rhetorical ability. Teodora has warned her cousin to avoid the company of men and, as mentioned above, Diana counters this admonition by quoting the commandment "Amarás a tu prójimo." (487) Teodora then shifts her tactics and warns of the deceitfulness of men, to which Diana responds that men are more often the ones deceived:

Teodora. Engañan las discretas y avisadas, que harán de vos?
Diana.   Por muchas engañadas,

en todos los estados,
siempre son más los hombres engañados.

(487)

[*Teodora*. They deceive intelligent and cautious women. What will they
do to you?
Diana. For all the women
who are deceived by men,
there are still more men betrayed by women.]

The comment of Teodora's servant, "Esto no sabe a mucha
bobería" [This doesn't sound like foolishness], is echoed by Laura's
aside to Diana that she has overplayed her hand and revealed too
much. Diana later attempts to justify her error by rationalizing the
vanity that inspired it:

No he podido
reprimir esta vez mi entendimiento;
que es luz, en fin, y sigue su elemento.

(487)

[I could not repress
my intelligence this time;
for intelligence is light, after all, and seeks its element.]

The second and more serious failure to maintain her strategic
advantage occurs near the end of act 2. After a series of private
interviews with Alejandro, Diana is convinced that he is both a
suitable and pleasing candidate for marriage. Unfortunately, the
first public meeting between the two is a disaster; Diana fails to
read between the lines of Alejandro's fictional account of himself
and of his reasons for coming to the court of Urbino. Accepting his
invention literally, she is offended by the romantic intrigue that he
has fabricated in order to hide his true identity and to elicit the
sympathy of Teodora and the courtiers. Diana is in possession of
the necessary contextual information, for she knows that he must
conceal his identity and invent a story for himself and she should
have recognized herself in his description of the imaginary Porcia.
But she fails to see the implications of the fiction and angrily sends
him away. The cause of this sudden inability to comprehend or even
to communicate effectively is, ostensibly, her own jealousy and the
conflicting emotions spawned by it. When chided by Fabio, Diana
acknowledges the emotional weakness that has clouded her judgment, then simply excuses her behavior on the grounds of her sex:

"Celos me dan. ¡Soy mujer" [I'm jealous. I'm a woman] (493). In a
later scene, she again attempts to excuse her jealousy as a feminine
weakness and, therefore, natural: "Es condición o flaqueza / de
voluntad de mujer" [It is woman's condition or her weakness of
will] (498).

Echoing Diana's own assessment of her behavior, Fabio again
rebukes her for having succumbed to a typically feminine vice in
giving way to suspicions and unfounded fears:

> Pero si este movimiento
> es condición de mujer,
> que dejan presto vencer
> su cobarde entendimiento
> de cualquier sospecha vana,
> dime si en haber traído
> a Alejandro te he mentido.
>
> (494–95)

> [But if this emotional outburst
> is due to your feminine nature,
> which allows your cowardly intellect
> to be overcome
> by any foolish suspicion,
> then tell me how I have deceived you
> in bringing Alejandro to you.]

The wider implications of this negative evaluation of feminine
judgment are suggested early in the play when Fabio advises Diana
to choose a wise and valiant husband. Offering to help her find an
appropriate candidate for the dukedom, he airs his own views
regarding the unsuitability of women as rulers:

> Señora, aunque gobernaron
> mujeres reinos e imperios,
> fue con inmensos trabajos,
> trágicos fines y medios
> sangrientos, que no dejaron
> ejemplo de imitación.
>
> (479)

> [My lady, even though
> women have governed kingdoms and empires,
> it was always with great effort,
> tragic ends and bloody

means, and is certainly not
worthy of imitation.]

The passages quoted above are noteworthy because of the emphasis on feminine rather than human limitations; the key term seems to be *entendimiento*. Fabio specifically identifies the weak intellect *(cobarde entendimiento)* that is easily overcome by destructive passions as a characteristically feminine attribute. Yet Diana repeatedly asserts the superiority of her own intellect and appears to substantiate her claims in the actual performance of her role. Even in her conventional portrayal of the jealous female, she has apparently engaged in a bit of self-conscious playacting. Having distracted Alejandro and Fabio with her pose as a capricious and unreasonable woman, Diana voices what are presumably her true sentiments in a soliloquy at the end of the scene. Expressing a desire to return to the safe haven of her native village, she reveals the fear for her life generated by the atmosphere of plots and schemes at court.

> No allí lisonjas, no engaños,
> no traiciones, no desprecios,
> adonde teme la vida,
> si no la espada, el veneno.
> Nunca yo supe en mi aldea
> de qué color era el miedo;
> agora, a mi sombra misma
> por cualquiera parte temo.
>
> (494)

> [There is no flattery or deceit there,
> no treachery or scorn;
> unlike the court where my life
> is threatened by poison, if not by the sword.
> Never did I know fear
> in my village;
> now I am terrified
> of my very shadow.]

In such a climate of distrust, even a misunderstanding between lovers takes on a sinister dimension; for if Alejandro's intentions are suspect, he must be viewed as a potential threat, as possibly in league with her enemies. Just as Diana has used and abused linguistic conventions in order to create the illusion of *bobería,* she likewise exploits conventional assumptions about her feminine role.

She excuses her behavior as feminine weakness in order to insure its misinterpretation. Her jealousy may be authentic, but its exhibition provides a protective smoke screen for the real source of her confusion: the fear of betrayal into the hands of her enemies.

Nor is Fabio the only male character to speak disparagingly of woman's place in the scheme of things. This issue is developed in a humorous context in act 2 where a similar sort of stereotyping occurs. In this scene, Teodora's suitors decide to switch allegiance to the newcomer. Blatantly admitting their desire for the dukedom, Camilo and Julio attempt to justify their change of heart by reciting clichés about the womanly virtues desirable in a wife. The sentiments are commonplace enough, but the obvious insincerity of the speakers, together with their gullibility, combine to produce a mirror image effect that is essentially comic:

> *Camilo.* que, por ser Duque de Urbino,
> no reparo en lo interior
> deste rústico edificio.
> Porque no la quiero yo
> para que me escriba libros,
> ni para tomar consejo:
> que de mujer no le admito.
>
> (488)

> [*Camilo.* I'm concerned with becoming the Duke of Urbino
> and not with the interior
> of this rustic edifice.
> I don't love her
> for her ability to write books
> or to give me advice;
> that I would never accept from a woman.]

Julio's speech provides an even more explicit example of the concern to put woman in her place:

> *Julio.* Más quiero boba a Diana,
> con aquel simple sentido,
> que bachillera a Teodora;
> pues un filósofo dijo
> que las mujeres casadas
> eran el mayor castigo
> cuando, soberbias de ingenio,
> gobernaban sus maridos.
> Lo que han de saber es sólo
> parir y criar sus hijos;

Diana es hermosa, y basta
que sepa criar los míos.

(489)

[*Julio.* I love Diana,
  simpleminded and foolish,
  more than Teodora with all her learning.
  A philosopher once said
  that married women
  are the greatest punishment
  when they are proud of their own cleverness
  and try to rule their husbands.
  All they need to know
  is how to give birth and rear their children.
  Diana is beautiful and it's enough
  for her to know how to rear mine.]

The expression of such smug sounding sentiments by young men who are themselves being duped by the protagonist lends a touch of dramatic irony to a situation that is inherently farcical. So striking is the discrepancy between misguided assumptions and visible evidence to the contrary in this scene that the underlying attitude of male superiority is made to seem as ridiculous as the speakers themselves.

The dramatist has clearly made use of very conventional notions regarding woman's inferiority only to turn them upside down in the course of this play. His heroine fails in significant ways to conform to the traditional feminine mold and yet she is never accused of usurping male prerogatives or of being unwomanly. She appears to play by the rules while, in fact, she simply makes her own. She succeeds in manipulating the other characters by exploiting their expectations; the courtiers are eager to welcome an ignorant country girl, easily flattered and deceived, and Diana presents them with a simpleton who thwarts their plots and schemes, making them look like fools in the bargain.

This heroine is representative of Lope's own tendency to exploit popular tastes and commonplace notions of human psychology along with literary and historical traditions in the creation of his plots and characters. In this play, the dramatist has apparently made use of the popular psychology of the period in order to create a distinctive woman who is at once a reflection and a negation of the stereotype.

Possibly the most useful source for many of the notions of faculty psychology prevalent in the seventeenth century is the *Examen de ingenios para las ciencias* [An examination of wits for the sciences] by Juan Huarte de San Juan. Dismissing the intellectual capacity of women in general in the final chapter, the author insists that women cannot attain great intelligence because of the cold and moist qualities appropriate to their sex. He goes on to admit that these very qualities, which are associated with the faculty of memory, dispose women to display a natural, though superficial, ability in the use of language.[5]

In Chapter 11 of the *Examen,* Huarte explicitly identifies rhetorical skill and the talent for language with the faculty of memory. He insists that these gifts are not a sign of intelligence, as they generally are incompatible with those skills associated with the intellect and the imagination (447). In the following chapter, however, he admits that nature occasionally endows a man with an equal measure of intelligence, imagination and memory; but he emphasizes the rarity of such gifted individuals because the strength of one faculty generally precludes equal vitality in the others (465).

Having concluded that intellectually gifted men are rare, Huarte expressly denies the possibility of a gifted woman.[6] Indeed, his insistence on the inferior nature of women is well in keeping with traditional views that are, in turn, echoed in the antifeminist sentiments expressed by the male characters in *La boba para los otros.*

It appears that Lope has simply made use of conventional wisdom to suit his particular ends and has, in effect, created the female equivalent of Huarte's exceptional man: a gifted heroine whose natural propensity for fluent expression is enhanced by a powerful imagination and considerable intelligence. She uses these remarkable talents in the service of goals that are acceptable to the extent that they are conventional; in this her performance is consistent with the norm for acceptable feminine behavior in Lope's theater. She attempts to fulfill her obligation as her father's heir and she accepts without question the need to choose a husband who possesses the attributes of a good ruler. Having made her choice, she appears to accept Alejandro's authority just as she accepts Fabio's guidance early in the first act. In this respect, it is worth noting that Fabio's one direct reference to Diana's intelligence occurs immediately after she has agreed to follow his counsel. He praises her *ingenio* because she is not like those women who scorn the advice and the authority of their fathers and husbands (479).

If Diana's performance conforms to the standard of womanly behavior exhibited in Lope's theater, the motivation for her actions is definitely not typical of his heroines. The love intrigue in this play is clearly subordinate to political concerns, for Diana's primary goal is to defend and secure her position as heir to the throne of Urbino. In this she is unlike the multitude of female protagonists who don male attire or who in some other way deviate from the traditional feminine norm in order to pursue an errant lover. Whether their motivation is the retrieval of lost honor or simply the pursuit of love and marriage, these young women are spurred to action by sentiments that for Diana are obviously secondary. Even her jealous outburst against Alejandro in act 2 is accounted for in terms of the larger political issue and attendant dangers.

Diana's preoccupation with an essentially political objective also sets her apart from the protagonist of *La dama boba,* the most likely subject for comparison. Although Finea progresses from *bobería* to discretion in that play, her misuse of social and linguistic conventions is in many ways similar to Diana's manipulation of language. Like the majority of Lope's heroines, however, Finea's efforts are motivated by a romantic attachment. Love provides the inspiration for her metamorphosis; whereas for Diana, love is a collateral issue rather than the mainspring of her actions.

Yet Diana is a conventional heroine to the extent that neither does she reject accepted standards of womanly behavior nor usurp male prerogatives. Instead, she makes intelligent use of a typically feminine attribute, her facility for language, while engaging in subterfuge and calculated deception, the ultimate defensive weapons. Pretending to embody to an extreme degree the intellectual deficiency traditionally ascribed to women, she eventually prevails over her more powerful adversaries by outmaneuvering and outsmarting them. In this respect, Diana recalls many of Lope's male protagonists who are forced to employ subterfuge in order to outwit higher ranking and more powerful antagonists. Like these figures, she manages to operate successfully within the system, never challenging the rules, but unobtrusively circumventing restrictive conventions, often turning them to her own advantage.

Having created the female counterpart of Huarte's gifted man, Lope endows her with exceptional linguistic talents and a flair for the dramatic that enable her to organize and direct the course of the play. By devising a series of effective smoke screens, she succeeds in distracting and ultimately disarming her enemies. To this end, she exploits the expectations of other characters regarding social and linguistic conventions. Her most notable accomplishment is her convincing portrayal of the simpleton. She further exploits the stereotype of the weak-minded, emotional female by adopting the capricious behavior of a jealous woman simply to mask the fear for her life. Then as cover for the mobilization of armed supporters, she stages the elaborate fiction of the crusade against the Grand Turk.

Diana's success in outmaneuvering her adversaries serves to highlight the disparity between her performance and the antifeminist rhetoric projected throughout the play. Like his heroine, Lope has exploited the expectations, assumptions, and sentiments of his audience and in this instance, the resulting contradiction between rhetoric and performance provides an ironic comment on the validity of the antifeminist sentiments.

Notes

1. Melveena McKendrick, *Woman and Society in the Spanish Drama of the Golden Age: A Study of the Mujer Varonil* (London: Cambridge University Press, 1974), p. 224.

2. Lope de Vega, *La boba para los otros y discreta para sí,* ed. Justo García Soriano, vol. 11, *Obras dramáticas* (Madrid: Real Academia Española, 1929), p. 475. All subsequent quotations are taken from this edition of the play. The English translations are my own.

3. Ronald E. Surtz, "Daughter of Night, Daughter of Light: The Imagery of Finea's transformation in *La Dama Boba,*" *Bulletin of the Comediantes* 33, no. 2 (Fall 1981): 163.

4. Kent Bach and Robert Harnish, *Linguistic Communication and Speech Acts* (Cambridge: MIT Press, 1979), p. 105.

5. ". . . las hembras, por razon de la frialdad o humedad de su sexo, no pueden alcanzar ingenio profundo; solo vemos que hablan con alguna apariencia de habilidad en materias livianas y faciles, con terminos comunes y muy estudiados, pero metidas en letras no pueden aprender mas que un poco latin, y esto por ser obra de la memoria. De la cual rudeza no tienen ellas la culpa, sino que la frialdad y humedad, que las hizo hembras, estas mismas calidades hemos probado atras que contradicen al ingenio y habilidad" [. . . women, because of the cold and moist qualities of their sex, cannot attain great intelligence; we see that they are only capable of speaking with some appearance of ability on simple, trivial subjects, using common terms acquired by much study; but as for serious learning, they can only master a little Latin, and that learned by heart. They are not to blame for their stupidity, however, but rather the cold and moist qualities that make them female, the very qualities that we have shown to be antagonistic to intelligence and cleverness]. Juan Huarte de San Juan, *Examen de ingenios, para las ciencias,* vol. 65 (Madrid: Biblioteca de Autores Españoles, 1953), vol. 65, p. 497.

6. ". . . ninguna mujer nace con ingenio . . ." [. . . no woman is born with intelligence . . .] Huarte, *Examen,* p. 497. For a helpful introduction to the work of Juan Huarte, I am indebted to the following: Malcolm K. Read, *Juan Huarte de San Juan* (Boston: Twayne, 1981); and to Carlos G. Noreña, "Huarte's Naturalistic Philosophy of Man" in *Studies in Spanish Renaissance Thought* (The Hague: Martinus Nijhoff, 1975), pp. 210–63.

Works Cited

Bach, Kent and Robert Harnish. *Linguistic Communication and Speech Acts.* Cambridge: MIT Press, 1979.

Huarte, de San Juan, Juan. *Examen de ingenios para las ciencias.* Madrid: Biblioteca de Autores Españoles, 1953, vol. 65.

McKendrick, Melveena. *Woman and Society in the Spanish Drama of the Golden Age: A Study of the Mujer Varonil.* London: Cambridge University Press, 1974.

Noreña, Carlos G. "Huarte's Naturalistic Philosophy of Man." *Studies in Spanish Renaissance Thought.* The Hague: Martinus Nijhoff, 1975.

Read, Malcolm K. *Juan Huarte de San Juan.* Boston: Twayne, 1981.

Surtz, Ronald E. "Daughter of Night, Daughter of Light: The Imagery of Finea's transformation in *La Dama Boba*" *Bulletin of the Comediantes* 33, no. 2 (Fall 1981): 161–7.

Vega Carpio, Lope de. *La boba para los otros y discreta para sí.* Ed. Justo García Soriano. *Obras dramáticas.* Vol. 11 Madrid: Real Academia Española, 1929.

Part 3
Rape, Politics, and Sexual Inversion

The Sources and Feminism of Lope's
Las mujeres sin hombres

MICHAEL D. McGAHA

Las mujeres sin hombres is the only one of Lope de Vega's eight mythological plays not based on Ovid's *Metamorphoses*. In the dedication of the play Lope poses as a classical scholar, citing no fewer than six classical writers in support of his statements about the Amazons. Menéndez Pelayo admiringly said that Lope's sources for this play "no fueron pocas ni vulgares, a no ser que las encontrase reunidas en alguna compilación de segunda mano, por ejemplo, en la *Officina* de Juan Ravisio Textor, que manejaba mucho, o en el libro de mitología de Natal Comes" [were neither few nor common ones, unless he found them all together in some secondhand collection, for example, Ravisius Textor's *Officina*, which he frequently consulted, or Natale Conti's book of mythology].[1]

Lope first cites the Babylonian author Berossus (third century B.C.) as having written about the Amazons of Africa. Menéndez Pelayo found no reference to the Amazons in the authentic fragments of Berossus, but did find a mention of warrior women who had conquered a king of Libya in the apocryphal Berossus forged by Giovanni Anio of Viterbo in the late fifteenth century. Lope states that Diodorus Siculus (first century B.C.) wrote about the Scythian Amazons, who killed their husbands and were conquered by Hercules. Diodorus Siculus discusses the Amazons in two sections of his *Bibliotheca Historica*.[2] The first section deals with the ninth labor of Hercules, which was to obtain the girdle of Hippolyta, queen of the Amazons. In order to do this Hercules declared war against the Amazons and defeated them in battle. The other section treats the Amazons' attempt to avenge themselves upon Theseus for having carried away their queen Antiope or, according to other sources, Hippolyta. Diodorus never mentions that the Amazons killed their husbands.

Lope cites Justinus (third century A.D.) as his authority for stat-

ing that Thalestris, queen of the Amazons, visited Alexander the
Great, accompanied by three hundred thousand of her women.
Menéndez Pelayo noted that the original text of Justinus speaks of
only three hundred women, but Jorge de Bustamante's Spanish
translation of Justinus's work mistakenly gives the three hundred
thousand figure. This would suggest that Bustamante's translation
may have been the principal source consulted by Lope. An examination of the translation, however, reveals disappointingly few parallels with Lope's version of the story, aside from the appearance of
several of the names he gives the Amazons in his play. Bustamante
does say that after most of the Amazons' husbands had been
slaughtered by neighboring tribes, the women decided to kill the
few remaining men "por que no paresciesse que entre ellas algunas
auia de mas preuillegio ni mejor libradas que las otras" [that it
might not appear that there were some among them more privileged
or favored than others].[3] He states that at the time of Hercules'
attack on the Amazons, they were ruled by two sisters named
Menalipe and Hippolyta. Orithya was away making war against
another kingdom, so Anthiopa led the defense of the Amazon
capital. Hercules took Menalipe prisoner but later released her in
exchange for the queen's girdle. Theseus took Hippolyta as his wife.

Lope also says in his dedication that Arrian and Xenophon
denied the existence of the Amazons: "se ríen de tal fábula" [they
laugh at that fable]. Menéndez Pelayo found that in fact in the
Anabasis Arrian denied the story of Thalestris' visit to Alexander
and stated that Xenophon had never mentioned the Amazons. Lope
concludes by saying that he has found the Amazons mentioned in
Virgil "y en todos los autores" [and in all the authors].

Pedro Mexía's *Silva de varia lección,* first published in 1540,
contains two chapters devoted to the Amazons. These chapters,
based on Diodorus and Justinus, contain all the same details in
which Lope coincides with Bustamante's translation of Justinus,
with the single exception that Mexía does not specify how many
women accompanied Thalestris to her meeting with Alexander.
Furthermore, Mexía's introductory remarks, in which he states his
reasons for writing about the Amazons, concur perfectly with
Lope's stated intention in writing *Las mujeres sin hombres:*

> Even though many men think it is clever to denigrate women's perfec-
> tion, noting that they are imperfect and weak because of their lewdness
> and other weaknesses, it is certain that if some of them indeed suffer
> some of these defects, they are much more common in men. For the
> truth is that in every kind of virtues women have the advantage over

men, or at least equal us, whether we choose to consider love, loyalty, charity, devotion, piety, meekness, temperance, mercy, or any of the other virtues. And if there be, or have been, some evils or sins in them, there are and have been much greater ones in men; and this is so notorious that there is no need to point out examples of it. It seems that men can boast only one thing in which they have a notorious advantage over women, which is arms and military activity; because, since this involves fierceness and cruelty and many other evils, they neither want to participate in it, nor did it please God to make them suitable for it. But, just so that men might know that even in this, if they wanted to take it up, they could equal and even excel them, many individual women have done many very singular things in warfare. And because it would be a long process to tell many outstanding stories about this, it will suffice to recount the history of the Amazons, women who were very bellicose and very courageous in warfare, who without any advice from men, won many battles, conquered great provinces and cities, and endured a very long time in sovereignty and power.[4]

Lope writes in his dedication that the story of the Amazons reveals that women

pudieron vivir solas en concertada república, ejercitar las armas, adquirir reinos, fundar ciudades y dar principio a una de las maravillas del mundo, que fue el templo de Diana en Efeso.

[managed to live by themselves in a harmonious republic, to carry on warfare, to acquire kingdoms, to found cities, and to begin one of the wonders of the world, which was the Temple of Diana in Ephesus.]

Mexía also mentions that the Amazons "poblaron y edificaron muchas y muy nombradas ciudades, y entre ellas aquella memoratísima Efeso, según opinión de muchos, do estaba aquel templo tan acatado de Diana" [populated and built many very renowned cities, and among them that most memorable Ephesus, according to the opinion of many, where stood that revered Temple of Diana].[5] Bustamante's translation of Justinus had mentioned the foundation of Ephesus but not the temple of Diana. Bustamante had stated that when the Amazons gave birth to male children, they killed them. Mexía gives a more humane version of the story: "y si era varón, enviábanlo a sus padres, que los criaban" [and if it was a boy, they sent him to his father to bring up].[6] This is the version followed by Lope:

> Si paren varón, le envían
> Al padre que fue su dueño . . .[7]

[If they bear a boy, they send him
to the father who begot him.]

Neither Bustamante's translation of Justinus nor Mexía's *Silva* contains the references to Berossus, Arrian, Xenophon, and Virgil cited by Lope. I am sure that Menéndez Pelayo was correct in suspecting that Lope culled these citations at the moment of writing the dedication from one of the handy miscellanies or reference books he was so fond of consulting. However, the book in question could not have been Ravisius Textor's *Officina* or Conti's *Mythologiae*. In the two chapters he devotes to the subject ("Mulieres bellicosae & masculae virtutis" and "Amazones") Ravisius Textor refers to Propertius, Virgil, Herodotus, Claudian, Valerius Flaccus, Statius, and Horace, but the names of Berossus, Diodorus Siculus, Justinus, Arrian, and Xenophon are conspicuously absent. Conti cites no classical sources whatsoever in his discussion of the Amazons (*Mythologiae*, book 7, chapter 9). The article "Amazones" in Stephanus' *Dictionarium*, another work frequently consulted by Lope, cites Sallust, Justinus, and Virgil, but none of the other authors mentioned by Lope. Lope found the classical citations he used in the dedication of another mythological play, *El Perseo*, in Vitoria's *Theatro de los dioses de la gentilidad*. However, in this case Vitoria's chapter "De como Hercules venció las Amazonas" (*Segunda parte*, book 2, chapter 8) also omits most of the sources cited by Lope.

The question of where Lope found the references to Berossus, Diodorus Siculus, Justinus, Arrian, Xenophon and Virgil is not very important, because these citations concern only the statements Lope makes about the Amazons in the dedication, not the plot of the play itself. The principal inspiration for Lope's treatment of the Amazon myth seems in fact to have come from Boccaccio's *Teseida delle nozze d'Emilia*, a long narrative poem in twelve books written around 1340–42. A brief resume of book 1 of the *Teseida* will suffice to show just how closely Lope follows Boccaccio.

Boccaccio describes the original rebellion of the Amazon women as follows:

In the days when Aegeus was king of Athens, there were wild and ruthless women in Scythia, to whom it probably seemed intolerable that their husbands should lord it over them. They banded together, therefore, and in a haughty proclamation announced that they would not be kept in subjection, but that they wanted to govern themselves. And they found a way to carry out their foolish design.

Each one spilt the life blood of her men with her own weapon, leaving him in the icy embrace of death as the stone cold victims of her spite, just the way the granddaughters of Belos dealt with their husbands in the still of the night. They liberated themselves in this way, but they were not able to remain free.[8]

The Amazons elected a queen, Hippolyta, who would correct their faults and give them rules and directives in right living. Any ship that arrived at their kingdom was forced to pay tribute. Theseus, Duke of Athens, hearing complaints about this, decided to avenge the women's crimes. The Greeks sailed for Scythia. Hippolyta, hearing of their approach, harangued her women and armed her lands. When Theseus arrived, he sent envoys to offer Hippolyta peace terms, which she rejected. Theseus angrily prayed to Mars and Minerva. His men came ashore and fought a long and bloody battle with the women. The women fled to the castle, and Theseus decided to besiege them. After several months, he began to excavate under the walls. Hippolyta sent a letter by two of her women, telling him that he had no reason to be at war with her and shaming him for fighting women. He replied, urging them to surrender. Hippolyta, deciding that the gods were very angry with her women, complied. When Theseus was notified of her decision, he offered to marry Hippolyta, and his knights married the other women. Book 1 concludes with a description of the marriage of the Greeks to the Amazons.

Lope took the outline of the plot from Boccaccio, then filled in the details with a reading of Mexía's *Silva* and, perhaps, Bustamante's translation of Justinus. He changes the name of the Amazon queen to Antiopía and includes the participation of Hercules and Jason—whom Boccaccio had not even mentioned—as secondary figures. He changes the name of Orithya, Antiopía's sister and rival to Deyanira, the woman whom Hercules ultimately married, according to Ovid. The play's first scene contains a fleeting reference to the fact that the campaign against the Amazons was one of the labors of Hercules, but Lope never mentions that Hercules was sent to obtain the Amazon queen's girdle. The motive for the campaign seems to have been merely to avenge

> . . . la crueldad de esta gente,
> Loca, bárbara, insolente,
> A quien Amazonas llama.[9]

[the cruelty of this insane,

barbarous, insolent race
whom they call Amazons.]

Lope's Theseus is much more gallant than Boccaccio's, and his
Antiopía turns out to be a more formidable enemy than Boccaccio's
Hippolyta. Hercules appears as an exponent of traditional *macho*
ideology, and Theseus is ultimately transformed into an enlightened
feminist. The play builds to a powerful climax in the middle of act 3
when both Theseus and Antiopía first choose honor over love and
then almost simultaneously realize the error of their decision.
While Boccaccio had presented Theseus as correctly reasserting
the role of the dominant male in the business of government and
warfare, Lope's Theseus ultimately sides with the Amazons against
his countrymen, thus acknowledging their claims to equality with
men. The war of the sexes ends in a truce in which neither side can
claim victory. The Amazons freely and with dignity choose to
accept the Greeks as their husbands.

Lope wrote *Las mujeres sin hombres* not long after he met the
woman who was to be the last great love of his life, Marta de
Nevares Santoyo. He dedicated the play to her, and it seems to have
been written with her in mind. We know that Marta had attended a
performance of Lope's *El laberinto de Creta,* because in an undated
letter to the Duke of Sessa, probably written in the spring or early
summer of 1617, Lope mentioned that "Ahora me dicen que va
Amarilis a la *Comedia del Laberinto:* del suyo quisiera yo salir, mas
no tengo hilo de oro, ni aun le quiero . . ." [Now they tell me that
Amaryllis is going to the *Play of the Labyrinth;* I'd like to get out of
hers, but I don't have a golden thread, nor do I really want
one . . .].[10] Marta may have complained to Lope of the rather
harsh treatment of women in that play, and *Las mujeres sin
hombres,* the most ardently feminist play ever written by Lope, may
well have been the poet's attempt to redress that grievance. He
begins the dedication by stating that

> No es disfavor del valor de las mujeres la *Historia de las Amazonas,*
> que, a serlo, no me atreviera a dirigirla a Vm.; antes bien las honra y
> favorece, pues se conoce por ella que pudieran vivir solas en concertada
> república, ejercitar las armas, adquirir reinos, fundar ciudades y dar
> principio a una de las maravillas del mundo, que fue el templo de Diana
> en Efeso.

> [The *History of the Amazons* is not a disparagement of women's worth,
> for, if it were, I would not dare dedicate it to you; rather, it honors and
> favors them, for one learns from it that they managed to live by them-

selves in a harmonious republic, to carry on warfare, to acquire kingdoms, to found cities, and to begin one of the wonders of the world,
which was the Temple of Diana in Ephesus.]

He goes on to say, however that, "el valor de mujeres determinadas
sólo con la blandura del amor podía ser vencido" [the valor of
determined women could only be conquered with love's gen-
tleness], and advises Marta that "no le ofrezco su historia para que
con su ejemplo desee serlo, antes bien para que conozca que la
fuerza con que fueron vencidas tiene por disculpa la misma naturaleza" [I don't offer you their history so that by their example you
might wish to be one of them, but rather so that you might know
that the force by which they were conquered has Nature herself as
excuse].

Besides being extraordinarily beautiful, Marta seems to have
been the most intelligent and talented of Lope's many loves. In
dedicating *La viuda valenciana* (1620) to her, Lope lavishly praised
her poetry, her talent as a musician and singer, her marvelous
command of the purest style in both written and spoken Spanish,
and her skill as a dancer. Marta had been married against her will to
the businessman Roque Hernández de Ayala when she was only
thirteen years old. The marriage had not been a happy one. The two
apparently had little in common and Roque treated Marta
abusively. However, Marta was a strong-willed person, a *mujer
determinada,* and by the time Lope met her, she seems to have won
a measure of independence from her husband. She was able to lead
a not unpleasant life as a woman about town, attending dinner
parties and musical and literary gatherings unaccompanied by her
husband. Small wonder, then, that she was reluctant to sacrifice her
freedom and her reputation for the love of a priest who was almost
twice her age. Lope himself tells us that "trabajo y cuidado me
costaron estos principios" [these beginnings cost me travail and
care][11] and he describes his arduous courtship of Marta in the
eclogue *Amarilis* as follows:

> Más fácil cosa fuera referiros
> las varias flores desta selva amena
> o las ondas del Tajo, en cuyos giros
> envuelto su cristal besa la arena,
> que las ansias, temores y suspiros
> de la esperanza de mi dulce pena,
> hasta que ya, después de largos plazos,
> gané la voluntad, que no los brazos[12]

[It would be easier to recount for you
the various flowers of this pleasant woods
or the waves of the Tagus, wrapped in whose crystal fluctuations
it kisses the sand,
than the anxieties, fears, and sighs
of the hope of my sweet pain,
until at last, after long delays,
I won her will but not her embrace.]

What better argument could Lope offer the elusive Marta than a play showing how even the valiant Amazons of old had finally surrendered to the force of love? Melveena McKendrick has written that the dedication, "with its careful combination of flattery and information, jocularity and didacticism, is a little masterpiece of innuendo."[13]

It would be unfair, however, to view this play as merely a cynical and calculated instrument of seduction. *Las mujeres sin hombres* reveals Lope's genuine sensitivity to the feminist viewpoint. In the play's first scene Montano recounts how the Scythian women first gathered together to discuss their husbands' outrageous behavior toward them:

> Cual contaba que su esposo
> Era por extremo necio,
> Que debe de ser la cosa
> Más triste del casamiento;
> Cual, que era celoso y loco;
> Cual, esquivo y avariento;
> Cual, descuidado de amor;
> Ya entendéis, pues sois discretos.
> Cual, levantando el cendal,
> Mostrando los brazos llenos
> De los golpes, y con ser
> Blanca nieve, jaspes hechos.
>
> (38b)

[One said that her husband
was extremely foolish,
which must be
the saddest thing in marriage;
another, that hers was jealous and crazy;
another, cold and stingy;
another, uninterested in love;
you get the point by now, for you are intelligent.
Another, lifting up her gauzy garment,

showed her arms full of bruises, and though they were
at first white snow, turned into jasper.]

It is surely no coincidence that Marta's chief complaints against her
husband Roque were of his stupidity and jealousy, nor that she
would eventually obtain a legal separation from him on the grounds
of wife-beating. What most enraged the Amazon women, however,
seems to have been not their husband's stupidity, jealousy, stingi-
ness, lack of sex drive, nor even their cruelty, but rather the hateful
double standard in sexual behavior. As they carried out the mas-
sacre of their men, they cried:

> ¡Mueran los hombres . . . ,
> Pues quieren, tiranos fieros,
> Que les guardemos la honra
> Que jamás nos guardan ellos!
>
> (39a)

> [Death to men,
> since those fierce tyrants want
> us to preserve the honor
> they never preserve for us!]

Echoing the sentiments voiced by Pedro Mexía, the play presents
women's supposed foolishness and fear of conflict as merely the
results of men's having denied them an education:

> Que el ser necios o cobardes
> No es defecto del sujeto,
> Sino que en las letras y armas
> No queréis darnos maestros.
> Treta es vuestra, viles hombres,
> Porque nos tengáis sujetos
> Que, estudiando letras y armas,
> Clara ventaja os hacemos.
>
> (49a)

> [Being foolish or cowardly
> is not an innate defect,
> but rather that they won't give us
> teachers of arms and letters.
> It is a trick of you vile men
> to keep us subjected,
> for when we study letters and arms,
> we are clearly better than you.]

Would Theseus have conquered the Minotaur if a woman hadn't
given him the golden thread? Would Jason have been able to win the
golden fleece without Medea's help? Who fought more valiantly in
the Trojan war than the Amazons Pantasilea and Camilla? These
are some of the questions Antiopía angrily hurls at the male chau-
vinist Greeks.

A speech by the Amazon Menalipe anticipates modern feminists'
demands for a revisionist "herstory." Menalipe urges that

> Haya mujeres soldados,
> Y mujeres escritores;
> Escribamos sus errores;
> Vivan también deshonrados.
> No siempre suya ha de ser
> La historia y la pluma.

(50b)

> [Let there be women soldiers
> and women writers;
> let us write their mistakes;
> let them too live in dishonor.
> History and the pen
> mustn't always be theirs.]

Lope's Amazons are neither lesbians nor man-haters. They simply
reject the unfair and unnatural inequality men have imposed upon
them. In a song in act 2 they propose a radically different sort of
relationship between the sexes:

> Como el sol a la luna
> Sus rayos tiende,
> Eso mismo los hombres
> A las mujeres.
> ¿De que sirven las galas
> Con que se adornan?
> Porque no hay hermosura
> Si no se goza.
> El ejemplo nos dieron
> Las altas palmas,
> Que no rinden sus frutos
> Si no se casan . . .
> Linda cosa es el hombre
> Sin libertades;
> Hombres y mujeres
> Fueron iguales.

(52b)

[Just as the sun extends its rays to the moon,
so are men to women.
What good is the finery
with which they adorn themselves?
For there is no beauty
if it is not enjoyed.
The lofty palm trees
have given us an example,
for they don't bear fruit
unless they marry.
Man is a lovely thing
when he doesn't take license;
men and women
were created equal.]

This sane and healthy attitude makes Hercules seem even more ridiculous when he blusters:

Que en esta tierra vil no quede viva
Una sola mujer, aunque no hubiera
Otras en todo el mundo, y la excesiva
Venganza de su fin la causa fuera.
Que en cuantos el linaje humano estriba
Valor no hallo que igualar pudiera
Vida de un hombre solo, y más si es bueno,
Que todo el mundo de mujeres lleno.

(53b)

[In this vile land let not a single woman
remain alive, even if there were
no others in the whole world, and the excessive
revenge brought it to an end.
For in all of the human race
I find no value that could equal
the life of a single man—and even more if he's a good one—
to the whole world full of women.]

In the introduction to the book *Editing the Comedia,* I argue that "If the *comedia* were indeed the mindless, unquestioning repetition of dramatic formulae whose content consisted of a ritualistic manipulation of worn-out concepts on love, honor, religion, and government that our textbooks so often describe, it would hardly merit our attention. In fact scholars are only now beginning to recognize that the *comedia* accurately reflects the teeming diversity, intellectual ferment, and social tensions of the milieu that gave it birth."[14] I believe that *Las mujeres sin hombres* is a good example of Lope's critical stance toward the accepted norms of the society he lived in and demonstrates the extent to which his plays were subversive of those norms. It is sad that we have made so little progress toward true sexual equality that this play remains as vital and relevant today as when it was written some 370 years ago.

Notes

1. Lope F. de Vega Carpio, *Obras de Lope de Vega.* Ed. Marcelino Menéndez y Pelayo, vol. 6 (Madrid: Real Academia Española, 1896), xxvi.

2. Book 2, chapter 45, book 4, chapter 28.

3. *Justino clarissimo abreuiador de la historia general del famoso y excellente historiador Trogo Pompeyo: en la qual se contienen todas las casas notables y mas dignas de memoria que hasta sus tiempos han succedido en todo el mundo; agora nueuamente traduzida en Castellano.* (Alcalá, 1540), 10.

4. Pedro Mexía, *Silva de varia lección,* ed. Justo García Soriano (Madrid: Sociedad de bibliófilos españoles, 1933), 61–62.

5. Ibid., 65.

6. Ibid., 64.

7. Lope, *Obras,* 39b.

8. Giovanni Boccaccio, *Teseida delle nozze d'Emilia,* trans. Bernadette Marie McCoy (New York: Medieval Text Association, 1974), 20–21.

9. Lope, *Obras,* 38b.

10. Francisco Asenjo Barbieri, *Ultimos amores de Lope de Vega Carpio.* (Madrid: Imprenta de José María Ducazcal, 1876), 59.

11. Cayetano Alberto de la Barrera, *Nueva biografía de Lope de Vega,* 2 vols., Biblioteca de Autores Españoles, 262–63. (Madrid: Atlas, 1973) 1, 179.

12. Ibid., 1, 183.

13. Melveena McKendrick, *Women and Society in the Spanish Drama of the Golden Age* (Cambridge: Cambridge University Press, 1974), 184.

14. Frank Casa and Michael McGaha, eds. *Editing the Comedia* (Ann Arbor: Michigan Romance Studies, 1985), i–ii.

Works Cited

Asenjo Barbieri, Francisco. *Ultimos amores de Lope de Vega Carpio.* Madrid: Imprenta de José María Ducazcal, 1876.

Barrera, Cayetano Alberto de la. *Nueva biografía de Lope de Vega.* 2 vols. Biblioteca de Autores Españoles. Madrid: Atlas, 1973.

Boccaccio, Giovanni. *Teseida delle nozze d'Emilia.* Translated by Bernadette Marie McCoy. New York: Medieval Text Association, 1974.

Casa, Frank, and Michael McGaha, eds. *Editing the Comedia.* Ann Arbor: Michigan Romance Studies, 1985.

Conti, Natale (Natalis Comes). *Mythologiae, siue explicationum fabularum, Libri decem.* Paris: Arnoldum Sittart, 1582.

Justinus clarissimo abreuiador de la historia general del famoso y excellente historiador Trogo Pompeyo: en la qual se contienen todas las casas notables y mas dignas de memoria que hasta sus tiempos han succedido en todo el mundo; agora nueuamente traduzida en Castellano. Translated by Jorge de Bustamante. Alcalá, 1540.

McKendrick, Melveena. *Women and Society in the Spanish Drama of the Golden Age.* Cambridge: Cambridge University Press, 1974.

Mexía, Pedro. *Silva de varia lección.* Edited by Justo García Soriano. Madrid: Sociedad de bibliófilos españoles, 1933.

Vega Carpio, Lope F. de. *Obras de Lope de Vega.* Edited by Marcelino Menéndez y Pelayo. Vol. 6. Madrid: Real Academia Española, 1896.

Vitoria, Baltasar de. *Theatro de los dioses de la gentilidad, Segunda Parte.* Salamanca, 1623.

The Politics of Rape and *Fineza* in Calderonian Myth Plays

THOMAS AUSTIN O'CONNOR

At first glance the theme of rape might not be considered relevant to the topic of this collection, the role of women in the *comedia*. Since rapists convert women into sexual objects upon whom power and violence are then exercised, any role ascribed to women would perforce appear to be a purely passive and uninteresting one. This view, however, is overly simplistic for it fails to address the complex depiction of rape in Calderonian theater.

While it would be anachronistic to credit Calderón with what we would call a feminist perspective on patriarchal society, nonetheless his varied dramatizations of the rape motif reveal fissures in sexist seventeenth-century Spain. Calderón, for whatever reason, saw that rape was indeed a political act, and Robert ter Horst, referring to tyrant princes in his theater, labeled "their rule as a politics of rape."[1] Since the phenomenon of rape occurs in comedies like *El galán fantasma* [The Phantom Suitor], the rape motif itself is not restricted to his serious theater. And, as is often the case, the mature view of rape comes into focus with the myth plays. For example, the politics of rape in *Fieras afemina Amor* [Love makes beasts effeminate], rather than a code that operates behind Hércules's back, becomes before his and our eyes a theme that must be probed.

Rape is a topic that has not yet been sufficiently surveyed nor properly understood,[2] and it is a significant motif in Calderonian theater, serving a variety of dramatic functions. The following taxonomy of rape is organized into three parts. First, I shall review the importance of the rape motif in some well-known Calderonian plays that are not dramatized versions of Greco-Roman myths. Second, I shall analyze seven of seventeen myth dramas in which rape plays a prominent role. In the third and final section, I shall consider those special cases in which children are born to mothers raped by

170

violent and ignoble males. In these instances, rape provides a window into the dynamics of Calderón's dramatic worlds. On examining the circumstances in which these children of violence develop, we shall come to an understanding of the generic conditions that characterize either tragic or comic results.

I

We are accustomed to view rape or the threat of rape as a proclivity of masculine nature, and modern psychology, sociology, and feminist writings have sharpened our awareness of the underlying motivations of this act. I see four principal manifestations in Calderonian theater. First, rape is presented as an evil act that dehumanizes the woman thus violated, but also leads to the death of the rapist, a just punishment for his attempt to steal what only love can confer. Don Alvaro de Ataide, the vain and duplicitous Captain of *El alcalde de Zalamea* [*The Mayor of Zalamea*] immediately comes to mind. No one laments his death, and even Felipe II appears on stage to ratify Pedro Crespo's judgment. Another example of the rapist's death occurs in *Los cabellos de Absalón* [Absalom's locks], where Tamar's rape by Amón allows Absalón to eliminate the heir apparent to the throne as he pushes King David's realm into civil strife. In both these plays broader social issues, the question of the administration of justice and, in the latter work, that of succession, loom larger than the victims' sufferings. These sufferings, therefore, are subsumed under a masculine set of assumptions that preoccupy patriarchal society. Rape is portrayed as a theft of what belongs to another male.

The second manifestation of rape occurs outside of what we normally consider its proper place; that is, serious drama, in what traditional scholarship has labeled a cape and sword play. *No hay cosa como callar* [There is nothing like silence] is unique in Calderonian theater because in this instance we find a rape without apparent dire consequences for either the rapist or the raped woman. Don Juan's rape of Leonor is potentially dangerous both to them and to their society, but the rapist remedies his offense with an offer to marry his erstwhile victim. Although in these *trances de honor* [honor's critical moments] timing is everything, we in our modern or postmodern consciousness feel uneasy for Leonor, just as we do for Leonor of *El médico de su honra* [*The Surgeon of His Honor*]. While marriage is viewed as just reparation for Leonor's stolen virginity, such a solution underscores a more horrible reality—marriage, in this case at least, is merely barter that justifies rape.

The third manifestation of rape escapes from the exclusivity of masculine preoccupations to reveal rape as the catalyst of a tragic concatenation of events with generational reach. In *La hija del aire* [The daughter of the air], based on Assyrian myth, Semíramis's mother was raped by a devotee of Venus, and we witness in consequence how Diana avenges this affront received from the goddess of love. To be born as a result of rape and not as an expression of conjugal love is to enter a fate-filled world. A child of violence, an "embrión de una violencia" [embryo of violence] (1998b), as Tetis describes her son Aquiles in *El monstruo de los jardines* [The monster of the gardens],[3] carries in his or her blood the inheritance of violence that always demonstrates its tragic valence. The social repercussions of rape affect even the unborn, who must somehow deal with the unnatural manner of their conception and its consequent guilt.

The fourth manifestation depicts the temptation to rape a vulnerable woman and the positive consequences of rape forsworn. The signal example occurs in *La vida es sueño* [*Life Is a Dream*] when Segismundo rejects the rape of Rosaura in order to restore her lost honor. This sign of having conquered himself translates into a dramatic statement concerning his suitability for kingship, but one not to be governed by a politics of rape.

II

Calderón's myth plays are by and large sophisticated depictions of dramatic worlds whose interpretative keys lie in our own experiential framework. Though the gods are frequently powerful and remote beings, they act more like crass members of the ruling classes than like ethereal beings removed from error and miscalculation. Although many scholars have approached this body of material from a historical framework that seeks to elucidate the allegorical meaning of the texts, my purpose is to address their narrative and symbolic significance. This strategy necessitates dealing with each play as a discrete work bearing distinct generic suggestiveness. The term "mythological plays" refers only to their source and not to any generic distinctiveness.

The myth plays that contain the rape motif may also be arranged according to the broad outline previously presented. For example,

in *Los tres mayores prodigios* [The three greatest prodigies],
Lidoro, Minos's captain-general, plans on abducting Ariadna. Allu-
sions to a punitive and vengeful attitude toward women characterize this violent man's motivation, because rape, for him at least,
is the proper response to Ariadna, who has rejected all his ad-
vances. He states clearly:

> Donde
> no puede el amor, consiga
> la osadía los favores.
>
> (1572a)

> [Where
> love cannot, let boldness
> obtain favors.]

Shortly afterwards he rationalizes his base plan as follows:

> Amor es dios, y no teme
> que lo sagrado le estorbe.
> De él te he de sacar huyendo
> a más remotas regiones,
> y hacer que agravios consigan
> lo que no pueden favores.
>
> (1572a)

> [Love is a god, and he is not frightened
> by a sanctuary's opposition.
> I will snatch you from it,
> fleeing to remote places,
> and will ensure that injuries obtain
> what favors could not.]

This situation is repeated in act 3 when Neso, after a year's delay,
determines to take by force what he could not win by persuasion.
Hércules appears and kills this abductor and putative rapist of his
beloved wife Deyanira. In both instances, whether to rape a disdainful woman or to rape a virtuous wife commands swift and
deadly retribution. A primary obligation of all noble males is to
protect all females from the predatory practices of ignoble men. It is
highly illustrative that, in this case, Deyanira is doubly victimized:
first by Neso's lustful objectification of her and secondly by her
husband Hércules's cowardly rejection of his possibly tainted wife.
Hércules's inability to protect and secure Deyanira's virtue brings
about tragic consequences for both of them.

A situation similar to the circumstances of *Alcalde's* and *Absalón's* plots obtains in *El monstruo de los jardines*. In Calderón's account of Aquiles's birth, he significantly altered the original myth. Although in Pérez de Moya's account of the marriage of Peleo and Tetis the human forced himself on the goddess, he did not rape her.[4] Not only does Calderón have Peleo, a mortal, rape Tetis, a goddess, he also has her avenge this affront by killing her attacker. The rape results in her being, however, impregnated with the future Greek hero who is destined to uphold Greek honor by laying waste to Troy. In *Fieras afemina Amor* we do not have the physical death of a rapist, rather the debasement, the effemination of Hércules, the greatest of all Greek heroes. This character tries to force Yole to marry him, or to be his concubine, a prime example of the politics of rape, in spite of his earlier rejection of her and all women. What he feels is not love but lust, and this passion brings him to a willing acceptance of effeminacy. Although Hércules does not technically rape Yole, his purpose is to force her to have intercourse with him in spite of her constant refusals. Hércules's demythologization occurs after he previously rejected the use of force in matters of the heart:

> ¡Qué bajo espíritu debe
> de tener quien se contenta
> con que lo que es voluntad
> lo haya de adquirir por fuera!
> Una mujer violentada,
> ¿es más, si se considera,
> que una estatua algo más viva,
> con alma algo menos muerta?

(2030a)

> [What a base spirit he must
> have who contents himself
> with what should be freely offered
> but is forcefully acquired.
> A woman done violence to,
> is she more, if carefully considered,
> than a statue somewhat alive,
> with a soul somewhat dead?]

In summary, in *Prodigios* [Prodigies] Lidoro dies because he attempts to abduct Ariadna in order to rape her; Neso dies because his attempted rape is a base expression of his frustrated passion, constantly rejected by the virtuous Deyanira. In *Monstruo* [Monster], a most novel situation occurs in which Tetis kills her rapist Peleo. And in *Fieras* [Beasts], although there is technically no rape, the consequence of Hércules's actions, his effeminacy, is worse than physical death. All these males attempt to steal "affection" that they have not earned through *finezas* [acts of kindness], affection, courtesy, and devotion motivated by either honor or love] or some other physical or moral virtue. Death is their penalty. While the rapist receives just punishment, the woman's dehumanization and suffering underscore the operative codes that lead to her victimization and open them to our inspection.

The case in which rape produces no dire consequence for the rapist or the raped woman, aside from some temporary injury to the female's reputation and fame, may be further complicated by our views that wish to transcend human suffering. In *El laurel de Apolo* [Apollo's Laurel] the latter attempts to rape the shy and fleet Dafne and avenge himself on the wiley god of love.[5] Dafne's metamorphosis before defilement presents a fact easily overlooked in prior rapes: though there may or may not be dire consequences for the rapists, there is always a horrible aftermath for the women thus debased and dehumanized. Dafne's metamorphosis is not an apotheosis, a tribute to Apolo's everlasting love, but a reminder, a dramatic statement about her loss of self. Only in this sense can *Laurel* and Dafne be related to Leonor of *No hay cosa como callar.* Rape demands that a severe penalty be paid, and frequently the woman pays the ultimate price with her life; the victim is doubly victimized. Calderón's plays entice us to deconstruct the traditional palliatives of marriage and metamorphosis by revealing marriage as barter and metamorphosis as loss.

By far the most challenging and significant use of the rape motif occurs as background to events dramatized on stage. A good example of this use is found in *Eco y Narciso* [Echo and Narcissus]. Liríope was raped by the impatient and powerful Céfiro, precipitating a series of events that eventually leads to the death of the offspring of this violent union. This act sets in motion a tragic concatenation that will only end with the deaths of the young and somehow guilty Eco and Narciso. Although not in the least responsible for his mother's rape, Narciso becomes tainted by his father's violence and his mother's excessive sense of shame, thereby inheriting a tragic patrimony.

Fortunas de Andrómeda y Perseo [The fortunes of Andromeda and Perseus] provides us with a very different view of these matters. The violent and crass rape of Danae by Júpiter precipitates a potentially tragic result both for her and her son Perseo. In this play one finds a deepening awareness and fuller manifestation of rape's terrible reach and dehumanizing consequence for women. Neptuno raped Medusa, turning her into a monster, a negative vision of the metamorphic phenomenon that denies transcendence. The text states that Neptuno

> no
> se valió de las finezas
> de rendido; que el amor
> de un poderoso no ruega,
> cuando puede la caricia
> valerse de la violencia.

(1651a)

> [He
> did not avail himself of the *finezas* (kindness and affection)
> of a devoted lover; for a powerful man's
> love does not entreat,
> when his caress is able
> to employ violence.]

Rape is diametrically opposed to *finezas,* the word that encapsulates honor's obligations both to men and to women, but in this latter instance the obligations become more acute, more evident. The nature and quality of male-female interactions may be graphically represented by the relation of "las finezas / de rendido" [the lover's kindness and affection] to violence and rape. The primary reason for Perseo's escape from the inheritance of Júpiter is his attentive regard for the male's obligation to perform mighty *finezas* for all women, particularly for the woman he loves. In a supremely masterful and ironic stroke, Calderón has Júpiter refer to his rape of Danae as a *fineza.* Among other significant differences between *Eco y Narciso* and *Fortunas,* Perseo's performance of *finezas* for his beloved Andrómeda directs his rite of passage from boyhood to manhood, signaling his avoidance of Júpiter's patrimony by his high regard for the true obligations of honor.

Rape produces social repercussions that primarily affect women in patriarchal society. By emphasizing the generational reach of rape, Calderón opens not only rape to inspection but also the larger society, its social structures, and the operative codes that contribute to the ideology of rape. Rape is a fateful inheritance of a warped society that endlessly reproduces itself until the individual consciously breaks its generational reach by adhering to the liberating ideology of *finezas.* In the third section I shall demonstrate the deep structure of these two plays, one leading to a tragic issue and the other, to a happy one.

The counterpart to *La vida es sueño's* depiction of rape forsworn occurs in the beautifully lyric and strangely melancholy *Ni Amor se libra de amor* [Even love cannot be rid of love]. Cupido, the god of love, finds himself in an amazingly similar circumstance to Segismundo's in which the latter is tempted to rape Rosaura. Cupido, too, does not rape the woman he loves, although his first impulse is to do so. The god of love makes clear what is ultimately at stake at this point in the play:

> Bien pudiera fozarte
> mi gusto, al ver que huyes;
> pero mis vanidades
> tan baja acción no sufren:
> que es baldón de lo noble,
> bajeza de lo ilustre,
> juzgar que con violencias
> los méritos se suplen.
> Oblíguete mi ruego,
> mi llanto te asegure,
> muévate mi fineza.

(1967a–b)

[To satisfy my lust, how easily
I could rape you once you flee from me;
but my pride
does not allow such a base action:
for it is a blemish on honor,
a base affront to my renown,
to believe that violence
may replace merit.
Let my plea oblige you,
my tears assure you,
my affection and kindness *(fineza)* move you.]

Cupido's love is true and in no way does he act as the powerful gods we have previously seen: Apolo, Júpiter, and Neptuno. Cupido's *finezas,* as well as Perseo's, provide us with the interpretative key that allows us to unlock and appreciate the Calderonian concept of nobility. True honor is motivated by the acceptance of *finezas'* demands as opposed to pleasures' promptings. Rape forsworn signals the transition from a masculine "politics of rape" to a conservatively informed "politics of *fineza.*"[6]

III

Those special cases in which a child is born to a woman raped by a powerful man or god present us with a unique opportunity to contrast two fundamentally opposing dramatic structures, one tragic and the other comic in its broad outlines. *La hija del aire* relates how Semíramis, the offspring of rape, inherits a violent horoscope that will lead to her destruction and that of many who come into contact with her. The details of this rape remind us of Tetis's rape in *El monstruo de los jardines*. First, the raped woman killed the attacker, avenging her wrong. Second, though in *Monstruo* the goddess brought up the "embrión de una violencia" in complete isolation, in *Hija* Semíramis was brought up by Tiresias after her mother's death in childbirth. In both instances, however, the child of rape is raised in an unnatural manner, cut off from human association. Both of these children face dire threats from a hostile fate that menaces them and those with whom they associate.

Calderón's beautifully lyric and dramatically moving play *Eco y Narciso* elaborates somewhat similar circumstances to those encountered in *Hija*. First, Céfiro raped Liríope and from this violent union Narciso was born. Though Liríope did not kill her attacker, she hid her child from human society and brought him up in seclusion, just as Semíramis was raised. Second, while both Semíramis and Narciso lived in fear of a fate that threatened them and others, their natural desires to be free and to participate in society eventually contribute to the fulfillment of what has been prophesied. Each case presents a unique dramatization of the confluence of what was predicted and what is determined by individual will.

These tragic plays can be contrasted with what I have labeled "divine comedy" in another study.[7] While *La devoción de la Cruz* [*Devotion to the Cross*] does not dramatize the stories of children of rape, it does narrate the lives of children born to a violent, cruel, and rigorous father and husband, one who was prepared to kill his wife, whom he mistakenly believed had betrayed him. These children of violence are capable of extricating themselves from their star-crossed past only by attending to the promptings of providence in their lives. What catches one's attention in this play is providence's effectiveness in bringing the three Curcio children to their divine destinies in spite of their father's deadly influence. We are compelled to ask: Where is this providential concern in the tragic plays mentioned above? Why has it been bracketed by the dramatist?

The myth play that markedly contrasts to *Hija* and *Eco y Narciso* is *Fortunas de Andrómeda y Perseo,* a work that contains all the elements that normally would be associated with tragic action. There is Júpiter's rape of Danae; Danae and her son are set adrift by her cruel father in a boat with a hole drilled in its hull. Somehow there is providential concern for these two that averts what would otherwise be a tragic issue. Danae, moreover, raises her son Perseo in normal society. Once his identity is revealed as "hijo vil de un adulterio, u de otra traición" [a vile son of some adultery, / or of some other betrayal] (1644a), however, his comfortable life becomes a torment to him. The intervention of Mercurio and Palas, his brother and sister, guides him through manifold difficulties to a form of *human* salvation symbolized by his adherence to the ideology of *fineza* and subsequent marriage to Andrómeda. Although the play is set in the mode of romance, its comedic outcome, in spite of the circumstances suggestive of tragedy, is due to Mercurio and Palas's intervention to thwart Perseo's inheritance of violence and rape. *Fortunas* depicts in clearly mythic terms what divine providence accomplished by analogy in *Devoción.*

Contrasting the elements that form the tragic structure of *Eco y Narciso* with those that form the "comedic" structure of *Fortunas,* one can discern the deep structures of Calderonian comedy and tragedy. These two myth plays that contain the rape motif depend on two fundamentally different conceptions of time that inform the characteristic substructures of Calderonian comedy and tragedy. In *Eco y Narciso, cyclical time* undergirds the dramatic action and traps the characters in human time so that Narciso somehow becomes tainted by the crimes of his father and errors of his loving but fearful mother.[8] I have designated this form of time *chronos* (lat. *tempus*). In *Fortunas,* on the other hand, teleological time informs the dramatic action and allows Perseo to escape his inheritance of violence and rape so that he is able to realize to the full his human potential.[9] While in this first instance the entrapment of Eco, Narciso, and Liríope is seen in purely human time, from which all mythic activity seeks escape through ritualized action,[10] in the second can be discovered a sacramentalized time that views both time and history as radically transformed by the New Covenant. *Eco y Narciso* dramatizes the deadly effects of *gusto* as the informing principle of human activity, whereas *Fortunas* dramatizes the liberating properties of *finezas* as the true guide to human conduct. Mercurio had advised the young Perseo:

> Ama, espera y confía;
> porque no puede

el que vence sin riesgo,
decir que vence.

(1667b)

[Love, hope, and be confident;
because he who conquers
without risk cannot
state that he conquers.]

Assumption of risk is, moreover, the prime attribute of *fineza*, for the noble person accepts all manner of danger for the other's sake. In contradistinction to the ignoble rapists Júpiter and Neptuno, each of whom "no se valió de las finezas / de rendido" [did not / avail himself of the *finezas* / of a devoted lover] (1651a) to satisfy his lust or *gusto* [pleasure], the noble Perseo wins Andrómeda through the performance of heroic *finezas*. He risks his life to save his beloved through the performance of *finezas* that are ultimately informed by the love principle:

Mas ¿qué mucho facilite
más que el hado dificulta,
amor, que en estas finezas
todos sus méritos funda,
para arrojarme a tus plantas?

(1678a)

[However, might love expedite
more than fate impedes,
for in these *finezas*
it (love) bases all merit,
so as to place me at your feet?]

Fortunas' teleological time I have labeled *kairos* (Lat. *opportunitas*). Fate is linked to *chronos* and providence, to *kairos*.

There is an ancient tradition that implicates children in the sins and crimes of their parents, and our notion of cyclical time assumes such a connection. Christ's disciples asked him concerning the man blind from birth: "Rabbi, who sinned, this man or his parents, for him to have been born blind?" (Jn 9:2).[11] And the Jews who cried out for Jesus to be crucified assumed a hereditary guilt that implicated their children: "'His blood be on us and on our children'" (Mt 27:26). St. Augustine pondered such issues in Ch. 46 of *The Enchiridion on Faith, Hope and Love:*

And it is said, with much appearance of probability, that infants are involved in the guilt of the sins not only of the first pair, but of their own immediate parents. For that divine judgment, "I shall visit the iniquities of the fathers upon the children," certainly applies to them before they come under the new covenant by regeneration. . . . and further, because there are other sins of the immediate parents, which, though they have not the same effect in producing a change of nature, yet subject children to guilt unless the divine grace and mercy interpose to rescue them.[12]

Even Ann Landers has broached the question of whether AIDS is a punishment from God that afflicts the innocent, such as the hemophiliac who receives a tainted blood transfusion, and the guilty by association, such as the infant born of a mother with AIDS.[13] In Calderón's tragic myths fate is linked to cyclical time in that, in this instance at least, the children of violent and erring parents somehow come under the influence of a "tragic inheritance."[14] St. Augustine's insight into these matters allows us to glimpse the inner workings of plays such as *Eco y Narciso* and *Fortunas,* for in the former tragic fate underscores the absence of "divine grace and mercy" that the latter makes clear in the roles of Mercurio and Palas. Fate symbolizes a de-Christianized world, or perhaps an "aChristian" world in terms of some myth plays, in which providential guidance is conspicuously absent. These plays dramatize a world outside of the pale of what we can call salvation history in Christian terms. In such works Calderón creates a dramatic world ruled by chance and fortune that become the hallmarks of his conception of tragedy, for there is no positive ruling presence to interpose itself between these children of rape and their tragic fates. Only in *Fortunas* is encountered an analogous force to that of providence in *Devoción;* that force signals human freedom from fateful heredity and anticipates liberation from the bonds of ensnaring time. The religious plays and the *autos sacramentales* [sacramental plays] are extended commentaries on the presence and efficaciousness of divine providence in human time. Calderonian tragedy is a lament for the absence of this caring presence bracketed by the Christian dramatist.

* * *

There is no such thing as heroic rape in Calderonian theater.[15] As a motif frequently employed both in myth plays and in secular plays, rape adapts itself to the overall dramatic design that in turn is related to the deep structures of his dramaturgy. Contrasting those structures manifest in *Eco y Narciso* and *Fortunas de Andrómeda y Perseo,* the essential features and inner workings of Calderonian comedy and tragedy are clearly seen: rape contains a tragic potential that only some form of providential guidance can counterbalance. Though that guidance and concern is found in *Fortunas,* one can only note its absence in *Eco y Narciso.* In no way has Calderón suggested why it is absent, and thus this tragic play, while it sensitizes one to the issues involved, remains mute regarding the fundamental mystery it seeks to dramatize.

Notes

1. *Calderón: The Secular Plays* (Lexington: University Press of Kentucky, 1982), p. 200. See also pp. 131–34, where he provides a brief survey of rape as a major Calderonian theme.

2. Of the many books on Calderonian theater that have been published in the 1980s, only ter Horst's addresses rape as a major theme.

3. Pedro Calderón de la Barca, *Obras completas: dramas,* ed. A. Valbuena Briones (Madrid: Aguilar, 1969). Citations refer to page and column. I do not agree with the interpretations of *Monstruo* put forth by Frederick A. de Armas, *The Return of Astraea: An Astral-Imperial Myth in Calderón* (Lexington: University Press of Kentucky, 1986), Sebastian Neumeister, *Mythos und Repräsentation* (Munich: Wilhelm Fink, 1978), and Everett W. Hesse, "Calderón's *El monstruo de los jardines:* Sex, Sexuality, and Sexual Fulfillment," *Revista Canadiense de Estudios Hispánicos* 5 (1981): 311–19.

4. Juan Pérez de Moya, *Philosophia secreta* (Madrid, 1928), 202–8. Original edition, 1585.

5. See Mary Barnard's *The Myth of Apollo and Daphne from Ovid to Quevedo* (Durham, N.C.: Duke University Press, 1987) for background information on Apollo's debasement.

6. This apparent social liberation of woman does not, however, change her subordinate position vis-à-vis man, rather it frees both of them from the oppression of rape. Calderón's positive view of *finezas'* power is conservatively motivated and societally prophylactic. Although his theater brings to the fore the consequences of what may properly be called a politics of privilege and abuse, the informing critique proceeds not from a liberational appreciation of woman's role in society, but from a hoped-for renewal of his conservative agenda that may be summarized as a politics of duty and responsibility.

7. Thomas A. O'Connor, "De tragedia a comedia en el teatro de Calderón: El tiempo como característica genérica," a paper given 18 August 1986 at the IX Congreso de la Asociación Internacional de Hispanistas, Berlin, Germany.

8. William R. Blue, in *The Development of Imagery in Calderón's Comedias* (York, S.C.: Spanish Literature Publications, 1983), employs the term "cyclical time" (p. 126 and pp. 136–7), but he does not develop the implications of this structure for Calderonian theater.

9. I am grateful to James A. Parr for suggesting that I label as "teleological" what was previously termed "progressive" time.

10. See Mircea Eliade, *Myth, Dreams and Mysteries: The Encounter between Contemporary Faiths and Archaic Realities,* tr. Philip Mairet (London: Harvill Press, 1960), p. 31.

11. *The New Jerusalem Bible* (Garden City, N.Y.: Doubleday, 1966).

12. *Basic Writings of Saint Augustine,* 1, ed. Whitney J. Oates (New York: Random House, 1948), 685n.

13. See Ann Landers, "Compassion Needed," *Manhattan Mercury,* 5 April 1987.

14. Francisco Ruiz Ramón, in *Calderón y la tragedia* (Madrid: Alhambra, 1984), refers to "la circularidad de la acción" (4) as a characteristic of Calderonian tragedy.

15. See Susan Brownmiller, *Against Our Will: Men, Women and Rape* (New York: Simon and Shuster, 1975), especially p. 289.

Works Cited

Augustine, St. *Basic Writings of Saint Augustine.* Vol. 1. Edited by Whitney J. Oates. New York: Random House, 1948.

Barnard, Mary. *The Myth of Apollo and Daphne from Ovid to Quevedo.* Durham, N.C.: Duke University Press, 1987.

Blue, William R. *The Develpment of Imagery in Calderón's Comedias.* York, S.C.: Spanish Literature Publications, 1983.

Brownmiller, Susan. *Against Our Will: Men, Women and Rape.* New York: Simon and Shuster, 1975.

Calderón de la Barca, Pedro. *Obras completas: dramas.* Edited by A. Valbuena Briones. Madrid: Aguilar, 1969.

de Armas, Frederick A. *The Return of Astraea: An Astral-Imperial Myth in Calderón.* Lexington: University Press of Kentucky, 1986.

Eliade, Mircea. *Myth, Dreams and Mysteries: The Encounter between Contemporary Faiths and Archaic Realities.* Translated by Philip Mairet. London: Harvill Press, 1960.

Hesse, Everett W. "Calderón's *El monstruo de los jardines:* Sex, Sexuality, and Sexual Fulfillment" *Revista Canadiense de Estudios Hispánicos* 5 (1981): 311–19.

Landers, Ann. "Compassion Needed," *Manhattan Mercury.* 5 April 1987.

Neumeister, Sebastian. *Mythos und Repräsentation.* Munich: Wilhelm Fink, 1978.

O'Connor, Thomas A. "De tragedia a comedia en el teatro de Calderón: El tiempo como característica genérica," a paper given 18 August 1986 at the IX Congreso de la Asociación Internacional de Hispanistas, Berlin, Germany.

Pérez de Moya, Juan. *Philosophia secreta.* Vol. 2. Madrid, 1928, Original edition, 1585.

Ruiz Ramón, Francisco. *Calderón y la tragedia.* Madrid: Alhambra, 1984.

ter Horst, Robert. *Calderón: The Secular Plays.* Lexington: University Press of Kentucky, 1982.

"The Rape of Deianeira" in Calderón's *El pintor de su deshonra*

MARCIA L. WELLES

Art historians have recently noted the need to return to textual sources in order to follow a narrative correctly.[1] By the same token, I believe that as students of literature we have undervalued visual sources available in a text. Because of its incorporation of a mythological painting in a secular drama, *El pintor de su deshonra* [The painter of his dishonour] offers a unique opportunity to study the interrelationship between the arts, as well as to appreciate the transformative power of myth. Yet, except for Susan L. Fischer's brief and thoughtful article on the meaning of the Hercules painting, little critical attention has been dedicated to the topic.[2] Further exploration at this time is, therefore, justified.

In 1982, a judge at the Cambridge Crown Court summarized his opinion on a rape case to the jury:

> Women who say no do not always mean no. It is not just a question of saying no, it is a question of how she says it, how she shows and makes it clear.[3]

Whether or not this judge was aware of it, the concentration on the issue of female consent harks back to St. Augustine, who in the *City of God* introduced the subtle, yet deadly distinction, between actual and "internal consent." Nuns who are violated are blameless, yet, he adds:

> And so whenever any act of the latter kind has been committed, although it does not destroy a purity which has been maintained by the utmost resolution, still it does engender a sense of shame, because it may be believed that an act, which perhaps could not have taken place without some physical pleasure, was accompanied also by a consent of the mind.[4]

The Rape of Deianeira from *Las transformaciones de Ovidio en lengua española.*
Trans. Jorge de Bustamante. Anvers: Pedro Bellero, 1595. (The Hispanic Society of
America)

Thus rape ceases to be an event definable in terms of public actions or statements; sexuality exists in the realm of "privacy and inward specificity,"[5] in the shadowy regions of "consent of the mind" known only to God according to the Church fathers, or, in our modern world, to the psychiatrist—perhaps. A woman can betray herself, however, in the involuntary manifestations of her body; the merest smile or unguarded gesture reveals her desire and becomes a certain sign of her "secondary" consent. In the betrayal of the body, the soul is revealed, as it were.

In *El pintor de su deshonra* the abducted Serafina is doomed when she responds, involuntarily after a nightmare, to the embrace of Don Alvaro, her rapist in intent, if not in fact: "Nunca fueron / tus brazos más agradables" [Never were your arms more agreeable] (3.3068–9).[6] All equivocations stilled "al verla en sus brazos" [upon seeing her in his arms] (3.3080), the aggrieved husband shoots them both, asking afterwards for his own death: "Ahora más que me maten; / que ya no estimo la vida" [Let them now kill me, / for I no longer value life] (3.3085–86). If language is the sign of the conscious, rational mind, the body is the sign of the irrational, unconscious self: the sexual sign. In an early article on this play, Bruce W. Wardropper noticed that "it is only in the critical moments of dream, swoon, confidence and *turbación* that it [the unconscious life of the mind] stands revealed in its true nature," which led him to conclude that Serafina "was not the victim of an heartless code, but of her own repressed sin."[7]

There is no doubt that the rape—in the Latin sense of "carrying off by force"—of Serafina constitutes the nucleus of the action of the play. Although the abduction does not result in sexual consummation, the general effect still is of contamination that determines a tragic outcome. The obvious unlawfulness of Alvaro's act of seizure encourages the reader to approach the text in the spirit of a prosecuting attorney, called to pass judgment on the guilt or innocence of Serafina according to the Augustinian concern with consent. Whatever judicial opinion is handed down determines an attitude of praise or blame for the husband's revenge, which in turn determines the interpretation of the author's opinion of the so-called "honor code"—approval or denial through irony. Does Don Juan Roca's act of murder invalidate his stated repudiation of the honor code? Does the playwright mean "pardon" when the Prince and fathers exonerate the murderer? Does Serafina mean "no" when she says "no"? Is Serafina guilty of secret desires, or is she "a victimized woman who is only to be esteemed for her steadfastness and virtue"?[8]

Because of the gaps between intention and utterance, utterance and performance, the text lends itself to multiple interpretations.

In order to move beyond the intricacies of "words, words, words," (2.2.194), Hamlet sought another source of evidence: "The play's the thing / Wherein I'll catch the conscience of the King" (2.2.616–17).[9] There is not a play-within-a-play in *El pintor de su deshonra,* but a painting is described, "The Rape of Deianeira," to which one can look to catch the conscience of Juan—the word *conscience* being used here is in its obsolete, but etymologically valid sense of "inmost thought or sense: knowledge of inner self." An example of ekphrasis, but by no means a mere rhetorical ornamentation, the painting functions as an "iconic enclave,"[10] which, by conveying information about the play and its players, helps clarify some of the ambiguities and determine a meaning. I recognize that by focusing on the painting I am committing a double act of displacement: I begin at the end of the play instead of at the beginning (the description appears in act 3), and I move the painting from its background position into the foreground. My justification is that the *historia* of the myth provides a narrative allegory mirroring in miniature the action of the play, which it infuses with moral energy.

Before discussing this rape (of Deianeira), it is important to place it in a context. Some fifty actual or attempted rapes, or "sexual extortions" are related in Ovid's *Metamorphoses,*[11] which led Charles Segal to suggest that the poem might be more properly considered an "epic of rape" rather than one of love.[12] Many of these, though by no means all, fall into the category of the so-called "heroic rape,"[13] perpetrated by the great Zeus himself. From its emergence in the fifth century B.C. as a popular subject for Greek vase painting and sculpture, depiction of the heroic rape has been characterized by an aura of nonviolence, a noteworthy absence of struggle or fear, and an elegance of posture and feature.[14] An example of a later, increasingly eroticized development of this tradition is Titian's *Danae* (1553–54). A counterpoint to this tradition are the scenes of amorous pursuit of the maenads by satyrs, or the pursuits of the centaurs. These depictions can acquire allegorical significance, as occurs in the Parthenon metope of the Centaurs, which, in juxtaposition with that of the Amazons, represents the invading army of barbarian Persians—a threat to the Athenian order.[15] For the sake of equilibrium, these may be called "bestial" rapes.

The rape of Hercules's bride Deianeira by the centaur Nessus falls unequivocally into the category of the bestial rape. This is the moment chosen for depiction by Juan, who, disguised as a painter, asks the Prince to look at his fable of Hercules, and see

> Como está la ira
> en su entereza pintada,
> al ver que se lleva hurtada
> el centauro a Deyanira:
> y con tan vivos anhelos
> tras él va, que juzgo yo
> que nadie le vea que no
> diga: "Este hombre tiene celos."
> Fuera de la tabla está
> y aún estuviera más fuera
> si en la tabla no estuviera,
> el centauro tras quien va.
> Este es el cuerpo mayor
> del lienzo, y en los bosquejos
> de las sombras y los lejos,
> en perspectiva menor
> se ve abrasándose, y es
> el mote que darle quiero:
> "Quien tuvo celos primero,
> muera abrasado después."

(3.2686–2705)

> [How ire
> is depicted in his whole body,
> upon seeing how
> the centaur is stealing Deianeira;
> and he pursues him with such eager longings,
> that it seems to me
> that there is nobody who sees him who will not
> say, "This man is jealous."
> He is outside the bounds of the panel,
> and would be even further removed
> if the centaur whom he pursues
> were not there.
> This is the main portion
> of the canvas; in the sketches
> of the shadows and distances,
> in diminishing perspective,
> he is seen burning,
> and the inscription that I intend
> to give it is:

"Let him who first was jealous,
afterwards die burned."]

The plot analogies are evident: the bride Serafina/Deianeira is abducted by Alvaro/Nessus, who is killed by the husband Juan/Hercules. The patterns of interaction and symbolic meanings of this ancient mythic discourse impinge upon the problematic areas of Calderón's society in ways that he obviously thought relevant to explore.

The characterization of the centaur is particularly relevant. These monstrous creatures, fathered by the transgressor Ixion, are noted by the mythographer Pérez de Moya for being, in addition to *ligerísimos e invencibles* [very swift and invincible]—*lujuriosísimos* [very lustful]. In his moral application, the commentator elaborates further:

En decir que estos animales eran lujuriosos, quisieron dar a entender haber hombres medio brutos entregados a sus vicios y sensualidades, regidos por el apetito y no por razón, que teniendo figuras de hombres viven como animales, rendidos a la sucia lujuria, a quien de tropel acompañan todos los los otros vicios.[16]

[In saying that these animals were lustful, they meant that there are men who are half beasts, given over to their vices and sensualities, goverened by appetite and not reason, who having the form of men live like animals, having surrendered to filthy lust, which all the other vices accompany in a mad rush.]

Hybrids who inhabit the mountains of Thessaly, centaurs live removed from the civilized society of the polis. One of their most celebrated outrages recounted in the *Metamorphoses* (2.12.210ff.) occurs when they try to carry off the women at the wedding of Pirithous, Theseus's companion, to a Lapith princess, Hippodameia.[17]

In the case of Nessus, too, the affront is associated with the marriage rite—Hercules is returning to his homeland with his new bride. The motif of violence marks the vulnerable moment of transition for the female as she moves from virginal childhood to married adulthood. If, according to Lévi-Strauss's *The Elementary Structures of Kinship,* legal marriage as an "exchange of women" epitomizes the rules of "right exchange" of gifts, governing the relations between the sexes and serving to integrate society,[18] so the centaurs show themselves hostile to this order, which they subvert.[19] Thus is established the line of demarcation between

culture and nature, between the "bestial sexuality of untamed in-
stincts and the structures of marriage exchange."[20] If marriage
involves a gift, rape is theft: Alvaro, violator of the marriage rules,
is called a *ladrón pirata* [pirate thief] (3.2118–19), and himself
recognizes the power of legitimate possession after his first secret
visit to Serafina, intimidated

> De haber visto
> la verdad de cuán valiente
> es en su casa un marido.
>
> (2.1486–88)
>
> [Having seen
> the truth of how valiant
> a husband is in his own house.]

In the Greek myths the acts of violence, allied as they are with
instinct, are perpetrated by other than adult Greek males—gods,
hybrids (centaurs, satyrs), barbarian enemies, or even adolescent
males.[21] In the play, Alvaro, defended by his sister because of his
youth (*la libertad de los años* [the freedom of early years] (3.2157);
hombre mozo [young man] (3.2160), is a "sea creature" miracu-
lously "resucitated" after he was assumed dead, a Protean being of
disguises who acquires the status of a demonic hybrid. Like the
centaurs excluded from the city center,[22] he inhabits the outskirts
of civilization, the sea and the woods.[23] In the final act he and the
distraught Serafina are in the environs of Naples in the family lodge,
which provides a respite from hunting, fittingly the traditional metaphor of male pursuit of the female.[24] This provides the perfect locus
for the conflation of venatic and erotic hunts, involving not only the
primary action, but also the secondary characters, the Prince and
Porcia, dressed *de caza* [for hunting] and armed with an *arcabuz*
[harquebus] (3.2348). In the final ironic twist of fate, the place of
refuge and rest from the exertions of the chase, becomes the place
of the enactment of violence. While it is expected that a hunt will
end with a killing,[25] here not animal, but human prey is trapped and
subjected to a literal and ritual death when Juan enacts his revenge.

If Alvaro's youth provides the stimulus, the enabling circumstances provide the occasion for the transgression. It is carnival
time, *Carnestolendas*, the privileged time preceding Lent marked
by laughter and confusion, gaiety and license, and a general relaxa-
tion in sexual and social mores, facilitated by the use of disguises.[26]
Alvaro plans to take full advantage of the disequilibrium:

> Notable fue
> la introducción destos días,
> pues aunque padre o marido
> las acompañen, han sido,
> Fabio, las galanterías
> permitadas.
>
> (2.1807–12)

> [The introduction of these days are notable,
> for although their father or husband
> may accompany them,
> gallantries, Fabio,
> have been permitted.]

The *gracioso* (lackey) Fabio, aware of those very passions normally unacknowledged by the refined upper classes, utters what has been termed an "ironic prophecy":[27]

> Y es de suerte,
> que con ser tan belicosa
> nación ésta y tan celosa,
> no ha sucedido una muerte.
>
> (2.1812–15)

> [It's a piece of luck
> that, considering what a bellicose
> nation this is and what a jealous one,
> a death has not occurred.]

In an atmosphere so different from the serious formality and hierarchical strictures that usually governed, vigilance is relaxed. The occasion presented itself to Alvaro, as it did to the centaur Nessus, who offered his help across the swollen river to Hercules's bride: "The Theban accordingly entrusted to Nessus' care the Calydonian maid, pale and trembling, fearing the river and the centaur himself."[28] So, too, does Juan entrust to the care of a stranger his own bride, who, had she been conscious, would have been even more "pale and trembling," more fearful of her caretaker, than was Deianeira. In both instances the females find themselves unprotected, outside rather than inside the home. The moral declaration of the *Philosophia secreta* is just as applicable to Juan as it is to Hercules:

Esta fábula nos amonesta que debemos mirar mucho cómo confiamos lo que bien queremos de otros, como Hércules confió mal a su querida Deyanira, de Neso.[29]

[This tale warns us that we should exercise caution when we entrust to others what we dearly love, as Hercules wrongly entrusted his beloved Deianeira to Nessus.]

In the words of Juan, "Matóme la confianza!" [Confidence killed me!] (2.2077).

Like Nessus, Alvaro will suffer the consequences of his action: as the centaur is pierced by Hercules's poisoned arrow, so is Alvaro pierced by Juan's bullet. Theirs have been acts of defilement; their deaths mark the expulsion of disruptive and alien elements and constitute the cleansing necessary to the reintegration of society, the restitution of the "right rules" governing the exchange of women.[30]

Another version of the moral explicitly connects the breaking of sacred boundaries with the role of women in society. Of the same incident in his translation of Ovid, Sánchez de Viana draws the following conclusion in his annotation:

Desta fabula podemos notar quan recatadamente deuen los hombres fiar de otros, aunque muy amigos sean las cosas que aman, mayormente en caso de mugeres que suelen ser escandalo de los muy sabios, por falta del qual recato se han visto y veen cada dia casos feyssimos.[31]

[From this tale we can note how cautiously men should trust in others, however friendly what they love may be, especially in the case of women, who are generally a cause for scandal to the very wise, for lack of which caution we have seen and see every day very ugly incidents.]

There is no possible doubt about Deianeira's innocence in the matter of her seizure; questions have been raised regarding her counterpart Serafina, who, unlike Deineira, had known and loved her abductor. Questions of culpability may not, in fact, be entirely relevant. The fault is not individual, but generic.

It is not the particular woman here, Deianeira or Serafina, but the symbolic force of the female sex that is acknowledged by the commentator. Her power lies not in her position in society, where she does not acquire importance; on the contrary, it has been noted that within myth woman is associated "with the wild and the sacred, with what is outside the limits of ordered civilisation, and with the forces of life. . . ."[32] The source of her power is beauty: of

Deianeira it is said that she "was once a most beautiful maiden and the envied hope of many suitors";[33]—Nessus also desired her. Serafina's beauty is such that all the suitable men, young and old, are drawn to her—Alvaro, Juan, the Prince. In fact, when Alvaro learns that the Prince, too, is smitten, he utters a despairing aside that is almost comical: "Esto me faltaba ahora" [This is all I needed now] (2.830).

Her physical perfection and her female alignment with nature impede Juan's ability to paint his wife: like nature, she exceeds the powers of human understanding and control. The artist says of her flawless proportions,

> y aunque ha sido
> mi estudio, he reconocido
> que no puedo desvelado
> haberlas yo imaginado
> como haberlas tú tenido"

(2.1136–40)

> [although the object
> of my study, I have acknowledged
> that in my state of rapt attention
> I could not have imagined
> that which you possess]

The critic Alan K. G. Paterson has written convincingly on the theme of painting in the play. He points to relevant passages in the *aesthetic excursus* of Albrecht Dürer that comment on the intractable mystery of nature, and concludes that, in the plight of Juan Roca, Calderón "caught, with precision, the central preocupation of the 'excursus' and the engraving: reason's defeat in the face of what lies beyond reason."[34] Like Apollo pursuing the wild Daphne whose hair is in disarray [*sine lege*] (477) and imagining, "What if it were arranged?,"[35] only in death can he impose upon her the desired control. The *deus artifex* topos is a prominent feature of the play and has merited much critical attention.[36] Art theory turns into parody when, in a travesty of this motif that he himself presents (2.1130–56), Juan cannot paint Serafina in life (2.1163–69), but only in death, not as *naturaleza* but as a *naturaleza muerta*—a still life. As Daphne is immobilized only when transformed into a laurel tree, so is Serafina's image captured only as a statue, as her sleeping, soon-to-be lifeless body is described ("pues ha hecho una escultura, / viniendo a hacer un retrato" [he has fashioned a sculpture, having come to compose a portrait] (3.3030–31]).

Woman's position in a patriarchal culture is inherently ambiguous: she is necessary at all levels of society for the purposes of reproduction; among the moneyed and noble classes she is required for the assurance of legitimate succession and inheritance. Juan marries late in life, finally succumbing to concern about "un mayorazgo que creo / que es ilustre y principal / y no de poco caudal" [an entailed estate that I believe / is illustrious and important, / not of little wealth] (1.61–63). In spite of his lackey's warnings against marrying so young and irresistible a woman, he is not mistaken in terms of settling his estate, for according to the humoral psychology of the day: "La facultad generativa tiene por indicio de fecundidad la hermosura de la mujer; y, en siendo fea, la aborrece . . ." [The generative faculty has as the indication of fecundity woman's beauty; and, if she is ugly, it abandons her. . . ,].[37] Yet she is by nature excluded from the governing force of that culture—the *logos*. To quote again Dr. Huarte de San Juan, all women are "frías y húmidas" [cold and humid], and, the good doctor adds, "la frialdad y humidad son las calidades que echan a perder la parte racional . . ." [coldness and humidity ruin the rational part].[38]

Woman, necessary to but different from the standard point of reference, the adult male, was as alien and threatening as that hybrid creature, the centaur, with the result that: "They came to represent a potentially dangerous, even poisonous force which was both within the city and outside it."[39] Their effect is to destabilize, to drive the settled Juan to say "que aún yo no sé, si soy yo [I no longer know, if I am myself] (1.83), to induce the Prince into a state of "violence" (2.1595), to completely derange Alvaro, according to Serafina: "que de ti mismo olvidado, / no te acuerdas de ti mismo" [having forgotten yourself, / you do not remember who you are] (2.1403–4). While Serafina seems to have adjusted gracefully and with pleasure to her state of adulthood (she has matured from a *girasol* [sunflower] to an *encina* [oak], (2.1312–68), she has nevertheless unintentionally created chaos around her. She has unleashed that dangerous force, *eros* (played out metaphorically in the fire imagery), which is quite unlike her peaceable state of contentment.[40] Juanete, by class and upbringing less discreet about bodily urges, alludes quite explicitly to the sexual drives (to be aroused or quieted, as the case may be) that propel the action of the play: "o él la refresque a ella, / o ella le caliente a él" [either he must cool her, / or she must warm him] (1.235–36), he warns of the May-December marriage of his master.

Thus Serafina, who was to bring order to Juan's life as guarantor of legitimate sucession, brings only destruction. She plays the role of *pharmakon,* both cure and poison—like Deianeira, in fact. It has been noted that "in the mythical theme of the 'don fatal,' it is commonly a garment of death that is the woman's gift: we have only to remember Eriphyle, Deianeira, Medea." Woman's weaving—one of her main functions—is shrouded in paradox: "The contribution to society has become the source of its destruction."[41] In Calderón's mythological *fiesta, Los tres mayores prodigios* (The three greatest prodigies) (1636), in which the same abduction by Nessus is portrayed, all three women characters (Deianeira, Medea, Phaedra) bring ruin to their heroic counterparts.

The representations of Hercules in the *fiesta* and in *El pintor de su deshonra* are similar. Juan characterizes the Hercules of his painting as the man "en quien pienso que el primor / unió lo hermoso y lo fiero" [in whom I think great care / joined the beautiful and the fierce] (3.2684–85). From this multifaceted hero Calderón chooses not the exemplar of virtue of the allegorical tradition that persisted in painting, an example of which is Zurbarán's "Labors of Hercules" series for the Buen Retiro Palace.[42] Instead, Calderón's Hercules is "demythified":[43] the playwright develops a salient facet of the classical literary tradition, which includes Euripides's *Heracles* and Seneca's *Hercules furens,* according to which the hero, overcome by an attack of madness, mistakenly kills his first wife, Megara, and children.[44] In these classical tragedies, as in Sophocles's *Women of Trachis,* the finality of the hero's death further emphasizes his human, as opposed to godly stature. The final sequel in the *Metamorphoses,* the apotheosis—Hercules's reward by Zeus for his labors and ascent to heaven (9.242–72)—is, therefore, significantly absent, as it is from both *El pintor de su deshonra* and *Los tres mayores prodigios.*[45] This focus on the hero's lack of control directly contradicts, in fact, the standard iconography, according to which one of his virtues, represented by a golden apple, is *nunca enojarse* [never to get angry].[46]

This rage, or madness of Hercules was eventually attributed to medical causes, and Hercules (as well as other Greek heroes) is cited as an example of melancholy by the psuedo-Aristotelian *Problemata* (30.1), a common source for the Renaissance books on humoral psychology: the characterization in standard reference works is as "Herculanus morbus."[47] As Teresa Scott Soufas has shown in her work on the subject, Calderón's wife-murderers are also figures of melancholy, as well as of distinction, as befits the fascinating question posed in the *Problemata:* "Why is it that all those who have become eminent in philosophy or politics or poetry or the arts are clearly of an atribilious temperament. . . ?"[48] Calderón uses the source material freely, imposing a curious role reversal. In the myth the direct cause of Hercules's fiery and agonizing death is not his own, but Deianeira's jealousy, which has prompted her to use the alleged love potion given to her by the dying Nessus. The complexities of her emotions are vividly portrayed in the classical sources; the earlier event, Hercules's killing of the centaur, is a minor incident—an uncomplicated, instinctive reaction of justified outrage, the serious consequences of which only become clear with the passage of time.

Calderón has conflated the sources; more importantly, he has deviated from them by attributing the hero's notorious rage to jealous passion, a state of irrationality reserved for the female by Sophocles (*Women of Trachis*) and Ovid (both in the *Metamorphoses* account and in Deianeira's letter (9) in the *Heroides,* concerning her jealousy of Omphale). Thus if Juan is the painter of his dishonor, he is also the writer of his madness: the inscription of the painting, "Quien tuvo celos primero, / muera abrasado después" [Let him who first was jealous, / afterwards die burned] deviates from the standard allegorical interpretation of this portion of the myth, and serves to reveal Juan's pathology—his conscience, as it were. Like the Hercules *furens,* however, Juan commits a terrible act when out of his mind, and if it is excused with uncomfortable readiness (in this and other such revenge plays), it is perhaps due to an implicit defense of not guilty by reason of temporary insanity. Like Hercules after the slaying of his wife and children, Juan Roca also remains alive after the act, but condemned to a state of suffering.

The abduction has contaminated all involved, and purification requires a catharsis.[49] As Deianeira is sacrificed, so is Serafina, and Juan is also expelled from the communal scene at the end. Society is indeed reconstituted; however, the ending of the play is not harmonious, but unsettling, with fathers staring at dead children and an unenthusiastic marriage in the offing between the Prince and Porcia. The cost of maintaining such pristine integrity has been too great, Calderón appears to suggest.

In her analysis of Sophocles's *Women of Trachis* Page duBois states: "The tragedy shows the attempt of civilizations to construct a circle within which culture exists, from which all elements of otherness, of difference, are excluded."[50] In part, as the critic suggests, this effort is doomed to failure because of the liminal position of women, outsiders needed within. In part, I should add, this attempt is also doomed because such efforts at perfect control are bound to fail.

If the mythological painting mirrors the play, so does the play mirror the society beyond it. The play interprets the myth in terms of sexual codes relevant to Calderón's era: in spite of the efforts of reason, the "beast" of sexuality has wreaked havoc. But sexual mores do not exist as a discrete element in a society; they too are a social artifact and coincide with other societal norms and preoccupations. Lawrence Stone has noted that periods of sexual repression (of adultery or homosexuality, for instance) are generally marked also by intolerance of racial, religious, and political deviance.[51] This is certainly true in the Spain of the Habsburgs, where neither Jew nor Arab nor Protestant was countenanced.

Calderón had written a play to celebrate Spínola's triumphant taking of Breda in 1625 (El sitio de Bredá [The seige of Breda]), only to see the city lost again in 1637. Of another time and place, William Butler Yeats wrote: "Things fall apart; the centre cannot hold."[52] How can Calderón not have perceived the futile sacrifice in lives and resources of Spain's mighty efforts to preserve a center that history no longer made viable? If the wasteland at the end of El pintor de su deshonra was the price exacted for the preservation of this particular culture, the cost was indeed too great.

Notes

1. Norman Bryson, "Two Narratives of Rape in the Visual Arts: Lucretia and the Sabine Women," in Rape, ed. Sylvana Tomaselli and Roy Porter (Oxford: Basil Blackwell, 1986), 162.

2. "Art-Within-Art: The Significance of the Hercules Painting in El pintor de su deshonra," in Critical Perspectives on Calderón de la Barca, ed. Frederick A. de Armas, David M. Gitlitz, and José A. Madrigal (Lincoln: Society of Spanish and Spanish-American Studies, 1981), 69–77.

3. Quoted in Jennifer Temkin, "Women, Rape and Law Reform," in Rape, ed. Sylvana Tomaselli and Roy Porter (Oxford: Basil Blackwell, 1986), 19.

4. Quoted in Bryson, "Two Narratives," 166–67.

5. Bryson, "Two Narratives," 169.

6. All translations from Spanish are my own. The translation and edition of The Painter of His Dishonor by K. G. Paterson (Aris & Phillips) was not yet available at the time this article went to press.

7. Bruce W. Wardropper, "The Unconscious Mind in Calderón's El pintor de su deshonra," Hispanic Review 18 (1950): 289, 300.

8. Fischer, "Art-Within-Art," 76–77.

9. The Tragedy of Hamlet, Prince of Denmark, ed. Edward Hubler (New York: New American Library), 1963.

10. Quoted in Emilie L. Bergmann, Art Inscribed: Essays on Ekphrasis in

Spanish Golden Age Poetry, Harvard Studies in Romance Languages 35 (Cambridge: Harvard University Press, 1979), 124.

11. Leo C. Curran, "Rape and Rape Victims in the *Metamorphoses,*" in *Women in the Ancient World: The "Arethusa" Papers,* ed. John Peradotto and J. P. Sullivan (Albany: State University of New York Press, 1984), 263.

12. Charles P. Segal, *Landscape in Ovid's "Metamorphoses": A Study in the Transformations of a Literary Symbol* (Wiesbaden: Franz Steiner, 1969), 93.

13. Susan Brownmiller, *Against Our Will: Men, Women, and Rape* (New York: Simon, 1975), 283–308.

14. Diane Wolfthal, "The Heroic Rape," unpublished essay, 1987, 2–4.

15. Page duBois, *Centaurs and Amazons: Women and the Pre-History of the Great Chain of Being* (Ann Arbor: University of Michigan Press, 1982), 54, 61–64.

16. *Philsophia secreta,* ed. Eduardo Gómez de Baquero, 2 vols., Los clásicos olvidados 6 and 7 (Madrid: Blass, 1928), 2: 123, 125.

17. Froma Zeitlin, "Configurations of Rape in Greek Myth," in *Rape,* ed. Sylvana Tomaselli and Roy Porter (Oxford: Basil Blackwell, 1986), 131–36.

18. Gayle Rubin, "The Traffic in Women: Notes on the 'Political Economy' of Sex," in *Toward an Anthropology of Women,* ed. Rayna Reiter (New York: Monthly Review Press, 1975), 171–77.

19. DuBois, *Centaurs and Amazons,* 27–29.

20. Zeitlin, "Configurations of Rape," 134.

21. Ibid., 125–26.

22. Du Bois, *Centaurs and Amazons,* 66–71.

23. Gwynne Edwards, *The Prison and the Labyrinth: Studies in Calderonian Tragedy* (Cardiff: University of Wales Press, 1978), 126–27; Alan K. G. Paterson, "The Comic and Tragic Melancholy of Juan Roca: A Study of Calderón's *El pintor de su deshonra,*" *Forum for Modern Language Studies* 5, no. 3 (1969): 254 n. 12.

24. Hugh Parry, "Ovid's *Metamorphoses:* Violence in a Pastoral Landscape," *Transactions and Proceedings of the American Philological Association* 95 (1964): 270–72.

25. Parry, "Violence in a Pastoral Landscape," 274–75.

26. Mikhail Bakhtin, *Problems of Dostoevsky's Poetics,* trans. R. W. Rotsel (Ann Arbor: Ardis, 1973) and Julio Caro Baroja, *El carnaval* (Madrid: Taurus, 1965).

27. A. A. Parker, "Henry VIII in Shakespeare and Calderón," *Modern Language Review* 43 (1948): 340, and Susana Hernández-Araico, *Ironía y tragedia en Calderón* (Potomac, Md.: Scripta humanística, 1986), 60.

28. *pallentemque metu, fluviumque ipsumque timentem / tradidit Aonius pavidam Calydonida Nesso, Metamorphoses* 2.9.111–12. All citations from Ovid refer to the Loeb Classical Library edition, trans. Frank Justus Miller (Cambridge: Harvard University Press, 1977).

29. Pérez de Moya, *Philosophia secreta,* 2.126.

30. DuBois, *Centaurs and Amazons,* 105.

31. *Las transformaciones* with *Anotaciones* (Valladolid: Diego Fernández de Cordoba, 1589), 173v.

32. John Gould, "Law, Custom and Myth: Aspects of the Social Position of Women in Classical Athens," *Journal of Hellenic Studies* 100 (1980): 52.

33. *quondam pulcherrima virgo / multorumque fuit spes invidiosa procorum,* Ovid, *Metamorphoses* 2.9.9–10.

34. "Juan Roca's Northern Ancestry: A Study of Art Theory in Calderón's *El pintor de su deshonra, Forum for Modern Language Studies* 7, no. 3 (1971): 208.

35. *quid, si comantur?,* Ovid, *Metamorphoses* 1.1.498.

36. See Ernst Robert Curtius, "Calderón's Theory of Art and the *Artes Liberales*," *European Literature and the Latin Middle Ages*, trans. Willard R. Trask (New York: Harper, 1963), 559–70; Paterson "Juan Roca's Northern Ancestry"; Robert ter Horst, "The Second Self: Painting and Sculpture in the Plays of Calderón," in *Calderón de la Barca at the Tercentenary: Comparative Views*, ed. Wendell M. Aycock and Sydney P. Cravens (Lubbock: Texas Tech Press, 1982), 175–92.

37. Juan Huarte de San Juan, *Examen de los ingenios para las ciencias*, ed. Estéban Torre (Madrid: Nacional, 1976), 323.

38. Huarte de San Juan, *Examan de los ingenios*, 318–19.

39. DuBois, *Centaurs and Amazons*, 5.

40. Edward M. Wilson, "Hacia una interpretación de *El pintor de su deshonra*," *Abaco* 3 (1970): 72–77.

41. Gould, "Law, custom and myth," 52. The first observation is credited by Gould to Louis Gernet, *Anthropologie de la Grèce antique* (Paris, 1968), (n. 46) 104ff., 197f.

42. Jonathan Brown and J. H. Elliott, *A Palace for a King* (New Haven: Yale University Press, 1980), 156–61.

43. Thomas A. O'Conner, "Hércules y el mito masculino: la posición 'feminista' de *Fieras afemina Amor*," in *Estudios sobre el Siglo de Oro: en homenaje a Raymond R. MacCurdy* (Madrid: Castalia, 1983), 171–80.

44. Seneca's two Hercules plays, *Hercules furens* and *Hercules Oetaeus*, were translated into Spanish by Francisco López de Zárate as the *Tragedia de Hércules furente y Oeta*, written by 1629, though not published until 1651 (see Edwin S. Morby, "The *Hércules* of Francisco López de Zárate," *Hispanic Review* 30 [1962]: 116–32). The radical departures from the originals (Megara is replaced by Deianeira throughout, for example, and Hercules's killing frenzy is eliminated) warrant its being considered an adaptation rather than a translation.

45. Frederick A. de Armas, *The Return of Astraea: An Astral-Imperial Myth in Calderón*, Studies in Romance Languages 32 (Lexington: University Press of Kentucky, 1986), 162–63.

46. Pérez de Moya, *Philosophia Secreta*, 2.102.

47. G. Karl Galinsky, *The Herakles Theme: The Adaptation of the Hero in Literature from Homer to the Twentieth Century* (Totowa, N.J.: Rowman and Littlefield, 1972), 232; Lawrence Babb, *The Elizabethan Malady: A Study of Melancholia in English Literature from 1580 to 1642* (East Lansing: Michigan State University Press, 1951), 59.

48. See in particular "Calderón's Melancholy Wife Murderers," *Hispanic Review* 52 (1984): 181–203. The citation from the *Problemata* is quoted in Babb, *Elizabethan Malady*, 59.

49. DuBois, *Centaurs and Amazons*, 100.

50. Ibid., 103–4.

51. Lawrence Stone, "Sex in the West," *The New Republic* 8 July 1985: 25–37.

52. Yeats, "The Second Coming," in *The Variorum Edition of the Poems of W. B. Yeats*, ed. Peter Allt and Russell K. Alspach (New York: Macmillan, 1971), 402.

Works Cited

Babb, Lawrence. *The Elizabethan Malady: A Study of Melancholia in English Literature from 1580 to 1642*. East Lansing: Michigan State University Press, 1951.

Bakhtin, Mikhail. *Problems of Dostoevsky's Poetics.* Translated by R. W. Rotsel. Ann Arbor, Mich.: Ardis, 1973.

Bergmann, Emilie L. *Art Inscribed: Essays on Ekphrasis in Spanish Golden Age Poetry.* Harvard Studies in Romance Languages 35. Cambridge: Harvard University Press, 1979.

Brown, Jonathan and J. H. Elliott. *A Palace for a King.* New Haven: Yale University Press, 1980.

Brownmiller, Susan. *Against Our Will: Men, Women, and Rape.* New York: Simon, 1975.

Bryson, Norman. "Two Narratives of Rape in the Visual Arts: Lucretia and the Sabine Women." In *Rape,* edited by Sylvana Tomaselli and Roy Porter, 152–73. Oxford, Basil Blackwell, 1986.

Calderón de la Barca, Pedro. *El pintor de su deshonra.* Edited by Manuel Ruiz Lagos. Colección Aula Magna 19. Madrid: Alcalá, 1969.

Caro Baroja, Julio. *El carnaval.* Madrid: Taurus, 1965.

Curran, Leo C. "Rape and Rape Victims in the *Metamorphoses.*" In *Women in the Ancient World: The "Arethusa" Papers,* edited by John Peradotto and J. P. Sullivan, 263–86. Albany: State University of New York Press, 1984.

Curtius, Ernst Robert. "Calderón's Theory of Art and the *Artes Liberales.*" In *European Literature and the Latin Middle Ages,* translated by Willard R. Trask, 559–70. New York: Harper, 1963.

De Armas, Frederick A. *The Return of Astraea: An Astral-Imperial Myth in Calderón.* Studies in Romance Languages 32. Lexington: University Press of Kentucky, 1986.

DuBois, Page. *Centaurs and Amazons: Women and the Pre-History of the Great Chain of Being.* Ann Arbor: University of Michigan Press, 1982.

Edwards, Gwynne. *The Prison and the Labyrinth: Studies in Calderonian Tragedy.* Cardiff: University of Wales Press, 1978.

Fischer, Susan L. "Art-Within-Art: The Significance of the Hercules Painting in *El pintor de su deshonra.* In *Critical Perspectives on Calderón de la Barca,* edited by Frederick A. de Armas, David M. Gitlitz, José A. Madrigal, 69–77. Lincoln: Society of Spanish and Spanish-American Studies, 1981.

Galinsky, G. Karl. *The Herakles Theme: The Adaptation of the Hero in Literature from Homer to the Twentieth Century,* Totowa, N.J.: Rowman and Littlefield, 1972.

Gould, John. "Law, Custom and Myth: Aspects of the Social Position of Women in Classical Athens." *Journal of Hellenic Studies* 100 (1980): 38–59.

Hernández-Araico, Susana. *Ironía y tragedia en Calderón.* Potomac, Md.: Scripta humanística, 1986.

Huarte de San Juan, Juan. *Examen de los ingenios para las ciencias.* Edited by Estéban Torre. Madrid: Nacional, 1976.

Morby, Edwin S. "The *Hércules* of Francisco López de Zárate." *Hispanic Review* 30 (1962): 116–32.

O'Conner, Thomas A. "Hércules y el mito masculino: la posición 'feminista' de *Fieras afemina Amor.*" In *Estudios sobre el Siglo de Oro: en homenaje a Raymond R. MacCurdy,* 171–80. Madrid: Castalia, 1983.

Ovid. *Metamorphoses.* Translated by Frank Justus Miller. Loeb Classical Library.

2 vols. 3d ed. Cambridge: Harvard University Press; London: William Heinemann, 1977.

Parker, A. A. "Henry VIII in Shakespeare and Calderón." *Modern Language Review* 43 (1948): 327–52.

Parry, Hugh. "Ovid's *Metamorphoses:* Violence in a Pastoral Landscape." *Transactions and Proceedings of the American Philosophical Association* 95 (1964): 268–82.

Paterson, Alan K. G. "The Comic and Tragic Melancholy of Juan Roca: A Study of Calderón's *El pintor de su deshonra.*" *Forum for Modern Language Studies* 5, no. 3 (1969): 244–61.

———. "Juan Roca's Northern Ancestry: A Study of Art Theory in Calderón's *El pintor de su deshonra.*" *Forum for Modern Language Studies* 7, no. 3 (1971): 195–210.

Pérez de Moya, Juan. *Philosophia secreta.* Edited by Eduardo Gómez de Baquero. 2 vols. Los clásicos olvidados 6 and 7. Madrid: Blass, 1928.

Rubin, Gayle. "The Traffic in Women: Notes on the 'Political Economy' of Sex." In *Toward an Anthropology of Women,* edited by Rayna Reiter, 157–210. New York: Monthly Review P, 1975.

Sánchez, de Viana, Pedro, trans. *Las transformaciones* with *Anotaciones.* By Ovid. Valladolid: Diego Fernández de Cordoba, 1589. (The Hispanic Society of America.)

Segal, Charles P. *Landscape in Ovid's "Metamorphoses": A Study in the Transformations of a Literary Symbol.* Wiesbaden: Franz Steiner, 1969.

Shakespeare, William. *The Tragedy of Hamlet, Prince of Denmark.* Edited by Edward Hubler. New York: New American Library, 1963.

Soufas, Teresa Scott. "Calderón's Melancholy Wife Murderers." *Hispanic Review* 52 (1984): 181–203.

Stone, Lawrence. "Sex in the West." *The New Republic* 8 July 1985: 25–37.

Temkin, Jennifer. "Women, Rape and Law Reform." In *Rape,* edited by Sylvana Tomaselli and Roy Porter, 16–40. Oxford: Basil Blackwell, 1986.

Ter Horst, Robert. "The Second Self: Painting and Sculpture in the Plays of Calderón." In *Calderón de la Barca at the Tercentenary: Comparative Views,* edited by Wendell M. Aycock and Sydney P. Cravens, 175–92. Lubbock, Texas: Tech Press, 1982.

Tomaselli, Sylvana, and Roy Porter, eds. *Rape.* Oxford: Basil Blackwell, 1986.

Wardropper, Bruce W. "The Unconscious Mind in Calderón's *El pintor de su deshonra.*" *Hispanic Review* 18 (1950): 285–301.

Wilson, Edward M. "Hacia una interpretación de *El pintor de su deshonra.*" *Abaco* 3 (1970): 49–85.

Wolfthal, Diane. "The 'Heroic' Rape." Unpublished essay, 1987.

Yeats, William Butler. *The Variorum edition of the Poems of W. B. Yeats.* Edited by Peter Allt and Russell K. Alspach. New York: Macmillan, 1971.

Zeitlin, Froma. "Configurations of Rape in Greek Myth." In *Rape,* edited by Sylvana Tomaselli and Roy Porter, 122–51. Oxford: Basil Blackwell, 1986.

A Time for Heroines in Lope

THOMAS CASE

One interesting aspect of Lope's historical plays is his treatment of women. They appear in many different roles and often, as studied by Melvenna McKendrick, they are self-asserting and *varonil* [manly].[1] Others adapt to male-dominant society by disguising themselves as men, as Carmen Bravo-Villasante has analyzed. Many women acquire the stature of heroine. In this study I would like to focus on the development and possible significance of two heroines in Lope's historical plays: Elvira, in *Las almenas de Toro* [The ramparts of Toro], and Sancha, in *Las famosas asturianas* [The famous Asturian women]. Both heroines are notable for their integrity and independence of spirit and, as Stephen Gilman says, for their *hombría* [manliness], without ceasing to be sensitive and discreet women.[2] They are leaders in times of national crises and they excel in upholding honor far better than the men around them and in securing the power of the monarchy.

While Lope drew his dramatic material from historical record, his portrayal of Elvira and Sancha are poetic creations meant to entertain the audiences of the *corrales* [the public theaters] (the *gusto* [pleasure] of his *Arte nuevo* [New Art]) and to confirm his, and their, belief in the Reconquest and the formation of the modern Spanish state. These heroines may also be statements of a sort in the intertextuality between the drama public and the play as a form of historical thought.

Both plays belong to the period of Philip III. *Las almenas* is dated 1610–19 by Morley and Bruerton, but that dating can be modified somewhat to 1615–19.[3] *Las famosas asturianas* is dated 1610–12, probably 1612, by Morley and Bruerton. Besides dramatizing what was for the public of the time a heroic past, the plays and their heroines have other significant characteristics. Elvira and Sancha are compelled to take control, first of their own lives and destinies, then of a political situation in which the male leadership is wanting. Elvira is a princess who rightfully defends her legally bequeathed city of Toro against the illegal siege of her brother.

After fighting valiantly and repulsing fierce attacks, she loses her city because of the treachery of Vellido Dolfos. She escapes to a nearby farm disguised as a peasant and there she meets Enrique de Borgoña, also disguised. After learning of her brother's death at Zamora and Alfonso VI's rise to the throne, she returns to Toro in triumph betrothed to the French nobleman. *Las famosas asturianas* dramatizes the times of Alfonso *el casto* [the chaste] of Leon in which the collective gallantry of Asturian women, destined to be the slaves and concubines of Moors as payment of annual *parias* [tributes], rebel under Sancha's leadership and force their king to revoke the treaty and to defend his kingdom. They shame their men into recognizing the iniquity of the tribute, even though it is a legal pact, and by taking up arms themselves, they lead their people to glory and a restoration of dignity and honor.

In *Las almenas,* Lope alters the historical events and historical characters known through the *Crónica general* [General chronicle], his main source, and the many *romances* [popular ballads] that treat the times of Fernando I, Sancho II, El Cid Campeador, Alfonso V, Urraca, Elvira and Vellido Dolfos. The background to the play is one of the most important periods of the Reconquest. After defeating Alfonso, Sancho II laid siege to Zamora, held by his sister Urraca. Vellido Dolfos murdered Sancho, and Alfonso returned from exile as king of Castile and Leon. Lope's play begins with a fictitious siege of Toro, held by his other sister Elvira. The account of the chronicle seems to be based on the lost epic, *El cantar de Sancho* [Song of Sancho]. Menéndez Pidal has demonstrated that Urraca and Elvira historically did not receive the cities of Zamora and Toro in Fernando I's will, but only the jurisdiction of certain monasteries (I: 140–41).

To invent the siege of Toro Lope borrows elements from the siege of Zamora. Part of his material, and the title of the play, are drawn from a *romance:*

> En las almenas de Toro,
> Allí estaba una doncella,
> Vestida de negros paños,
> Reluciente como estrella;
> Pasara el Rey don Alonso,
> Namorado se había de ella,
> Dice: —si es hija de rey,
> Que se casaría con ella,
> Si es hija de duque,
> Serviría como manceba—
> Allí hablara el buen Cid,

Estas palabras dijera:
—Vuestra hermana es, señor,
Vuestra hermana es aquélla.
—Si mi hermana es, dijo el Rey,
Malo fuego encienda en ella.

[On the ramparts of Toro,
there was a damsel,
dressed in black clothes,
shining like a star,
King don Sancho passed by
and fell in love with her.
Says he: —if she is the daughter of a king,
I would marry marry her,
if she is daughter of a duke,
she could be my concubine—.
Then spoke the good Cid,
these words he said:
—Sire, she is your sister,
that damsel is your sister.
If she is my sister, said the king,
may an evil fire burn her to a crisp.]

This *romance* was first published by Timoneda in 1573. In the play, it is expanded considerably (ll.532–671). Lope may have been familiar with the Timoneda edition, and he may have known others of the same subject, or, as Menéndez Pelayo suggests, he composed parts of the poem himself to be part of his play.[4] Both the Timoneda *romance* and the extended poetic passage in the play have the same theme: the king falls in love with his own sister without recognizing her. When his advisor (the Cid in the *romance,* Pedro Ançures in the play) tells him who she is, the king vows not to let anyone else have her and orders her killed. In the *romance,* the brother is Alfonso; in the play he is Sancho.

History says very little about Elvira, so Lope enjoyed complete freedom in handling her character. In the play, she assumes Urraca's strong-mindedness as illustrated in the chronicle and several *romances.* She is a full dramatic personage through her steadfastness as a ruler and warrior and as a witty, deft, and tactful woman in her disguise as a peasant girl while hiding from Sancho's army. Her charms enamor the disguised Enrique de Borgoña. Historically, this duke married Elvira's niece, Teresa, and with her created the royal house of Portugal. Lope's public was tolerant of such license, and if it was aware of these changes may have applauded even more because the pieces fit so well dramatically.

Elvira, the protagonist, dominates both the main plot, that is, the political strife of Sancho II's reign, and the secondary action, the scenes that take place at don Vela's farm. No male character challenges Elvira's dominance. Lope created the role of Elvira to suit the histrionic range of the celebrated actress, Jusepa Vaca, the wife of the *autor de comedias* [stage director] and director of this play, Juan de Morales Medrano. Elvira's character and her portrayal in the *romance* and the play have been the subject of two important studies, one by Stephen Gilman, and the other by Marsha Swislocki. Both critics note her obscurity in history and the attempt to attribute to her a sensuous and provocative personality in artistic creation. Swislocki concludes that Lope "hace de ella una mujer fuerte y dinámica como las mujeres de Lope suelen ser; una mujer que no *está en* sino que *se pasea por* las almenas de Toro" [makes of her a strong and dynamic woman as Lope's women usually are; a woman who *is* not *on* but who *strolls about* the ramparts of Toro].[5]

Besides falling in love with his sister, King Sancho is seen to be a determined ruler who will stop at nothing to keep his kingdom intact. His obsession drives him to excesses, such as the siege of Toro, and the employment of Vellido Dolfos as his advisor. Robert A. Lauer states: "The king is damned in his attempt to unite the kingdom, however, for stooping to the lowest means to do so."[6] Enrique de Borgoña is an undeveloped personage who serves to inflate Elvira's importance by seeing through her peasant disguise to recognize her qualities of a noblewoman. Old don Vela also falls in love with her, but his function is mainly comic. The Cid merely plays out his role as vassal to Sancho:

> Obedecer al mayor
> Y no replicar al rey
> no sólo fue justa ley,
> pero es lealtad y es amor.

(ll.288–91)

> [To obey one's superior
> and not talk back to the king,
> not only was a just law,
> but is loyalty and is love.]

Sancho sends the Cid as ambassador to Elvira during the siege. Elvira confronts him and asks him to own up to reality: "¿cómo bos, Cid, me engañáis?" (1.473) [How can you, Cid, deceive me?] She pleads for fairness. The Cid can only respond:

Elbira, quanto a tener
disculpa de enbajador,
sirviendo al rey, mi señor,
no ay más que satisfacer;
quanto a ser hijo de Diego
Laínez, el de Bibar,
de otra suerte os quiero hablar.

(ll.496–502)

[Elvira, as far as having
pardon as an ambassador
by serving the king, my lord
it is my duty to satisfy his wishes;
as far as being the son of Diego
Lainez of Bivar
I wish to speak to you in other terms.]

Lope dedicates *Las almenas* to his friend, Guillén de Castro, a playwright today best known for dramatizing the Cid in *Las mocedades del Cid* [The Young Exploits of the Cid], Parts One and Two. Menéndez Pelayo thought that Lope deliberately avoided competing with his Valencian friend because of his care in "huir de la materia épica" [fleeing from epic subject matter].[7] In his dedication, he makes no reference to Castro's Cid plays and instead praises him for *Dido*, which he confesses he had seen in Valencia (probably in 1616). Besides having seen the play on the stage (it did not appear in print until 1625), Lope's choice to exalt *Dido* in connection with *Las almenas* seems appropriate. Both Dido and Eneas must sacrifice their personal interests to protect national honor and to further the destinies of the people they lead. Castro's *Dido* is a tragedy, and Lope's *Las almenas* could have been one also, because of the death of King Sancho. As Lope discusses in his dedication, his play is a tragicomedy and it ends with Elvira's triumphal return to Toro. He displays his knowledge of classical learning regarding the theories of drama prevalent at that time and of which his enemies accused him of being ignorant. There is another link. Venus provokes Dido's tragic end. Gilman shows us that Elvira is poetically associated with Venus.[8]

The other play, *Las famosas asturianas,* is based on the legend, of thirteenth-century origin, of the *cien doncellas* [The Hundred Women], paid as tribute to the Moorish kings of Cordoba. Menéndez Pelayo studied the various versions of the legend (BAE 195.56–63) and believed that Lope availed himself of a poem by Pedro de la Vezilla Castellanos, published in 1586, as his direct source (73–81). Another Lope play, *Las doncellas de Simancas* [The Maidens of Simancas], based on the same legend, deals with an earlier period.

Las famosas asturianas opens with a discordant note, a rebellion against King Alfonso *el casto* in Leon. The king takes refuge in a monastery and is later rescued by Nuño Osorio. This opening scene serves to indicate the weaknesses of the king and the strength and loyalty of Nuño Osorio. At court, the payment of the one hundred women is considered. Nuño Osorio strongly objects to the outrage, but Alfonso's advisors insist on compliance: "¿Qué importan cien mujeres / si por negallas mueren cien mil homes?" [What do one hundred women matter / if by denying their delivery / one hundred thousand men die] (BAE 41.). Women make better martyrs because audiences feel outraged by wronged innocence.[9] Nuño Osorio responds:

> Antes por una sola non cuidara
> Que cien homes el moro cautivara,
> Digan tantas fazañas en historias
> El valor de las fembras en el mundo.
>
> (470)

> [Rather I would think that for just one woman
> the Moor would have to capture one hundred men.
> Let the many brave deeds in history
> proclaim the bravery of women in the world.]

Nuño is given the task of delivering the women to the Moors, which places him in personal conflict between his loyalty to the king and his love for Sancha, one of the chosen women. Led by Sancha, the women rebel by having recourse to a unique stategy: first, they cast aspersions on their men for their cowardice; then they appear naked before the Christian knights, but cover themselves for the Moors. Sancha explains to Nuño:

> Atiende, Osorio cobarde,
> Afrenta de homes, atiende,
> Porque entiendas la razón
> Si non entenderla quieres.
> Las mujeres non tenemos
> vergüenza de las mujeres;
> quien camina entre vosotros
> Muy bien desnudarse puede,
> Porque sois como nosotras,
> Cobardes, fracas y endebles,

Fembras, mujeres y damas.
Y así, no hay por que non deje
De desnudarse ante vos,
Como a fembras acontece.
Pero cuando vi los moros
Que son homes, y homes fuertes,
Vestíme; que non es bien
Que las mis carnes me viesen.

(480)

[Listen carefully, coward Osorio,
you insult to manhood, listen carefully
so you may hear my speech,
even if you do not wish to understand it.
We women do not feel
embarrassment in front of other women;
one who strolls among you
can very well remove her clothing,
because you are like us,
cowards, weaklings and feeble,
females, women and ladies.
Therefore there is no reason why a woman
cannot be naked in your presence,
as it happens to other women.
But when I saw Moorish men,
who are real and strong men,
I put my clothes on; for it is wrong
for them to see my naked flesh.]

Nuño and his soldiers are shamed by their tolerance of such an abomination and decide to disobey their king and fight to the last man. Sancha and the other women also take up arms (*armadas de espadas y rodela* [armed with swords and buckler]) (481). The Moors accuse King Alfonso of breaking a pact, but after Sancha and Nuño explain what an affront to individual and national honor the tribute was, the king himself rescinds the treaty.

While *Las famosas asturianas* has a weak dramatic structure, it has good characterizations of King Alfonso, Nuño Osorio, and Sancha, and a powerful poetic impact. Sancha redeems herself and the Asturian women from dishonor and slavery and the Christian nation from its ignominious subjugation. As a free and independent spirit, she also liberates Nuño from his dishonor and enables him to be a suitable match for her.

Sancha fits into McKendrick's *cazadora* [huntress] type of heroine. She does not come directly from Lope's source. In act 1 she appears "sola, con montera de caza, vaquero y venablo" [*alone, with hunting cap, shepherd gear and lance*] (467), having just killed a bear. She opposes her father's desire to marry her to Laín de Lara, who believes women should be passive:

> Cuida Laín de Lara,
> Que en estrado le atiendo
> En cuadras de mi casa,
> Porque con él me casa
> Mi padre; y yo, que aun de le ver me ofendo,
> Ando por estas flores
> Cazando fieras y olvidando amores.
> Non al que el verme libre
> Piensa mi pensamiento;
> Lo al arrojo de mi alma lueñe.
> El dardo el brazo vibre,
> Y al oso corpulento
> En tierra el cuento la cuchilla enseñe.
> Laín de Lara sueñe
> Sus fingidos placeres;
> Que yo por bosques quiero
> Teñir el blanco acero;
> Que non se amañan todas las mujeres
> A desfilar vainillas,
> Que facen a los homes lechuguillas.
>
> (467)

> [Lain de Lara thinks
> I am waiting for him in my sewing room
> in the chambers of my house,
> because my father is marrying me to him;
> and I, though I am offended to see him,
> I walk among these flowers,
> hunting wild beasts and forgetting about love.
> My thoughts are only
> on my own freedom;
> all the rest I cast far from my soul.
> My arm readies the shaft
> and may its blade show its tip
> clean through the bear on the ground.
> Let Lain de Lara dream
> his pretended delights;
> for I wish to stain my
> blade in the forest;
> for not all women want to settle down
> to making hemstitch
> for ruffs to adorn men's necks.]

Laín thinks women should tend to their sewing *[estrado]* or "el cultivado jardín," [flower garden] but Sancha answers:

> Más precio esperar aquí
> Que un jabalí fiero asome
> Que oir blanduras de un home
> Puesto que fembra nací.

(468)

> [I esteem here much more
> seeing a wild boar appear
> than to hear soft words from a man
> simply because I was born a woman.]

Although not studied by McKendrick, Sancha is the ideal *bella cazadora* [beautiful huntress]. Her abilities as a "Diana" and love of physical freedom at first make her refuse love and marriage:

> En libertanzas de soltera vida
> Pasé lo joven de mis verdes años
> Enojos fue al tiempo, a amor regaños
> Que non me tuvo por jamás rendida.
> Cuidaba yo que era pasión fingida
> Cuando sentía encaramar sus daños.

(473)

> [In the joy of freedom of single life
> I spent the youth of my early years
> not giving time any care, scorning love,
> which never held me in its grip.
> I thought that it was a faked passion
> when I heard its dangers brought up.]

Sancha evolves into the perfect heroine, the *mujer esquiva* [woman who avoids love] who later yields to nature to love a man of virtue and nobility of spirit; the woman who can lead men and women and can teach men what their responsibilities are and forces them, in this case through shame, to assume them. Sancha redeems herself, the other women, Nuño Osorio, and finally the Spanish nation. Harriet Boyer associates her with Artemisa of mythology and with Laurencia of *Fuenteovejuna* and attempts to show that *Las famosas asturianas* exemplifies the Jungian principle of the masculine and the feminine: "En términos generales, la trama se reduce al conflicto entre los sexos o, mejor dicho, entre lo masculino y lo femenino" ["In general terms, the plot comes down to the conflict between the sexes, or rather, between the masculine and the feminine].[10]

Did Lope create these plays just for the entertainment of the Madrid *corrales* or are there ideas besides their appealing marketability? *Las almenas de Toro* and *Las famosas asturianas* are entertaining because they feature women of superior wisdom and integrity of the Reconquest who were instrumental in leading a male-dominant society to victory in situations where the male leaders had failed. After they succeed, power is returned once more to the men. Elvira and Sancha complete the process by marrying suitable husbands. Unlike Castro's *Dido,* history did not provide the heroine.

Lope was an avid reader of histories, chronicles, and other records, not only because they provided him the raw material for his dramas, but also because he had a grasp of their importance for the Spanish nation. He was a supporter of monarchy and the Catholic faith, but he was also a patriot who longed for strong government and a clear national purpose. Jameson has shown that he was sufficiently well grounded in classical studies to understand the moral and rhetorical uses of history, and he thought enough of himself as a historian to aspire to the post of Royal Chronicler in the years immediately after his establishing permanent residence in Madrid in 1610.[11] In 1617, he wrote *El triunfo de la fe* [The triumph of the faith], an historical treatise. As a new, and repentent, priest, according to Cummins, Lope was anxious to establish himself in his new vocation as a promotor of the Catholic faith and to justify his position as Procurator Fiscal and Notary Apostolic.[12] "He asserted his right to be considered a sacred historian,"[13] and in such a way attempted to outshine his rival, Suárez de Figueroa, as a historian by composing a work of inspiration and religious stimulation.[14] From 1617 to 1625, he supervised the publication of 144 of his plays in *Partes IX–XX,* for which he wrote some cogent prologues, and in *Partes XIII–XX* he wrote dedications for the ninety-six plays of those collections. His personal life, his interpretations of art, and his vision of history frequently are topics in these discourses. His concern over how history would regard him was one of his reasons for printing his old plays, for profit was not a motive.[15] Many had to be rewritten because of the alterations of stage directors. Unscrupulous printers were putting his name on others' works. In *Egloga a Claudio,* [Eclogue to Claudio] he complains:

Mas ha llegado, o Claudio, la codicia

a imprimir con mi nombre las ajenas,
de mil errores llenas.

(BAE38.434)

[Oh Claudio, greed has gone so far as
to print the works of others,
full of mistakes,
with my name.]

In other words, Lope was concerned about future interpretations of his plays. History was a serious matter to him and his plays were a form of historical thought, not merely instruments of propaganda for the status quo, as Maravall and Diez Borque have maintained.

Lope was no less zealous in using history to inspire nationalism in his plays. The *corrales* audiences were much larger and more diverse than the reading public of his *Triunfo de la fe* and his prologues and dedications. As Díez Borque has amply shown, the performance in the Madrid *corrales* were commercially successful and lucrative, attended by noble and commoner alike. This broad spectrum of society was an excellent forum for relaying messages.

Madrid era una ciudad esencialmente política, donde estaban concentrados todos los organismos de la administración central, lo que suponía una variadísima escala de cargos públicos, desde los puramente "políticos y de alta categoría que ejercía la propia nobleza—pues esta desdeñaba los puestos de secretario, pero aceptaba cargos en el Consejo de Castilla, Consejo de Estado . . . , etcetera—hasta todos los puestos intermedios que desembocaban en el abundantísimo grupo de la "gente de capa negra," como se denominaba a los funcionarios de los tribunales, secretarías, consejos, etc.[16]

[Madrid was essentially a political city, where all the organisms of the central administration were concentrated, which supposed a quite varied gamut of public posts, from which the purely "political" and of upper category which the nobility itself operated—for it despised the posts of secretary, but accepted posts in the Council of Castile, Council of State . . . , etc.—to all intermediate posts which flowed into the most crowded group of "those who wore the black cape," as the public employees of the courts, secretariats, councils, etc. were called.]

The *corrales* were structured along the lines of social class, from the expensive *aposentos* [box seats] for the nobles and rich middle class, to the cheap area for the *mosqueteros* [groundings], who watched standing up. Again, Díez Borque elaborates:

Por todo esto, la comedia del XVII no pertenece, privativamente, a
ninguno de los grupos sociales existentes, sino que, recogiendo la
conciencia colectiva de un solo grupo social: la nobleza, pertenece a
todos y no a ésta en exclusiva; por las especiales características del
XVII, de las que—en la práctica social—sobresale la superposición de
los modos de pensar y actuar de la nobleza sobre la conciencia colectiva del grupo que es prácticamente anulada por esta superposición que,
a mi juicio, y como trataré ampliamente más adelante, tiene mucho de
compensación.[17]

[In spite of all this, the theater of the seventeenth century does not
belong in particular to any of the existing social groups, but rather,
gathering together the collective consciousness of a single social group:
the nobility, which belongs to all groups and not exclusively to itself;
because of the special circumstances of the seventeenth century, from
which circumstances that—in social practice—the superposition of the
ways of things and acting of the nobility excels over the collective
consciousness of the group which is practically cancelled out by this
superposition which, in my judgment, is a great compensating factor.]

For such a crowd, then, historical plays, and social plays as well,
could have a special meaning, both in the transmission of signs and
in their reception, since the public was not just a consumer of the
text but operated in its production as well. Lope was not attempting
to reconstruct the past but was addressing his own times, although
he glorified the Reconquest and appropriates its language through
the *romancero* [ballad collections] and the chronicles. Lindenberger notes that "it is commonplace to take historical plays as a
comment on the playwright's own period."[18]

With that in mind, what comment could Lope be attempting in
Las almenas and *Las famosas asturianas,* if any? How influential
could historical plays be in the *corrales* of the second decade of the
seventeenth century? The court of Philip III may hold part of the
answer. Historians agree that the weak and withdrawn Philip III
was not ruling the country. A trend of national failures ushered in
toward the end of Philip II's reign (for example, bankruptcy and the
Armada of 1588) grew worse. Philip III, as his father had fore-
warned, placed power in the hands of nobles headed by don Francisco de Sandoval y Rojas, Marquis de Denia, elevated to Duke of
Lerma in 1599. Philip III's reign was characterized by loss of
prestige abroad and mismanagement of Spain and its empire. There
set in, in the words of J. H. Elliott, "a deadening inertia which
crippled both the capacity and the desire to act."[19] Compounded
with this aboulia, "financial stress, favoritism, and maladministra-

tion eventually led to protest even among the upper classes."[20] This was especially true after 1612, when Lerma assumed almost complete control of the government.

Lope was a witness to this deplorable state of affairs. He now lived permanently in Madrid, associated with nobility and courtiers, attended meetings of the academies, and even traveled with the court on certain occasions, such as in 1613 and 1616.[21] In fact, the publication of his *comedias* supplied him with a convenient platform from which to address many different court figures on a variety of subjects.

Las famosas asturianas was dedicated to don Juan de Castro y Castilla, Gentilhombre de la boca de Su Majestad, Corregidor de Madrid. The subject of the dedication is *fabla* [archaic language], the artificial medieval language of the play: "quise ofrecer a V. M. esta historia, que escribí en lenguaje antiguo para dar mayor propiedad a la verdad del suceso, y no con pequeño estudio, por imitarla en su natural idioma" [I wished to offer this story to you, which I wrote in archaic language, in order to render greater naturalness to the truth of the event, and it took some effort for me to imitate its natural language].[22] Menéndez Pelayo praised the play but frowned on the use of *fabla,* declaring "semejante *fabla,* que no se *fabló* nunca" [Such archaic language was never spoken].[23] The eminent critic, however, failed to recognize Lope's seriousness in attempting a vivid portrayal of the Reconquest in more than one dimension. The "verdad del suceso" [the truth of the event] is Sancha's strategy to force her king to change his policy and disregard the bad advice of his counselers. *Las famosas asturianas,* written around 1612, was published in *Parte XVIII* in 1623, with its dedication to a prominent member of the court, don Juan de Castro.[24] The dedication in the same *Parte* of *La campana de Aragon* to the young Fernando de Vallejo, also deals with the impact of history on the stage. History, says Lope, is better appreciated in drama:

> La fuerza de las historias representada es tanto mayor que leída, cuanta diferencia se advierte de la verdad a la pintura y del original al retrato; porque en un cuadro están las figuras mudas y en una sola acción las personas; y en la comedia hablando y discurriendo, y en diversos afectos por instantes, cuales son los sucesos, guerras, paces, consejos, diferentes estados de la fortuna, mudanzas, prosperidades, declinaciones, de reinos y períodos de imperios y monarquías grandes. De la historia, dijo Cicerón, que no saber lo que antes de nosotros había pasado, era ser siempre niños; conocida es su utilidad, tan encarecida de tantos.[25]

[The impact of histories performed on the stage is all the greater than when read, just as one notices the difference between a real scene and a painting of it, and of subject compared with the portrait; because in a painting the figures are speechless and the persons are in a single action; in a play, by speaking and discoursing, and in diverse emotions without interruptions, such as are the events, wars, peace, advices, different states of kingdoms and periods of empires and great monarchies. About history, Cicero said that not to know what had happened before us was to always remain as children; the lessons of history are well known, and are greatly esteemed by many.]

History, then, has its lessons (*su utilidad*) and they must be heeded. Historical drama can teach those lessons better than written history. The lesson of *La campana de Aragón* [The bell of Aragon] is obedience and loyalty to the king, another play which Morley and Bruerton date in the reign of Philip III (1596–1603), probably 1598–1600. The lesson in *Las almenas* seems to be King Sancho's unwillingness to live up to the law (his father's will) and the price he pays for following the treacherous advice of Vellido Dolfos. As the Cid remarks to Elvira: "Guardaos, Elbira, quel rey / no está bien aconsejado" [Be careful, Elvira, for the king / is not well advised] (ll.504–5). *Las famosas asturianas* reveals a king who also is subject to the abominable advice of Teudo and Meledón in agreeing to abide by the *parias* of the hundred Christian women. To defend the concept of monarchy, the blame of evil is cast on the advisors and not on the king. Lope, of course, would not criticize his king nor the institution of monarchy.[26]

Elvira and Sancha are artistic creations of exceptional women who become heroines by their integrity and bravery. They surpass the male leadership of their times and exemplify the great virtues of the Spaniards of the Reconquest. Lope is hardly a feminist in creating these outstanding female roles, for he is not promoting equality of the sexes nor rule by women. He does show, on the other hand, that despite their subservient role in Spanish society, women can take action that forces men to undertake the duties assigned to them. Laurencia and the women of *Fuenteovejuna* demonstrate this very well. Ruth Kennedy and J. C. J. Metford have studied Tirso's carefully veiled comments about the court of Philip IV.[27] After all, the public that witnessed these historical plays could easily see a mirror for their times as well as for the past. In her article on historical drama, Carol Bingham Kirby demonstrates how the Reconquest on the stage portrayed the providential plan for man, and in *El último godo* [The last gothic king] dramatized Spain's fall and redemption. She suggests: "Es posible que así

Lope haga una crítica de la corte de su época, pero no es una crítica profunda [It is possible that that was Lope's way of criticizing the court of his day, but it is not a profound criticism].[28] Maybe it was not a profound criticism, but certainly an indirect statement to courtiers in the audience. Lope's plays, after all, are not propaganda, but works of art. In her key study, Charlotte Stern clarifies this point: "Art, however, conveys ambiguous and polysemous meaning, embraces short-term and long-term functions, and encompasses a variety of aesthetic modes."[29]

Spain always triumphs in the historical plays of the Golden Age. In spite of the crises dramatized, Lope turns away from tragedy to produce triumphs of the Reconquest in *Las almenas de Toro* and *Las famosas asturianas*. The heroines, Elvira and Sancha, feminine characters who are exceptionally well portrayed and well rounded for a *comedia,* bear the strength and integrity of the Spanish people the public wished to see on the stage. Women of integrity who were warriors, avengers, rebels, and other types of *mujer varonil,* were popular figures in Golden Age drama, and, as McKendrick has shown, there was no lack of classical and historical sources to draw from.[30] The *mujer varonil* was a product of her age, and Lope exploits her popularity in Elvira and Sancha. He also places them in moments of national crisis in which they rise to the occasion and find suitable solutions. Regarding the dramatists' use of strong women, McKendrick concludes: "That they regarded her as a good commercial proposition, and that they were governed by theatrical conventions and considerations of plots does not mean that they did not infuse into their presentations their own ideas and views concerning women in general."[31] Elvira and Sancha also match the fondness of the baroque period for extremes of personality. Beyond Lope's view of women, there is a glimmer of hope they can provide for times of stress and crisis. Heroines are especially optimistic figures in a male-dominated social structure, for they form a sort of reserve of additional resources when all else fails. The message is indirect and veiled, but it is possible to infer that Lope, witnessing the troubles of the reign of Philip III, was hoping to rebuke the advisors of his king and to jar the court into acting in the best interests of the country.

Notes

1. Melveena McKendrick, *Woman and Society in the Spanish Stage of the Golden Age: A Study of the "mujer varonil,"* (Cambridge: Cambridge University Press, 1974).

2. Stephen Gilman, "Poetry and History: *Las almenas de Toro*," *Essays in Hispanic Literature in Honor of Edmund L. King,* Ed. Sylvia Molloy and Luis Fernandez Cifuentes (London: Tamesis, 1983), 81.

3. Thomas E. Case, "The Early Date of Lope's *Las almenas de Toro.*" *Romance Notes* 6: 156–59.

4. M. Menéndez Pelayo, "Observaciones preliminarres" a *Obras de Lope de Vega,* reprinted in *Biblioteca de Autores Españoles* 197, 16. All further references to this work are identified by the abbreviation *BAE.*

5. Marsha Swislocki, "Una aproximación al romance 'En las almenas de Toro'," *Hispanic Studies in Honor of Joseph H. Silverman,* 233.

6. Robert A. Lauer, "The Killing of the Tyrannical King in the Spanish Theater of the Golden Age (1582–1671)" (Diss. University of Michigan, 1983), 266.

7. BAE 197, xxii.

8. Gilman, "Poetry and History," 86–90.

9. Herbert Lindenberger, *Historical Drama: The Relation of Literature and Reality* (Chicago: University of Chicago Press, 1975), 48.

10. Harriet P. Boyer, "*Las famosas asturianas* y la mujer heroica," *Lope de Vega y los orígenes del teatro español,* ed. M. Criado de Val (Madrid: Edi-6, 1981), 482.

11. Henry N. Bershas, "Lope de Vega and the Post of Royal Chronicler," *Hispanic Review* 31 (1963): 109–17.

12. A. K. Jameson, "Lope de Vega's Knowledge of Classical Literature," *Bulletin Hispanique* 38 (1936): 444–501; J. S. Cummins, ed., *El triunfo de la fee en los reynos del Japon* (London: Tamesis, 1965), xxxviii.

13. Cummins, *El triunfo de la fee,* xxix.

14. Ibid., xl.

15. José María Díez Borque, *Sociedad y teatro en la España de Lope de Vega* (Barcelona: Bosch, 1978), 100–101.

16. Díez Borque, *Sociedad,* 123–4.

17. Ibid., 139–40.

18. Lindenberger, *Historical Drama,* 5.

19. J. H. Elliott, *Imperial Spain* (New York: Meridian, 1963), 263.

20. Stanley Payne, *A History of Spain and Portugal,* 2 vols. (Madison: University of Wisconsin Press, 1973), 1.308.

21. H. Rennert y A. Castro, *Vida de Lope de Vega,* 2d. ed. (Salamanca: Anaya, 1967), 203, 215.

22. *Dedicatorias, Las famosas asturianas,* 202–3.

23. BAE 196.77. In the play only the Christians speak *fabla.* The Moors Audalla, Amir and Celin speak modern Spanish, perhaps to indicate that they are speaking Arabic.

24. Lope published the *Primera parte* and *Segunda parte de don Juan de Castro* the following year in *Parte XIX.*

25. *Obras,* reprinted in BAE 38, 52.203–4.

26. Lope praised Philip III in plays such as *El Perseo* (1611–15, probably 1611) and *San Diego de Alcala* (1613).

27. Ruth Kennedy, "Tirso's *La prudencia en la mujer* and the Ambient That Brought It Forth" *PMLA* 63 (1948): 1131–90. J. C. J. Metford, "Tirso de Molina and the Conde-Duque de Olivares" *Bulletin of Hispanic Studies* 36 (1959): 15–27.

28. "Observaciones preliminares sobre el teatro histórico de Lope de Vega." *Lope de Vega y los orígenes del teatro español,* 335.

29. Charlotte Stern, "Lope de Vega, Propagandist?" *Bulletin of the Comediantes* 34 (1982): 14.
30. McKendrick, *Women and Society*, 276–310.
31. Ibid., 323.

Works Cited

Bershas, Henry N. "Lope de Vega and the Post of Royal Chronicler." *Hispanic Review* 31 (1963): 109–17.

Boyer, Harriet P. "*Las famosas asturianas* y la mujer heroica." In *Lope de Vega y los orígenes del teatro español,* edited by M. Criado de Val. Madrid: Edi-6, 1981.

Case, Thomas E. "The Early Date of Lope's *Las almenas de Toro.*" *Romance Notes* 6: 156–59.

———, ed. *Las dedicatorias de Partes XIII–XX de Lope de Vega.* Madrid: Hispanofila, 1975.

Castro, Guillén de. *Obras.* Edited by E. Juliá Martíanez. 3 vols. Madrid: Rev. de Archivos, Bibliotecas y Museos, 1925.

Cummins, J. S., ed. *El triunfo de la fee en los reynos del Japon.* London: Tamesis, 1965.

Díez Borque, José María. *Sociedad y teatro en la España de Lope de Vega.* Barcelona: Bosch, 1978.

Elliott, J. H. *Imperial Spain.* New York: Meridian, 1963.

Gilman, Stephen. "Poetry and History: *Las almenas de Toro.*" In *Essays in Hispanic Literature in Honor of Edmund L. King,* edited by Sylvia Molloy and Luis Fernández Cifuentes, 79–90. London: Tamesis, 1983.

Jameson, A. K. "Lope de Vega's Knowledge of Classical Literature." *Bulletin Hispanique* 38 (1936): 444–501.

Kennedy, Ruth. "Tirso's *La prudencia en la mujer* and the Ambient That Brought It Forth." *PMLA* 63 (1948): 1131–90.

Kirby, Carol Bingham. "Observaciones preliminares sobre el teatro histórico de Lope de Vega." In *Lope de Vega y los orígenes del teatro español.*

Lauer, A. Robert. "The Killing of the Tyrannical King in the Spanish Theater of the Golden Age (1582–1671)." Diss. University of Michigan, 1983.

———. "The Use and Abuse of History in the Spanish Theater of the Golden Age: the Regicide of Sancho II as Treated by Juan de la Cueva, Guillén de Castro, and Lope de Vega." *Hispanic Review* 56 (1987): 17–37.

Lindenberger, Herbert. *Historical Drama. The Relation of Literature and Reality.* Chicago: University of Chicago Press, 1975.

Maravall, José Antonio. *La cultura del barroco.* Barcelona: Ariel, 1975.

McKendrick, Malveena. *Woman and Society in the Spanish Drama of the Golden Age: A Study of the "Mujer Varonil."* Cambridge: Cambridge University Press, 1974.

Menéndez Pelayo, M. "Observaciones preliminares" a *Obras de Lope de Vega,* reprinted in BAE 195 and 197.

Menéndez Pidal, R. *La España del Cid.* 2 vols. Madrid: Espasa Calpe, 1955.

Metford, J. C. J. "Tirso de Molina and the Conde-Duque de Olivares." *BHS* 36 (1959): 15–27.

Morley, S. G., and C. Bruerton. *Cronología de las comedias de Lope de Vega.* Translated by María Rosa Cartes, Madrid: Gredos, 1968.

Payne, Stanley. *A History of Spain and Portugal.* 2 vols. Madison: University of Wisconsin Press, 1973.

Rennert, H. y A. Castro. *Vida de Lope de Vega.* 2d ed. Salamanca: Anaya, 1967.

Stern, Charlotte. "Lope de Vega, Propagandist?" *Bulletin of the Comediantes* 34 (1982): 1–36.

Swislocki, Marsha. "Una aproximación al romance 'En las almenas de Toro'." In *Hispanic Studies in Honor of Joseph H. Silverman,* edited by Joseph V. Ricapito, 227–33. Newark: Juan de la Cuesta, 1988.

Vega Carpio, Lope. *Las almenas de Toro.* Edited by Thomas E. Case. Chapel Hill: University of North Carolina Press, 1971.

———. *Obras,* reprinted in BAE 38, 41.

Paradox and Role Reversal in
La serrana de la Vera

RUTH LUNDELIUS

In recent years critics of the Spanish *comedia* have shown a lively interest in a popular stock character: the *mujer varonil* [masculine woman], who, as the very antithesis of the traditional heroine, was totally at odds with the expected mores of feminine behavior.[1] Deriving from a long and widespread literary tradition, and lent actuality by an occasional historical example, this type took on renewed popularity in the Golden Age. She appeared in the repertory of virtually every dramatist, beginning with Lope de Vega, whose sensitivity to the dramatic appeal of the masculine woman was expressed in his dictim ". . . con acciones de hombres / no agradan mal las mujeres" [women do not displease with manly actions],[2] and sustained her vogue in a long line of potboilers turned out quickly to satisfy popular demand. For Vélez de Guevara, however, she had a particular fascination, perhaps because the frequently impecunious dramatist hoped to fill the theater with a character of proven attraction. My own count indicates that in one form or another she appeared in about a fourth of his plays as listed by Spencer and Schevill.[3] They themselves remarked on Vélez's predilection for this character, and, as I have found, the evidence fully supports B. B. Ashcom's observation that "Vélez is much the greatest exponent of the *mujer varonil*" among the Golden Age dramatists.[4]

The guises of the *mujer varonil*—the *esquiva* or woman averse to love and marriage, the *serrana* [mountain girl], the *bella cazadora* [beautiful huntress], and the *bandolera* [female bandit]—that richly populate Vélez's' theater are also exemplified in one way or another in Gila, the protagonist of *La serrana de la Vera*. Gila comes before the audience as a rough tomboy, physically superior to men, inclined to masculine pursuits and diversions—from war and hunting to contests of strength—answering for the most part only to her own unbridled aspirations, and contemptuous of love and marriage.

As such, she is typical of many of Vélez's creations of this type, but she is also portrayed as rejecting the ordinary feminine roles, attitudes, and goals with such radical vehemence that she becomes the most masculine of all the *serranas*. The audience is given to understand that she has been a *serrana* by birth, by her chosen lifestyle, by her uncouth language, by her amazing physical strength, and even by her very name, which evoked a similar character in the well known ballad of the "serrana de la Vera," which inspired Vélez's play.[5] From the ballad he retained the pattern of conflict between the *serrana* and society and the ensuing atmosphere of violence, but he embedded his plot in an intuitively penetrating social and psychological matrix that interpreted Gila and her behavior in terms of concerns and values of his own age. One way Vélez accomplished this was through the use of paradox and reversal—the familiar Baroque devices of showing how things should not be.

The schism in Gila's nature is clearly revealed early in the play when her father praises both her feminine beauty and her masculine strength. Initially untroubled by the paradox of her being he describes her thus:

> que fuera de la presencia
> hermosa, tan gran valor
> tiene, que no ay labrador
> en la Vera de Plasencia
> que a correr no desafie,
> a saltar, luchar, tirar
> la varra, y en el lugar
> no ay ninguno que porfie
> a mostrar valor maior
> en ninguna cosa destas,
>
> . . . .
> De bueies detiene un carro,
> de un molino la violenzia;
> corre un caballo mexor
> que si en él cosida fuera . . .[6]
>
> [for, besides her beautiful appearance,
> she has such great valor
> that there is no rustic
> in the Vera de Plasencia
> that she does not challenge to race,
> to jump, to wrestle, to throwing contests,
> and in the locale
> there is no one more determined

> to demonstrate great courage
> in any of these things . . .
> she can stop an ox-drawn cart;
> she can stay a windmill;
> she races a horse better
> than if she were sewn on it . . .]

Vélez masterfully underlines this word picture with a stunning theatrical scene in which Gila appears on stage on horseback, ". . . el cabello tendido, . . un cuchillo de monte al lado, botín argentado y puesta una escopeta debaxo del caparazón del caballo" [. . . her hair loose, . . . a hunting knife at her side, silver striped boots, and a gun beneath the trappings of the horse] (10). From this vantage point—her long hair flowing in the wind and brandishing the accoutrements of war and the chase—she recounts the fierceness of the just-concluded hunt. The juxtaposition of disparate characteristics was surely not lost on the audience. The modern reader must remember that this was not just literature but living theater, and Vélez was always solicitious to extract the maximum dramatic effect from his stagecraft. He never lost an opportunity to put on a spectacle, with *apariencias* and *tramoyas* [stage machinery], in which he specialized, to the annoyance of Cervantes, who refers to "el rumbo, el tropel, el boato, la grandeza de las comedias de Luis Vélez de Guevara" [the pomp, the bustle, the pageantry, the sheer sweep of the plays of Luis Vélez].[7] The part of Gila must have demanded an uncommonly gifted actress, a player who must both project a bold masculine manner yet subtly protect a certain femininity. By the seventeenth century the *mujer varonil* had become so much in demand that certain actresses specialized in the role. One such was Jusepa Vaca, and, indeed, Vélez tells us that he wrote the part of the *serrana* for "la señora Jusepa Vaca." In Act 1, he even inserted a token of his admiration for her talent: "que lo hará muy bien la señora Jusepa" [for Jusepa will do it very well] (16).[8]

The difficulty of the part only reflected the troubled nature of Gila, who is repeatedly shown as identifying, not just verbally, but totally, with that constellation of attributes and expectations that defined and maintained masculine predominance in society. As her character emerges, Gila would today be recognized as a transsexual; that is, a person who feels born on the wrong side of the gender distinction and who longs for the fulfillments of the other sex.[9] From such ambiguous spectacles as the preceding one, from the comments of other characters, and from her own declarations, the

audience is soon made to realize that Gila's self-image is indeed far
from feminine:

> Si imagináys
> que lo soy [muger], os engañáys
> que soy muy onbre.
>
> (350–52)

> [If you imagine
> that I am a woman you are mistaken,
> for I am very much of a man.]

And

> Por inclinación soy onbre.
>
> (1833)
>
> [By inclination I am a man.]

> Muger soy solo en la saya.
>
> (773)
>
> [I am a woman only in my skirts]

Though she continually asserts and flaunts her masculine pro-
clivities, as if the wish would transfigure the reality, she does not, as
some of Vélez's *mujeres varoniles,* appear in masculine clothing,
probably due to the tradition of the ballad. But she repeatedly calls
herself "hombre" and the other characters in the play concede that
it would have been better if she had indeed been a man. As Magdelena said:

> Erró la Naturaleza,
> Gila, en no herte varón.
>
> (659–60)

> [Nature erred,
> Gila, in not making you a man.]

Although the dramatist and his audience were probably more interested in the *mujer varonil,* as her long-playing popularity in the
theater would attest, from the sensational or scenic points of view,
Vélez has instinctively incorporated into his portrait of Gila many
of the behavioral and emotional conditions that modern personality
theory recognizes as significant in the formation of unconventional
behavior. Gila was born, as she puts it, with excessive *altibez*

[pride] (1566), which she, however, in keeping with the cultural assumptions of her age, attributes to the stars. The preference of modern critics for the analytic or the sociological points of view, which I will shortly discuss, over the astral interpretation in no way obscures the fact that Vélez, with keen intuitive insight, depicted Gila as so psychologically structured along masculine lines that she unself-consciously assumes the male attitudes of aggression, dominance, and self-assertive strength in work and play.

Her physical strength was equal to her inclinations for masculine pursuits. At the local fair in Plasencia she had defeated a fencing master as well as some local bullies in a "juego de armas" [arms contest] and then taunted them as "gallinas mojadas" [wet chickens] (834, 1887, 1900). She had delivered a blow to the jaw of one Andrés that, he complained, knocked his teeth out (1885). Her tongue was nearly as formidable as her fists. She could outswear the proverbial trooper. And so with threatening oaths she evicted the Captain, don Luis, who had insolently insisted on billeting himself at her father's house despite the latter's protests. While hunting she had killed a wild boar, a wolf, and even a bear. In the presence of the *Reyes Católicos* she had bulldogged a steer to the ground. Obviously nothing was further from her nature than the passivity and submissiveness—the self-effacing virtues—of conventional women.

Instead she identified with the attitudes that supported masculine predominance in society; accordingly, she put women very low on the scale of things, juxtaposing "alimañas y mugeres" [animals and women] (1081), and reiterates her determination "por no parezer muger, / que es lo que yo más desseo" [to not seem a woman, which is what I wish most] (1086-87). Once again one is reminded of certain phases of psychoanalytical theory, such as Freud's rather biased explanation for the inferior status of women and general deprecation of the female sex. Moreover, if not guided by positive role models, some girls, in an attempt to identify with the "superior" sex, launch into exaggerated masculine patterns of behavior. Vélez's insight into the psychological dynamics of his heroine is further demonstrated when he assigns much of the blame for Gila's lack of femininity to the failure of her parental role models. Gila's mother was remembered as being much like the aberrant Gila herself: "que de tan biçarra polla / fue otra igual el cascaɾon" [for of such a bizarre chick, another such was the shell] (941-42), which suggests that she may not have been properly integrated into the conventional feminine role model either. One is to understand that Gila could derive little or no guidance from that quarter. That her upbringing, crossing gender distinctions as it did, was a travesty for a Spanish girl is made equally clear when she is described as ". . . es polla, / que entre sus gallos crió" [that chick, who grew up among the roosters] (493-94). And although Gila's father rebukes her when her masculine excesses get completely out of hand, he also, especially early in the play, is openly proud of her, and compares her with male forebears;

> una hija me dio el zielo
> que podré dezir que vale
> por dos hijos, porque sale
> a su padre y a su agüelo . . .
>
> (129–32)

> [Heaven gave me a daughter
> that I can say is worth
> two sons, for she takes after
> her father and grandfather . . .]

It is evident from the beginning, as her father Giraldo admits later on, that he has culpably contributed to her growing gender confusion. For Giraldo, Gila, though a beloved daughter, also filled the role of son.

Vélez shows us that from the conventional viewpoint the sex-typed division of labor and authority within her family was a shambles, and this disarray carried over into the work outside the house as well. Here, also, Gila rejected the private domain of women—the inner, enclosed, domestic space of the house—for the public, social world of men, from hunting to acts of bravado in the plaza. Mere housework, the ancient yoke of women, she leaves to her cousin Magdelena, while she goes off to dice with the local bloods (1826). Gila was at home everywhere except at home. When she is at work in Act 2 she is out plowing in the fields and goading on the oxen (1055). When her father asked her to clean house and prepare supper for the soldiers quartered there she retorts:

> Vamos primero que nada
> a ver del modo que ponen
> . . . la vandera y armas . . .
>
> (1818–20)

> [Let's go first of all
> to see how they are setting up
> the flag and the arms . . .]

Again, how far Gila deviates from the social norm can be seen
when her father congratulates her on her marriage (which he had
imprudently arranged to the false-hearted Captain don Lucas) with
the significant words: "tu remedio" [your remedy] (1570). But all
Gila was able to reply dwelt on the honors reserved for men:
"¿Anme elegido / por general, por rey, obispo o papa?" [Have they
elected me general, king, bishop, or Pope?] (1555-56). An obvious
attraction of a masculine stance for Gila was the independence
inherent in the social position of males. For Gila, who had appropri-
ated that freedom early on, the constraints imposed by matrimony
on a wife were abhorrent. Marriage for a woman, in her opinion, as
in that of her sister types, was only another form of slavery. In such
subordination she found an irrefragable reason for refusing marriage:

> 　　　　　Hasta agora
> me imaginaba, padre, por las cosas
> que yo me he visto her, honbre y mui onbre.
> ·　·　·　·　·　·　·　·　·　·　·　·　·
> 　　　　　No me quiero casar, padre, que creo
> que mientras no me caso que soy onbre.
> No quiero que nadie me sujete,
> No quiero que ninguno se imagine
> dueño de mía; la libertad pretendo . . .

> 　　　　　　　　　　　　　　　　　　(1584–88)

> [Until now
> I imagined, father, by the things
> that I have seen myself do, that I was a man, and very much of a man
> . . .
> I do not want to marry, father, for I believe
> as long as I don't marry that I am a man.
> I don't want to be subordinated to anyone;
> I don't want anybody to imagine
> that he is my master; I want freedom . . .]

The immobilizing constriction of feminine clothing was another
reason for her antipathy to the conventions imposed on her sex:

> 　　　　　　　. . . y no quiero
> meterme agora a cavallera y herme
> muger de piedra en lo espetado y tiesso,
> encaramada en dos chapines, padre,
> y con un verdugado hecha campana.
> ·　·　·　·　·　·　·　·　·　·　·　·　·

aprendiendo do nuebo reverenzias
que será para mí darme ponzoña . . .

(1593–1600)

[I don't want
to be a made-up gentlewoman and become
a woman of stone through such stiffness and rigidity,
set atop two high heels, father,
and with a hoop skirt like a bell

. . .

learning to make curtseys,
for it will be like giving me poison . . .]

These lines are redolent of the comic incongruity as well as the contradiction between what she aspires to be and what society decrees she should be. Fashion, as a sign of feminine subordination, was a symbolism not lost on Golden Age audiences, and Gila's sartorial recalcitrance was a clearly understood aspect of her role inversion. The Captain, when his mind turns to it, quickly reads these signs for what they are. He wastes no time complimenting her dress and other feminine graces. For whatever his faults, he understands Gila's deviant temper and subtly casts his snares along the natural paths of her inclinations. Thus his flattery is irresistibly persuasive, as when he remarks to Gila:

que abéys de ser al lado de don Lucas
. . . . otra Semíramis,
otra Evadnes y Palas española.

(1610–12)

[for you will be at the side of don Lucas
. . . another Semiramis,
another Evadnes and Spanish Pallas.]

And Gila, overwhelmed to hear her fondest fantasies echoed from another, enthusiastically replies:

Esa razón me puede obligar sola,
por imitar a vuestro lado luego
a la gran Isabel, que al de Fernando,
emprende heroycos hechos . . . .

(1613–16)

[That reason alone can persuade me
to imitate at your side

the great Isabel, who, beside Fernando,
undertakes heroic deeds. . . .]

Gila, however, forgot, as Professor McKendrick points out, that
Isabel never turned her back on the feminine roles of wife and
mother.[10] Furthermore, *heroycos hechos,* naturally accruing to a
queen, are eccentric, perhaps impertinent, in an ordinary woman.
True, the term *varonil* applied even to ordinary women was, up to a
point, a commendation, and it was so used in reference to women in
the *comedia.* In the once in a lifetime crises that engulfed the
heroines of the *comedias* it obviously was desirable for them to
transcend the traditional weaknesses of their sex—moral, mental,
and physical—to meet the emergencies at hand. But as a settled
nature the infringement of male prerogatives, and even more the
habitual flaunting of such encroachment, was condemned on all
sides.

The characters in *La serrana de la Vera* at first express mixed
amazement and admiration for the *valor* and *varonía* [manliness] of
Gila. King Fernando himself, upon encountering her for the first
time, exclaims:

> ¡Qué valerosa muger!
>
> (931)

> [What a brave woman!]

And Isabel adds:

> No he visto maior valor.
>
> (932)

> [I have not seen such valor.]

The Captain affirmed:

> No e visto en onbre jamás
> tan varonil biçarría.
>
> (249–50)

> [I've never seen in a man
> such dashing courage.]

The fencing master even conceded that:

> En toda mi vida vi

> una muger tan valiente.
>
> (801–2)

> [In all my life I never saw
> such a brave woman.]

Her *brío* is often extolled and her strength admired. On the other hand, her masculine excesses eventually evoked comments which paired astonishment with condemnation. Her father rebukes her:

> Gila ¿en qué has dado?
>
> (721)

> [Gila, what have you done?]

Another man is disconcerted:

> ¿una muger
> toma la espada?
>
> (725–26)

> [¿A woman
> takes up a sword?]

And even Isabel expresses reservations:

> Loca aquella labradora.
>
> (923)

> [That girl is crazy.]

Although moments later she exclaims:

> Enamora
> verla tan valiente y bella.
>
> (937–38)

> [It is wonderful
> to see her so brave and beautiful.]

However, the final judgment of disapprobation of her masculinity is unmistakable. At the end Gila herself bites her father's ear and upbraids him for indulging her whims:

> que esto mereze quien pasa
> por las libertades todas

de los hijos. Si tú usaras
rigor conmigo al principio
de mi inclinación gallarda
yo no llegara a este estremo.

(3251–56)

[for this is what one deserves
who allows total liberty
to his children. If you had
restrained me more at the beginning
of my masculine inclinations
I would not have reached this extreme.]

Even in contrition her impudence bursts out. The idea of laying hands on, of all people, her own father is shocking and, in its manifestation here—biting his ear—traditionally comic. Yet her father himself finally admits some responsibility for her aberrations when he laments: "Confiesso que es justa paga / a mi descuido" [I confess that it is a just payment for my neglect] (3259-60). Gila's speech would also seem to be an explicit condemnation of her father for not bringing up his daughter in a manner befitting a woman. Clearly, the qualities of *varonía* in the appropriate circumstances evoke admiration for a woman, but the excesses of Gila ultimately incur universal disapprobation.

Again and again this paradox of Gila's being is explored by Vélez. The opposition of antitheses—a favorite Baroque topos—is welded by Vélez into a dramatic strategy as he developed his portrait of Gila, juxtaposing masculine and feminine, aggression and passivity, strength and beauty into a character so tautly deviant from accepted cultural norms that a dramatic explosion, given the slightest external provocation, seems inevitable. As Vélez goes about building up the contradictions in Gila's character, each scene adds to the total sense of unease and to an ever augmenting realization of just how bizarre a social misfit she really is. Her pride lies in showing off her masculine attributes, yet her feminine appeal (what we would call her sex appeal) is ever on display, despite herself.

The erotic element—the ambiguous bisexual aura—implicit in the masculine woman, was a salient aspect of Gila's appeal and, indeed, of the lasting popularity of all these characters throughout the Golden Age. Thus Gila, in keeping with the tradition prescribed by Lope, was, as we have seen, a bewitching blend of the most attractive attributes of both sexes. This counterpoint of qualities— *hermosa* [beautiful] and *valerosa* [brave]—which has had an enduring appeal even into our own unisex times is repeatedly emphasized by all the characters. Vélez, both verbally and visually, imparts a sense of tense, even twisted, sexuality when he focuses on Gila's feminine side. Despite the emphasis on the masculine temperament of Gila, and even though she herself shows only indifference or hostility to romance, nothing should obscure the point that Vélez equally emphasizes Gila's feminine gifts. Her seductive combination of disparate qualities and, not a little, the challenge of a difficult conquest all intrigued and then inflamed the Captain:

> porque venze can valor,
> con hermosura y amor.
>
> (452–53)

> [because she conquers with valor,
> with beauty and love.]

The passage from Gila's contrary qualities to ambivalent behavior to the suspicion of deviant sexuality was one ploy Vélez counted on to attract and hold his audience.[11] For instance, innocently enough Gila expresses great admiration for Queen Isabel: "después de dezir que es bella, / dizen que es braba muger" [in addition to saying that she is beautiful, they say that she is a courageous woman] (633–34).[12] Such was also how Gila wanted to see herself:

> en viendo yo
> mugeres desta manera
> me buelbo de gusto loca.
>
> (642–44)

> [On seeing
> women of this type,
> I go mad with pleasure.]

From an expression of admiration and a longing for identity, Gila's language takes on a warmer tone, imbued with erotic feeling, and ambiguous in its context, when she blurts out before remembering herself:

> . . . si onbre huera,
> por vos sola me perdiera,
> y aun así lo estoy,
> ¿por Dios!
>
> (888–90)

[. . . if I were a man,
to you alone I would lose my heart,
and by God, even so,
I am lost!]

In other verses the amorous assertions are even more direct: "Que
de vos / alta señora, a muchos días que estoy / enamorada . . ."
[Because, / great lady, for a long time / I have loved you] (871–73).
Gila also hopes to impress the Queen with her great feats, as she
says, into a reciprocal sentiment: "y yo a Isabel enamoro" [and I
will inspire love in Isabel] (908).

Such extravagant language, is not usual in the *comedia* from one
woman to another, and while on the face of it probably does not go
beyond the bounds of mere exaggeration, would in this context
surely have tended to suggest unconventional sexuality—parallel-
ing, perhaps even motivating, her errant behavior. Although as a
rejected suitor his remarks are not completely disinterested, the
gracioso [jester] also hints at this when he repeats gossip from the
townspeople:

> ven que no tienes cuidado,
> han dicho que lo has dexado
> por faltas secretas tuyas.

(1168–70)

> [they see that you have no cares of love,
> and they say that you have avoided it
> because of secret defects of yours.]

Gail Bradbury, who has discussed the frequent appearance of
various aspects of irregular sexuality in the *comedia,* writes:
"Clearly the scientists of the age were not at all reluctant to associate the masculine woman and the effeminate man with at least two
abnormalities—sex change and mixed sexuality . . . . It would
therefore be unreasonable to suppose that seventeenth century
dramatists avoided, of necessity, the more sensational aspects of
the strong woman/weak man topic, or that their audiences were less
aware than we are of the blurred boundaries between inverted and
irregular sexuality."[13] In addition, the classical tradition, peopled as
it was with all manner of deviant behavior, sexual metamorphoses,
hemaphrodites, heroic or mythical superwomen, such as the Amazons or Semiramis, and, in fact, with the whole underworld of
human sexual behavior, supplied both inspiration and legitimacy to

the handling of such themes in the seventeenth century.[14] The aura of unconventional sexuality surrounding these masculine women afforded the playwrights of that age an unusual opportunity to exploit the dramatic potentialities inherent in juxtaposing nature and convention, appearance and reality, sensationalism and instruction in paradoxical modes especially pleasing to Baroque sensibilities. The opportunities to treat erotic themes beyond the horizons of conventionality must be considered among the more important reasons for the enduring popularity of the role reversal type throughout the Golden Age. In the case of Gila, Vélez, too, well aware that these themes would entice his audience, has explored the many guises of the erotic ambiguities inherent in the *mujer varonil* figure.

Another concern for the conservative society mirrored in the comedia were the anti-social implications of Gila's behavior.[15] It is a fine psychological insight that in Gila the blocking up of the normally sanctioned erotic outlets—romance and marriage—was replaced by a furious individual aggressiveness: "Todo es fiereza y rigor" [all fierceness and harshness] (1114), turned against the other sex but potentially liable to rampage in any number of illicit directions. Gender confusion and individual aggressiveness such as Gila's, which already connoted a refusal to abide within prescribed limits, could be linked quite naturally by the popular mind with forms of social subversion and decay. Gila's uncompromising repudiation of marriage struck at the very heart of the traditional ideology of the function of the family and its members in society. When she finally was persuaded to marry by the treacherous Captain don Luis, who in character was revealed as the negative of everything that was positive about Gila, she accepted his false suit, paradoxically, not for love or out of feminine weakness—the sanctioned reasons—but instead in anticipation of the heroic deeds and glory the Captain promises. Her very masculine aspirations led her right into the snares of her betrayer. Both are false to the ideal of matrimony as defined by their society; for the Captain it is a trick to enjoy a sexual conquest, while Gila sees it as a step toward the fulfillment of her masculine ambitions of martial conquest. Thus seduced and seducer—stock figures of these plays—the one a disdainful heroine, the other a swaggering soldier, are brought together by motives conventionally creditable to neither. And the dialectic of moral aberration is drawn out with grim symmetry. The Captain is shown as a don Juan—faithless, boasting, arrogant, and imprudent, and set over against him is a woman equally violent, proud, and rash. Both are paragons of the social rebel, and both are ultimately made to pay dearly for their transgression of the social code.

Vélez, having counterposed his two flawed protagonists, highlights the dramatic tension of his plot by introducing a symmetrical structure of crime and retribution, played out both conceptually and linguistically.[16] The Captain is as twisted in his way as Gila is in hers.[17] Both became obsessed with extracting a personal revenge for the humiliations they inflict on one another. Although of noble station, don Luis was morally depraved: "muy traidor y muy galán, / muy noble y muy fementido, / muy falso y muy bien nacido . . ." runs the antithetical refrain. [very deceitful and very gallant, very noble and very unfaithful, very false and very well-born] (3008–10). Rebuffed and even manhandled by Gila when she ejected him from her father's house, he, like Gila later on, sets out to get even. After seducing Gila, he gloats: "que ya coxió la venganza / lo que sembró mi esperanza" [what my hopes sowed has now been reaped in vengeance] (2023–24), and Gila, searching for her seducer, vows: "mi venganza solicito" [I seek revenge] (3060). Seduction and abandonment—the triumph of a don Juan—universally were considered as morally reprehensible and socially threatening for they breached the ideals of honor and chastity, two bastions of a woman's status in the family and of the family in society. The Captain was well aware that his pleasure was a betrayal of his trust, of the law, and of society: "que siendo ofizial del rey, / no es justa razón causar / alboroto en un lugar. / Mas yo romperé esta ley" [for, being an official of the King, it is not right to cause disorder in a town. But I will break this law] (515–18). But don Luis's earlier resolution, made with more prescience than he realized—"Esta serrana valiente / he de rendir si me cuesta / mil vidas . . ." [I am going to conquer this brave *serrana* if it costs me a thousand lives] (vv. 486–88) is matched against Gila's furious and indiscriminate vengeance which, before she tracks down her seducer, included "dos mil vidas" [two thousand lives] (3240). And Gila, also, was headstrong and heedless of society in declaring her defiance: ". . . que si me acomete / el mundo no importa" [for if the whole world assails me, it doesn't matter] (2755–56).

Vélez, playing out the paradoxical opposition of his character, interestingly, does not invoke a double standard of retribution, for if Gila was in the end executed at the hands of the law, so too, did the Captain perish by the hand he had wronged. Justice was meted out to both. However, Vélez's attitude toward Gila was uncommonly severe, more so than that of any dramatists toward their characters of this type who revolt against society and take to a life of crime. As McKendrick points out, the other young women are reintegrated into society in one of two ways.[18] One pattern was set by Lope de Vega's earlier *La serrana de la Vera* (1595–98) as well as his later *Las dos bandoleras y fundación de la Santa Hermandad de Toledo* (1597–1603), where the girls, after a few token murders, renounce the error of their ways, marry their suitors, and thus are accepted back into conventional society. The other ending parallels the other sanctioned path of life for women, namely, repentance and spiritual salvation, as in Tirso de Molina's *La Ninfa del cielo,* Valdivielso's *auto sacramental La serrana de Plasencia,* as well as plays of the type of *El esclavo del demonio* and *La devoción de la cruz.* But Gila, unrepentant and murderous to the end, was the too extreme exception for the usual happy resolution of her actions.

While her actions are shown to flow logically from her natural inclinations, Vélez leaves no doubt that it is just these inclinations that are radically flawed and misdirected. To her unconventional self Gila remains true from first to last. Maria Grazia Profeti's view that Gila's behavior is only a pose of bravado and blustering until she carries the role too far and loses control of both her honor and her life is invalidated, I believe, by accumulation throughout the play of masculine behavior.[19] Gila is, in fact, the only *serrana* in the Golden Age theater whose behavior seems thoroughly grounded psychologically and whose reaction to betrayal is unwaveringly consistent with her errant character. A male viewpoint and masculine values dominate her reaction to the Captain's betrayal. Violent crime and war have always been the male domain in society. The disaster strikes primarily at her pride and sense of personal dignity, not to mention her extravagant dreams of adventure and glory. She was overwhelmed by intense personal humiliation, and not by the more customary agonies of dishonored females, namely public censure, the loss of reputation and marriageability, and familial loss of face.

Dramatically, Gila was too spectacularly violent and antisocial to permit less than a completely punitive climax. For Vélez never absolved her of a just share of responsibility for what she became or for what she did. And what she did was an intolerable deviation from the traditional dispensation of women in Spanish society. She flouted every institution that structured the lives of conventional women. Her very being subverted the ideological validation of the established view of women in nature and society. Women were, according to this tradition, naturally subordinate to masculine— that is, rational—authority and purposes, both in mind and body.

Gila stood in diametrical contradiction to all this; she rebelled against her destiny as a woman. Gila's quarrel with her femininity was not based on a reasoned dissatisfaction with women's lot.[20] Neither she, nor Vélez in creating her, were moved by libertarian values. She is not an ideological revolutionary.[21] She has no aspiration to raise the status of women; instead she wants to raise her status to that of men in society. Although Gila, as a *bandolera,* after her seduction describes herself as an avenger of women and appeals to the King: "y al que mugeres agrabia / castigad . . ." [and punish the man who dishonors women] (2572–73), the play cannot be viewed as a defense of women. It is traditional society and its values that are vindicated in the end.[22]

Too fiercely independent, willful, aggressive, and inordinately proud—a primal sin in itself but even more culpable in a woman— she never accepts her femininity, never assents to the subordination expected of a woman. Her seduction, as has been remarked, was a double fault—a fall from virtue and worse, a fall for all the wrong reasons. And her response to this calamity was even more inappropriate and anomalous. She took the matter into her own hands, seeking vengeance directly, and so, by actions unnatural to her sex, only sank into greater dishonor.[22]

Gila tries to reaffirm her pride and dignity, paradoxically, by ways that only alienate her more from society. The fact that she kills men indicates that she is rebelling against a predominantly masculine society and the value system that supports it. Her indiscriminate slaughter of every man who crosses her path, two thousand, as we are told, until she comes upon her seducer, is a turn toward anarchy. She is both breaking through the framework of social prescriptions laid down for women and repudiating society itself.[23] However, the plot of *La serrana* was constructed in such a way that realistically Gila has no other alternative than to take the matter of her honor into her own hands. Her weak and aged father was not one to avenge her nor did anyone else come forth in this village of *gallinas* (chickens). In this way Vélez is able to play upon another paradox: the injustices that were apt to befall a woman in contemporary society are matched against the dilemma of a woman without protectors who is obliged to either suffer injustice quietly or to act in her own behalf and suffer even greater dishonor. Critics have noted certain unresolved ambiguities and tensions in the play— qualms about justice having been done.[24] And indeed Gila does receive some sympathy. Her father, who helped hunt her down, is yet moved to grief: "el viejo / sangre y lágrimas derrama" [her old father weeps tears and blood] (3262–63). Queen Isabel laments her plight: "A mí me eterneze el alma" [it grieves my soul] (3287), and "Pena me a dado / sabiendo que es muger" [it has saddened me knowing that she is a woman] (3173-74). Pascuala says of Gila: "Rasgan . . . el corazón / sus razones" [her words . . . break your heart] (3241–43). Some compassion, but no mercy, is shown to Gila and her predicament. But, sympathy aside, social convention and the law are upheld.

King Fernando refused to rescind the death penalty, "por razón de estado" [for reasons of state] (3171). It must have seemed important to Vélez to uphold the precedence of the central authority to pass judgment as against the medieval pretensions to private vengeance or to exculpate individual feuds. The preservation of social unity, of the *res publica,* so recently won in the days of the *Reyes Católicos,* and so threatened (at least in conservative views) in Vélez's age, was too important to permit a disruptive force of the magnitude of Gila. It was through the arrows of the *Santa Hermandad* (the country constabulary), established by the *Reyes Católicos* expressly for the purpose of suppressing violence and brigandage in the countryside, that the sentence was executed.[25] The gruesome display on the stage of the dead *serrana,* tied to the stake and pierced by arrows—a sacrifice to the social order—must have produced a profound moral impression as well as sensational theater. In this way Vélez mixed preachment with entertainment.

The pronouncement of King Fernando: ". . . a sido / justo castigo" [it was a just punishment] (3284-85) was the concurrent judgment of author and society. This was echoed in the words of a sacristan, who was reported to Gila to be *descomulgándote* [excommunicating you[(2712). Her own father disowned her (3090-91). Her actions are thus condemned by both secular and religious authorities. Gila herself, concurring in the justice of her sentence: "No la [muerte] tengo por desgracia" [I don't consider it unjust] (3229), affirms her identity, even in death, with the masculine ethos. Such words from the lips of a man are appropriate, even a heroic defiance, but from a woman, they are absurdly incongruous. And as if Vélez wished to make the statement more explicit he has Gila repeat: "nadie de mí se lastime" [no one should feel pity for me[(3226).

The legend of the *serrana* lent itself to the dramatic exploration of the role reversal theme. Paradox, theatricality, illusion, spectacle—all staples of Vélez's lavish Baroque stagecraft—swirled around Gila in scene after scene, replete with ambiguous social implications, until in the end the established social order was overwhelmingly reaffirmed. The dual nature of Gila, her feminine beauty and mascuine bravado, enticing to both sexes of the audience, was an obvious invitation to view the relation of the sexes in society from new perspectives and to exploit for dramatic purposes the deviant sexuality implicit in this figure and the situations arising around her. In this way the play made it possible to consider matter too sensitive to handle except in a fictive and indirect manner. Such imaginative adventures also afforded the audience an escape from the hardening rigidities of everyday social stratification into an afternoon's entertainment in a world turned upside down—a *mundo al revés*, an especially popular Baroque topos.[26] Maravall describes the monolithic, conservative, controlled nature of seventeenth-century Spanish society, with all its secular and religious institutions to maintain the status quo.[27] But obviously not all individuals fit into such rigid social molds. Especially interesting is Vélez's exploration of unusual women who were not accommodated within the limits of an authoritarian society. The function of the *comedia* as a temporary release or safety valve which Wardropper proposes in his important study, *Teoría de la comedia,* seems especially applicable in the role reversal plays, for here not only society but the very view of society generally depicted in the *comedia* is turned upside down.[28]

In these plays, we may catch a faint echo of current concerns and controversies concerning women and their place in society. There is contemporary evidence that this question was not cut and dried.[29] In addition, the authors had every opportunity to have their say through their characters and their dramatic destinies. It is curious that Vélez, who dwelt on this theme so often, was never again so harsh as in this play. The overwhelming impression one gets from these plays is the vindication of popular prejudices and the affirmation of the traditional place of women in society. The plays featuring the transposition of social roles are not so radical as they might appear, including, as we have seen, *La serrana de la Vera.* They do not ultimately question the basic relations of the sexes, or the division of roles in society; rather they uniformly end by upholding society against eccentric individuality. Wardropper has noted that in the serious plays of the Golden Age it is always society that is vindicated, never the individual.[30] And this is the calamity that unfolds in *La serrana*—individuality, when eccentrically developed, as in Gila, crashes head-on into the social norms with fatal consequences for the unyielding heroine. The reactionary environment of Spanish society of this period is described by Maravall: "Traducida en los severos intentos de restablecer una estratificación cerrada con carácter aristocrático y tradicional, venciendo para llegar a ello los impulsos individualistas."[31] [Expressed in strict attempts to reestablish a closed stratification of society, aristocratic and traditional, and suppressing, in order to achieve this goal, individualistic impulses.] It is little surprising, then, that Vélez, working in the *comedia*—the genre par excellence of popular collective sentiment—carried the legend of the *serrana* to a conservative and expected end. The role reversals may furthermore be seen as indicative of a world shaken out of its natural order. And in light of the increasing destabilization of the social order of Counter-Reformation Spain, with the concomitant growing repression and authoritarian reaction, the dramatization of these sex-role inversions may take on a certain importance in shoring up the traditional social fabric.[32] The breakdown of role distinctions could easily come to be associated with the general cultural and political failure of the times.

It is well to remember that these plays centering around the masculine woman were first and foremost popular entertainment. As such, to be acceptable to the public, and to be permitted by the authorities, they were under constraint to offend neither. In the increasingly closed and static society of Counter-Reformation Spain the *mujer varonil* offered the public, for the course of the *comedia,* an unfettered fantasy, rousing action, and erotic excitement. That the plays often spiced action with the excitement of aspects of deviant sex was no matter, for the punitive ending of these plays, and *La Serrana* especially, reestablishes the rightness of the established norms—so the audience could have some added excitement, while the authorities could leave satisfied that vice was punished and society was safe, even if the play did start off with some dangerous ideas and situations. The liberation from inhibitions and restrictions, with the ultimate triumph of the social order, produced very good theater.

Notes

1. The most comprehensive study is Melveena McKendrick's *Woman and Society in the Spanish Drama of the Golden Age: A Study of the "Mujer Varonil"* (Cambridge: University of Cambridge Press, 1974); see also Carmen Bravo-Villasante, *La mujer vestida de hombre en el teatro español* (Madrid: Revista de Occidente, 1955): Barbara Matulka, "The Feminist Theme in the Drama of the Siglo de Oro," *Romanic Review* 26 (1935): 191–231; and my "The *Mujer Varonil* in the Theater of the *Siglo de Oro*" (unpublished diss. University of Pennsylvania, 1969).

2. *Dios hace reyes* in *Obras de Lope de Vega, Ac.,* 608b.

3. *The Dramatic Works of Luis Vélez de Guevara: Their Plots, Sources, and Bibliography* (Berkeley: University of California Press, 1937).

4. B. B. Ashcom, "Concerning 'La Mujer en hábito de hombre' in the *Comedia*," *Hispanic Review* 28 (1960): 57.

5. For brief resumés see editions of *La serrana de la Vera* by Ramón and María Goyri de Menéndez Pidal, *Teatro Antiguo Español"* vol. 1 (Madrid, 1916), pp. 134–46, and by Enrique Rodríguez Cepeda, 2d ed. (Madrid: Ediciones Cátedra, 1982), pp. 16–20. Rodríguez Cepeda discusses at length the polygenesis of the *serrana* in "Fuentes y Relaciones en *La serrana de la Vera*," *Nueva Revista de Filología Hispánica* 23 (1974): 110–11. A very interesting anthropological-literary study by François Delpech, "La leyenda de la serrana de la Vera: Las adaptaciones teatrales" *(La mujer en el teatro y la novela del siglo XVII: Actas del IIo Coloquio del Grupo de Estudios sobre Teatro Español* [Toulouse: Université de Toulouse, 1979], 25–38), traces archetypal elements from the mythic cycle of the strong woman to the dramatic adaptations in the Golden Age.

6. Ed. Ramón and María Goyri de Menéndez Pidal, 133–50. All subsequent references are to this edition.

7. *Comedias y Entremeses*, 1.8, cited in Ruth Lee Kennedy, *Studies in Tirso, I: The Dramatist and His Competitors, 1620–26* (Chapel Hill: North Carolina Studies in the Romance Languages and Literatures, 1974), p. 221.

8. Lope's *Las mocedades de Roldán* was also written "a devoción del gallardo talle, en hábito de hombre, de la única representante Jusepa Vaca" (*Obras, Ac.* N., 13, 205), as well as *Las almenas de Toro*. Another actress who specialized in masculine roles was Juana de Villalba, for whom Lope wrote his *La serrana de la Vera* and also *La varona castellana*. She was described as a "mujer varonil, Diana cazadora, Hércules, gigante hecho de nieve y de rosas" (Thornton Wilder, "Lope, Pinedo, Some Child Actors, and a Lion," *Romance Philology* 7 [1953]: 19).

9. Shirley Weitz, *Sex Roles: Biological, Psychological, and Social Foundations* (New York: Oxford University Press, 1977), pp. 52–54.

10. McKendrick, *Woman and Society*, p. 116.

11. Delpech refers to her "almost homosexual veneration" of the Queen (29), and Matthew D. Stroud points out that "she uses terminology usually reserved for a suitor referring to his lady" ("The Resocialization of the *Mujer Varonil* in Three Plays by Vélez," in *Antigüedad y Actualidad de Luis Vélez de Guevara*, ed. C. George Peale [Amsterdam/Philadelphia: John Benjamin's Publishing Co., 1983], p. 122). Ashcom states: "The Lesbian motif is implicit in most of the plots involving masculine women" (59). McKendrick, however, considers at length and then rejects the possibility of a lesbian motif in the *mujer varonil* plays in general. After numerous other arguments she concludes: "If seventeenth century moralists and critics of the theatre never used the so-called lesbian motif as ammunition in their denunciations of the theatre as a corrupting influence, this must have been because it simply did not occur to them to regard the *mujer vestida de hombre*, and the complications she sometimes gave rise to, in this light. And if it did not occur to over-vigilant moralists, one wonders whether it occurred to anyone" (319).

12. Queen Isabel, incidentally, is compared to the same archetypes of feminine bravery: "¡Evadnes! ¡O Semíramis cristiana / O invencible católica española!" (1928–29). She is addressed also as "católica Diana" (1041) and "dibina amazona" (884), and was habitually described by Vélez as a *mujer varonil* in this and other plays as well.

13. Gail Bradbury, "Irregular Sexuality in the Spanish *Comedia*," *Modern Language Review* 76 (1981), 573.

14. See Bradbury, "Irregular Sexuality." Ovid's *Metamorphoses,* both the original and translations, were well known as well as other Spanish histories of mythology. Numerous examples of sex-change and hermaphroditism are included by Antonio de Torquemada in his *Jardín de cosas curiosas* (ed. A. G. de Amezúa y Mayo [Madrid: Sociedad de Bibliófilos Españoles, 1943] pp. 77–81). The hermaphrodite could be regarded with amazement and admiration, as a prodigy who had exceeded Nature, while homosexuality was severely punished as demonstrated by the examples (all male) in Jerónimo de Barrionuevo's *Avisos (1654–1658) Biblioteca de Autores Españoles,* vols. 221–22, ed. A. Paz y Melia [Madrid: Ediciones Atlas, 1968], nos. 72, 101, 168. Medical theories from Aristotle to the contemporary Juan Huarte de San Juan described woman as an imperfect replica of man, and Huarte gives a "scientific" explanation of the basically similar biology between man and woman in his *El Examen de ingenios para las ciencias* (ed. Rodrigo Sanz [Madrid: Imprenta la Rafa, 1930], 2. 370).

15. McKendrick, *Woman and Society,* pp. 109–41; see also Stroud, "Resocialization," pp. 11–26.

16. There are numerous other examples of symmetrical structure in the play. Just as Gila's pride and vanity made her vulnerable so is Giraldo blinded by vanity and ambition. In his desire for social status he believes the Captain's deceitful promises to honor the family by marrying Gila and bestowing "merced" (1515) and "ocasión de que onrréys la sangre vuestra" (1464).

17. For an interesting discussion of characterization see E. Rodríguez Cepeda, "Sentido de los personajes en *La serrana de la Vera,*" *Segismundo* 9 (1973): 165–96.

18. McKendrick, *Woman and Society,* pp. 109.

19. Maria Grazia Profeti, "Note critiche sull'opera di Vélez de Guevara," in *Miscellanea di Studi Ispanici* 10 (1965): 70, 103–04.

20. McKendrick, *Woman and Society,* p. 116.

21. See Rita Hernández-Chiroldes, "Nueva interpretación de los problemas político-sociales en el teatro de Vélez" (unpublished diss., University of Texas, 1982). Although the author makes many interesting and valid points, I do not agree with her general focus or conclusions that Vélez questions the system of hierarchies and values and defends the socially oppressed *[villanos]* as well as those both socially and sexually oppressed (women). Postrevolutionary and especially twentieth century ideology can be misleading when applied to the seventeenth-century world view.

22. Julian Pitt-Rivers tells us that even in this century among the *pueblo* the woman who usurps the male prerogative of violence forfeits the last shred of shame ("Honour and Social Status," in *Honour and Shame: The Values of a Mediterranean Society,* ed. J. G. Peristiany [Chicago: University of Chicago Press, 1966], p. 42).

23. A. A. Parker first pointed out the positive quality of revolt from the standpoint of the aggrieved individual, but its negative aspect from the point of view of society. ("Santos y bandoleros en el teatro español del Siglo de Oro," *Arbor* 13, nos. 43–44 [1949]: 395–416). McKendrick has studied very comprehensively the serious implications of the antisocial behavior of the female bandits in "The Bandolera of Golden Age Drama: A Symbol of Feminist Revolt," *Bulletin of Hispanic Studies* 46 (1969): 1–20, and also *Woman and Society,* pp. 109–41.

24. See Rodríguez Cepeda, Introduction to his edition of *La Serrana de la Vera,* pp. 13–22 and his "Temática y pueblo en *La Serrana de la Vera,*" *Explicación de Textos Literarios* 3 (1974): 169–75. Delpech finds conflict between patriarchal and

matriarchal values at a deeper or archetypal level: "Negación de todo feminismo, pero negación trágica que infunde dudas inconfesadas y angustiosos malestares" (29).

25. Gila's comparison to San Sebastián was probably prompted by the similarity in the method of execution. In addition, there may have been some symbolic significance attached to the use of the arrow as the weapon of the chaste Diana. Furthermore, San Sebastián, once a soldier in the Roman army according to legend, was often associated with soldiers and hunters. See the *New Catholic Encyclopedia* (New York: McGraw-Hill, 1967) and *Lexikon für Theologie und Kirche* (Freiburg: Verlag Herder Freiburg 1965), sub. Sebastian.

26. See Helen F. Grant, "The World Upside-Down," in *Studies in Spanish Literature of the Golden Age Presented to Edward M. Wilson*, ed. R. O. Jones (London: Tamesis Books, 1973), pp. 103–35; also E. R. Curtius, *European Literature and The Latin Middle Ages* (New York: Pantheon Books, 1953), pp. 94–98.

27. *José Antonio Maravall, La cultura del Barroco* (Barcelona: Editorial Ariel, 1975).

28. Bruce W. Wardropper, *Teoría de la comedia. La comedia española del Siglo de Oro* (Barcelona: Editorial Ariel), pp. 232.

29. McKendrick, *Woman and Society,* pp. 282.

30. Wardropper, *Teoría de la comedia,* p. 224.

31. José Antonio Maravall, *Teatro y cultura en la sociedad barroca* (Madrid: Seminarios y Ediciones, 1972), pp. 49–50.

32. Natalie Z. Davis points out that the subordination of the woman to a father or husband was especially useful in expressing the relationship of all subordinates to their superiors in early modern Europe. "The nature of political rule and the newer concept of sovereignty were very much at issue. In the little world of the family larger matters of political and social order could find ready symbolization" (Women on Top," in *The Reversible World: Symbolic Inversion in Art and Society,* ed. Barbara A. Babcock [Ithaca: Cornell University Press, 1978]).

Works Cited

Ashcom, B. B. "Concerning 'La Mujer en hábito de hombre' in the *Comedia.*" *Hispanic Review* 28 (1960): 45–62.

Bradbury, Gail. "Irregular Sexuality in the Spanish *Comedia.*" *Modern Language Review* 76 (1981): 566–80.

Bravo-Villasante, Carmen. *La mujer vestida de hombre en el teatro español.* Madrid: Revista de Occidente, 1955.

Cervantes, Miguel de. *Comedias y Entremeses* in *Obras Completas.* Edited by R. Schevill and A. Bonilla, Madrid, 1915.

Curtius, E. R. *European Literature and the Latin Middle Ages.* New York: Pantheon Books, 1953.

Davis, Natalie Z. "Women on Top." In *The Reversible World: Symbolic Inversion in Art and Society,* edited by Barbara A. Babcock. Ithaca and London: Cornell University Press, 1978.

Delpech, François. "La leyenda de la serrana de la Vera: Las adaptaciones teatrales." In *La mujer en el teatro y la novela del siglo XVII: Actas del IIo Coloquio del Grupo de Estudios sobre Teatro Español* pp. 25–38. Toulouse: Université de Toulouse, 1979.

Díez Borque, José María. *Sociología de la comedia española del siglo XVII.* Madrid: Ediciones Cátedra, 1976.

Grant, Helen F. "The World Upside Down." In *Studies in Spanish Literature of the Golden Age Presented to Edward M. Wilson,* edited by R. O. Jones, pp. 103– 35. London: Tamesis Books, 1973.

Hernández-Chiroldes, Rita. "Nueva interpretación de los problemas político-so- ciales en el teatro de Vélez." Unpublished diss., University of Texas, 1982.

Kennedy, Ruth Lee. *Studies in Tirso, I: The Dramatist and his Competitors,* 1620– 26. Chapel Hill: North Carolina Studies in the Romance Languages and Liter- atures, 1974.

Lundelius, Ruth. "The *Mujer Varonil* in the Theater of the *Siglo de Oro.*" Un- published diss., University of Pennsylvania, 1969.

Maravall, José Antonio. *La cultura del Barroco.* Barcelona: Editorial Ariel, 1975.

———. *Teatro y literatura en la sociedad barroca.* Madrid: Seminarios y Edi- ciones, 1972.

Matulka, Barbara. "The Feminist Theme in the Drama of the *Siglo de Oro,*" *Romanic Review,* 26 (1935), 191–231.

McKendrick, Melveena. "The *Bandolera* of Golden-Age Drama: A Symbol of Feminist Revolt." *Bulletin of Hispanic Studies* 46 (1969): 1–20.

———. *Woman and Society in the Spanish Drama of the Golden Age: A Study of the "Mujer Varonil."* Cambridge: University of Cambridge Press, 1974.

Parker, A. A. "Santos y bandoleros en el teatro español del Siglo de Oro." *Arbor* 13, nos. 43–44 (1949): 395–416.

Pitt-Rivers, Julian. "Honour and Social Status." In *Honour and Shame: The Values of a Mediterranean Society,* edited by J. G. Peristiany, pp. 19–77. Chicago: University of Chicago Press, 1966.

Profeti, Maria Grazia. "Note critiche sull' opera di Vélez de Guevara." *Mis- cellanea di Studi Ispanici* 10 (1965): 47–174.

Rodríguez Cepeda, Enrique. "Fuentes y relaciones en *La serrana de la Vera.*" *Nueva Revista de Filología Hispánica* 23 (1974): 100–111.

———, ed. *La serrana de la Vera.* 2nd ed. Madrid: Ediciones Cátedra, 1982.

———. "Sentido de los personajes en *La serrana de la Vera,*" *Segismundo,* 9 (1973), 195–96.

———. "Temática y pueblo en *La serrana de la Vera,*" *Explicación de Textos Literarios,* 3 (1974): 169–75.

Spencer, F. E., and Schevill, R. *The Dramatic Works of Luis Vélez de Guevara: Their Plots, Sources, and Bibliography.* Berkeley: University of California Press, 1937.

Stroud, Matthew D. "The Resocialization of the *Mujer Varonil* in Three Plays by Vélez." In *Antigüedad y Actualidad de Luis Vélez de Guevara,* edited by C. George Peale, pp. 111–26. Purdue University Monographs in Romance Lan- guages. Amsterdam and Philadelphia: John Benjamin's Publishing Co., 1983.

Vega, Lope de. *Obras de Lope de Vega publicadas por la Real Academia Es- pañola.* Edited by M. Menéndez y Pelayo. 15 vols. Madrid, 1890–1913.

———. *Obras de Lope de Vega publicadas por la Real Academia Española.* Edited by E. Cotarelo y Mori. 13 vols. Madrid, 1916–1930.

Vélez de Guevara, Luis, *La serrana de la Vera.* Edited by Ramón and María Goyri de Menéndez Pidal. Teatro Antiguo Español, Vol. I, Madrid, 1916.

Wardropper, Bruce W. *Teoría de la comedia: La comedia española del Siglo de Oro.* Barcelona: Editorial Ariel, 1978.

Weitz, Shirley. *Sex Roles: Biological, Psychological, and Social Foundations.* New York: Oxford University Press, 1977.

Lope's *El anzuelo de Fenisa:* A Woman for All Seasons

ANITA K. STOLL

One of Lope's little-known plays, *El anzuelo de Fenisa [Fenisa's Hook]* provides us with two most interesting female characters who lead us into several intertwined areas of inquiry: female sex-role inversion, generally studied as the various permutations of the *mujer varonil* [woman with male characteristics], the significance of this inversion and the picaresque elements in the play. It reflects an upside down world, one in which such inversions denote a rejection, albeit temporary, of authority and of normal social categories.[1] Mikhail Bakhtin's study of the presence of the carnival spirit in *Rabelais and his World* helps to clarify the goal of the oppositional patterns represented by the picaresque and the *mujer varonil*. The temporary lifting of usual societal restraints provides an exhilarating freedom after which all return renewed to the routine of the world right side up. We can also observe these various elements as they travel through time within this exceptional vehicle by Lope through the study of three adaptations of this play dating from 1801, 1912, and 1961.[2]

In Lope's play, Fenisa is a beautiful woman who, by her own testimony, was once deceived by a man. Now she devotes her beauty and wiles to deceiving men for pleasure and money. She is, in contemporary terms, a con artist. She seeks out her prey along the docks of the port city of Palermo, Sicily. She strings him along with professions of love and gifts until he is duped and then takes him to the cleaners. Her victim in the play is Lucindo, a Spanish merchant who has just arrived with goods to sell. She gains his confidence through lavish gifts and then, when he has the profit from the sale of his merchandise she tells him she must ransom her brother and asks his help. His money in hand, she casts him aside. A month later Lucindo returns from Valencia with a counter-con, swindling Fenisa out of his money plus 50 percent. This main plot revolves around these lower- and mercenary-class characters. The secondary plot introduces the upper-class element. While Lucindo was away Fenisa fell in love with a beautiful youth, Don Juan de Lara, really the disguised noble Dinarda searching for her love Albano, who had to flee from Sevilla because of a duel with her brother Felix. Fenisa learns both of Lucindo's counter-con and that Don Juan is a woman in the last scene, as all leave her metaphorically holding the bag.

The two characters Fenisa and Dinarda provides us with two examples of Melveena McKendrick's *mujer varonil,* that is, a woman who displays characteristics of male behavior, even though she may not appear in masculine dress.[3] Dinarda is the typical girl page whom McKendrick describes as *guerrera* [woman warrior]: she adopts male dress to facilitate her pursuit of her lover who has disappeared.[4] This "mujer vestida de hombre" [woman dressed as a man] was a sure attention-getter on the stage of the period, given the erotic suggestion provided by a woman in men's tight-fitting clothing of this era, and particularly when coupled with such suggestive comments as Fenisa's appreciative notice of (Dinarda's) Don Juan's charms after this first meeting: "Fuera de la cara hermosa, / me matan piernas y pies/. . .que del hombre la hermosura/ consiste en piernas y brío."[5] [Besides a pretty face, legs and feet attract me . . . because in a man beauty consists of legs and spirit.] While Fenisa does not employ men's clothing, she behaves like a man in many other ways, since it is more typically masculine behavior to verbalize such an unequivocally physical observation. She also is very independent, enunciating clearly her rights:

> pero no es razón que viva
> quien nació libre también
> de un hombre cautiva.

(23)

> [it is not right that a being
> who was born free also should live
> as captive of a man.]

Fenisa has characteristic features of several of McKendrick's types: for example, the *mujer esquiva,* for she shuns love and marriage. She says very early in the play that she was once deceived by a man and now she was making a career of paying back all men for his blow. For this she also fits McKendrick's avenger category. She could also be seen as the *bandolera* [female bandit] as she makes her living through stealing. This character is more complex than Dinarda, who is a repetition of many other adventurer-women of the Spanish *comedia*. The reason may be found in the source for the main action of this play.

The play is based on one of the stories from the *Decameron,* "Astucia por astucia" [Trick for trick].[6] The picaresque setting is taken directly from Boccaccio's story, as are the many picaresque elements to be found in the person of the protagonist. The play preserves some of the amoral tone of the genre until the very end. The protagonist may be perceived as both right—she must earn her living—and wrong—she deceitfully dupes Lucindo out of his necessary working capital. She has no lineage, belongs nowhere except the dock and like the *pícaro* lives by her wits, moving from adventure to adventure, from victim to victim. She is in a permanently liminal state and will never be integrated into society, since she mistrusts men and victimizes them (except Dinarda-Don Juan), therefore foregoing marriage, which is woman's only acceptable role within society in seventeenth-century Spain. Again like the *pícaro* she lives for purely material and physical pleasures. These picaresque elements are the opposite of the values held by society in general, just as the sex role deviations are contrary to societal expectations. These inversions provide a liberation from accepted norms as outlined by Barbara Babcock.[7] "Liberty's a Whore: Inversions, Marginalia, and Picaresque Narrative," in *The Reversible World: Symbolic Inversion in Art and Society.* As Babcock indicates, one of the effects of inversions and reversals is to break down preconceived notions. In *Fenisa* this applies both to woman's role vis-à-vis man, and to class differentiation, because the two women and the two plots represent two distinct and separate classes in society.

These two classes are carefully delineated, as Nancy D'Antuono explains in her study of the play in *Boccaccio's "Novelle" in the Theater of Lope de Vega.* The lower class is represented through the clever use of the concept of the *anzuelo;* to evoke both the port (fishing literally), and Fenisa's con game (fishing metaphorically). It is also presented in clever dialogue in which, for example, Lucindo the merchant declares his love in terms of precious cargo. There are multiple occurrences of certain symbols: *cadena* is used repeatedly both concretely and figuratively to underscore the mercenary, materialistic or "un-noble" aspects of the play. Lucindo has Tristán hide his gold chain before he goes to Fenisa's house; she pointedly looks for it and inquires what happened to it. Lucindo begins his speech describing his love for Fenisa in merchant/mercenary terms:

Cadenas de obligaciones
me acordarán mi ventura,
pues sin las de tu hermosura
en las que llevo me pones, . . .

(24)

[Chains of obligations
will remind me of my fortune,
for without those of your beauty
you put me in those which I wear . . .]

At the end of the play Fenisa gives Osorio a gold chain as token of
her appreciation for his role in bringing about her engagement to
Don Juan.

The words *gato* [cat] and *gatazo* are also very often used: *gato* is
the animal/purse of money obtained by Fenisa from Lucindo, and
gatazo is used for the trick or con. In the verses "este ratón al
revés/ nos ha cogido este gato" [this mouse in reverse has caught
this cat for us] (34), Fenisa is characterized as the mouse who
reverses normal expectations by seizing the cat (purse). *Gato* also
has the meaning of clever and deceptive thief. The centrality of this
word in its multiple meanings is underscored by its use in a sonnet
spoken by the gracioso Tristán as he and Lucinda leave to return to
Valencia. The last six lines are

A dios Fenisa, a Dios gato delgado,
a Dios cabo de gato, cuyo espejo
puede servir de exemplo, y de recato.
Pero permita Dios que tu pellejo
antes de un mes por tu vellaco trato
sirva de gato a un avariento viejo.

(35)

[Goodby Fenisa, goodby slender cat,
goodby cat's tale, whose image
can serve as example and as warning.
But may God permit that your hide
before a month for your villainous treatment
serve as purse for an avaricious old man.]

Here, the idea of commerce and money is something animalistic,
of the lower class: or the opposite of the highest level of human
existence, that of the nobility. Another symbol of the animalistic
side is the frequent evocation of that famous *femme fatal* Circe,
who charmed men and then turned them into pigs, echoing the

seductive and victimizing nature of Fenisa. The banquet-gaming scene in act three is yet another animalistic-Carnivalesque feature. D'Antuono concludes that the nobility subplot, added by Lope to the original story plot, ends by glorifying the nobility represented by Dinarda and her brother Felix (who appears only briefly) and establishes (or reestablishes) a hierarchy of values for the viewer and censor. Other aspects of this carnivalesque spirit are the languge already described and several comic dialogues in macaronic Italian mocking Spaniards.

The ideas of commerce and money, anathema to the nobility, also serve to promote this image of the world upside down. This complicated series of inversions suggested and carried out in various human interchanges serve to free the audience momentarily from the strict categories of masculine / feminine, peasant / noble. Mikhail Bakhtin describes this carnivalesque and contradictory state of affairs in *Rabelais and his World*. The celebratory festivals of medieval and Renaissance times provided an occasion for throwing off the fetters of society, written and unwritten, turning it upside down. Bakhtin pointed out that

> During carnival time life is subject only to its law, that is, the laws of its own freedom. It has a universal spirit; it is a special condition of the entire world, of the world's revival and renewal, . . . and this universal renewal was vividly felt as an escape from the usual official way of life.[8]

That is what we find here. The reimposition of organization and law comes at the end, with the arrival of the noble Felix and the punishment of Fenisa. Lope has captured the picaresque nature and carnivalesque spirit of the underside of society, which serves as a renewing force for the audience. This accomplished, he turns it back again at the end, providing the genial touch of glorifying officialdom, that is, those in power, the nobility. Babcock concludes her introduction stating

> The *mundus inversus* does more than simply mock our desire to live according to our usual orders and norms; it reinvests life with a vigor and a *Spielraum* attainable (it would seem) in no other way. The process of symbolic inversion, far from being a residual category of experience, is its very opposite. What is socially peripheral is often symbolically central, and if we ignore or minimize inversion and other forms of cultural negation we often fail to understand the dynamics of symbolic processes generally.[9]

Even though punished, Fenisa remains free and able to continue her former life on the periphery of society. Therefore Lope leaves an element of liberty represented by Fenisa, and we might say that in her case the inversion, rather than being righted, remains, the true picaresque, a permanent departure from societal norms, a subversion of the values of the dominant group and a revolutionary idea for the time.[10]

The breaking of societal strictures during the play and the ultimate return to the status quo, except for Fenisa's extrasocietal freedom, is maintained in the adaptations of the play in many respects and is even amplified in one case. These adaptations in later periods allow one to observe the modifications deemed necessary for later centuries and societal imperatives and to take account of these later treatments of the *pícara-mujer varonil*.

Cándido María Trigueros prepared the version printed in the year 1803. He also included an *Advertencia* to his version which explains the reasons behind the changes he introduced, providing insight into his understanding of the play as a later eighteenth-early nineteenth-century reader and dramatist. Significantly, he changes the name of the play to *La Buscona*, picking up an epithet used early in the original to describe the *gracioso* Tristán's wise perception of Fenisa's business: "Pudo salir a pescar / buscona debe de ser" [She was able to go out fishing, she must be a con lady].[11] He notes that this title more accurately reflects his moralistic and didactic reading of the play: Oxalá no fueran las busconas tan abundantes en nuestros dís como en los de Lope . . . pero las hay a millares . . . . "La risa y mofa que aquí las castiga puede convertirse en antídoto muy efectivo." [I wish the con artists were not so abundant in our days as in those of Lope . . . but there are thousands of them . . . the laughter and mocking which punishes them here can be a very effective antidote] (A2). In keeping with the preoccupation of his period with classical theater he notes a similarity to the Roman *tabernarios* and compares it with those of Terence. He says that he has changed the play from three to five acts in order to preserve sufficient unity of place. The scene changes at the beginning of each act but in such a way that "aun con la misma vista se percive estar muy cerca de donde se acabó [Even with the same view one perceives being very near where it ended] (A2) In order to conserve the unity of time, he leaves out Lucindo's return to Valencia: "Este viage no era necesario, y ahora se ha dispuesto todo de manera que puede vengarse en el mismo día" [This trip was not necessary, and now everything has been arranged so that he can avenge himself in the same day] (A2). (In the original a month passes between trick and revenge.) However, this change necessitated other minor changes so that everything turns out well ordered. He also noted having shortened some long speeches he considered repetitive and scenes he considered accessory or episodic. He further comments that the action is, although complicated, unified, and that there is unity of interest; that is, it keeps the audience always intent on learning the final outcome for the protagonist. His summary judgment is:

> "La facilidad con que he podido reducir esta comedia, me ha convencido de la sólida bondad de la invención de Lope: y no sería culpa suya si yo no lo he desempeñado bien." (A5)

> [The ease with which I have been able to adapt this play, has convinced me of the solid value of Lope's creation: and it would not be his fault if I have not carried it out well.]

He thus views the play as we would expect, given the prevailing orientation of the time, and makes changes to emphasize a didactic purpose and alters it to conform to the unities.

Specific changes related to the inversion pattern are the employment of a *gallo-gallina* [rooster-hen] wordplay, used to amplify the comic aspect of Dinarda's dress as well as the idea of the upside down world. In the opening scene of the original there is a casual, never-repeated, one-line comment before any gender issues are raised suggesting that males typically relate sexually to multiple females: "que viven cien gallinas con un gallo" [that a hundred hens live with one rooster] (19). Trigueros picks up the *gallo/gallina* opposition and expands it into a comic play regarding Dinarda's gender, suggesting that her appearance is ambivalent; "que es gallo ingerto en gallina, / o gallina ingerta en gallo" [that he is rooster inside a hen or a hen inside a rooster] (18). The wordplay is carried through the scene and then returned to at the end of the play when Dinarda reveals herself as a woman: "Fabio: Volvióse el gallo gallina" (39). [The rooster turned into a hen.]

Another similar motif popular in the medieval world is also introduced by Trigueros, that of the wheel of fortune, which represents a reversal of fortunes at the end of the play. Lucindo delights in the success of his trick:

> Para, fortuna, tu rueda
> que yo no te pido nada,
> . . . pues ya queda
> la Buscona rebuscada.

(35)

[Fortune, stop your wheel
since I don't seek anything,
. . . since now
the Con Lady has been conned.]

In the following scene Fenisa, who has not yet discovered her loss
although the audience has, employs the same motif: "la suerte a mi
bien atenta/ sobre su rueda me sube" [luck attentive to my good/
lifts me on her wheel] (35). The juxtaposition of the two scenes with
equivalent messages ironically underscores the reversal of Fenisa's
fortunes.

The last scene is of particular note and in keeping with the
moralizing tone. This author has Dinarda revealed not as the fiancée
of Albano who traveled to Sicily from Seville to find him, but as his
wife, certainly a more proper state for a Spanish noble woman
pursuing a man so far from home. He also adds a few lines at the
end that emphasize the unrepentance of the tricked Fenisa:

> Huyamos, Celia, de todos,
> encerrémonos aprisa;
> que si nos están mofando,
>
> . . . .
>
> no faltarán otros bobos,
> que desquiten esta risa.

(39)

[Let's flee, Celia, from everyone,
let's hide ourselves quickly;
for if they are mocking us
. . . other fools will not be far away
who will belie this laughter.]

Lope stops with the exposure of the deceptions. Trigueros read and
produced it as a didactic tale warning gullible men about predatory
women and sharpened Fenisa's punishment and exile from society.
Changes made in the text reflect his preoccupation, as well as the
period's desire to observe the unities. But in the meantime, he took
the idea of the world upside down and actually expanded Lope's
original idea regarding sex role reversal with comic imagery.

The 1912 adaptation was done by Cristóbal de Castro and opened
in the Teatro Español on 25 November, "siendo director artístico
Don Benito Pérez Galdós" [being artistic director Don Benito
Pérez Galdós], as the title page tells us. This adaptation in three
acts, each divided into two *cuadros,* follows the original much more

closely, for there is not the same preoccupation with the unities as in the 1803 version. There are several departures from the original, however. In keeping with the passage of time, there is a general modernization of language. Lope's sonnets are left out, although an entirely new one is created, perhaps because of audience expectations for Golden Age Drama. There is also a general cleaning up of the play, with suggestive aspects omitted, reflecting the Victorian period. Banished from this version is the scene of Celia's checking Lucindo's bed, she says, on orders from Fenisa to find out if there is any sign of another woman. In another excision Dinarda/Don Juan and Fenisa disappear into a back room together so that Dinarda can dispel doubt about her sexual identity. The ending is also changed, reflecting a general softening of tone from the original. Fenisa's financial losses are reduced, the tone of Lucindo's letter telling of the trick is softer, Dinarda's revelation as woman is more realistic—here she leaves the stage in man's clothes and reappears in woman's clothing—and most interestingly, her noble brother Felix appears for the first time and to Fenisa's "¿Que he de quedar tras de pobre, / burlada y escarnecida?" [besides remaining poor, must I also be made fun of and mocked] he answers "Pobre no, que yo os acojo . . ." [Poor no, for I will take you in . . .] thereby offering the renegade *pícara* an entrance back within the bounds of society. Thus an entirely new reading of what in the original was a sensual romp ending with a clever sting, and became in the early nineteenth century a didactic story, here in the early twentieth is modernized, sanitized, less carnivalesque, and less picaresque, reflecting the society of the time.

The 1961 version by Juan German Schroeder, divided into two parts, opened in the Teatro Nacional María Guerroro on 3 March, 1961. In his foreword the adaptor classes Lope's play as "una de las más perfectas y magistrales de su época de madurez" [one of the most perfect and magistral of his epoch of maturity].[12] He responds to the sensuous elements in the play: "La galería de pícaros, amantes, vividores, rufianes, los propios tipos de Fenisa y Celia, están más próximos del popular y recio retrato de los entremeses cervantinos que del incorrecto aire de Boccaccio. . . ." [The gallery of picaros, lovers, high-livers, ruffians, the types of Fenisa and Celia themselves, are closer to the popular and sharp portrait of the Cervantine entremés than the incorrect air of Boccaccio . . .]. He has attempted to adapt the scenic elements "al gusto e imperativos estéticos de nuestro día para que con ellos alcanzase una acogida que nos la devolviese del injusto olvido" [to the taste and aesthetic imperatives of our day so that it will achieve a reception which will return it for us from an unjust rejection]. Consequences of the adaptor's reading of the play as sensuous, even using the term *dolce vita,* are stage directions that encourage this interpretation by the actress who plays Fenisa. In her first scene on stage the direction indicates "Pide a Celia su bolso, se retoca y contempla en el espejo y en 'arreos de bizarría se adorna ostentosamente con un collar" [She asks Celia for her pocketbook, she touches up her face and looks at herself in the mirror and she adorns herself ostentatiously with a necklace].[13] Later in a scene where she hosts a party of several gentlemen gambling in her house, the stage directions read "Quítase el vestido y queda en ropa interior. . . . [she takes off her dress and remains in her underclothes . . .] (66), a definite adaptation to the more permissive code of attire on stage in the twentieth century, and well suited to the permissive and suggestive tone of carnival.

Again, the ending provides a brief glimpse into one of the variations. Like the 1912 version, the ending of the play is made more realistic than the original in which Don Juan becomes Dinardo by saying "Pues sabed que soy Dinarda" [Well know that I am Dinarda] (45). In both twentieth-century adaptations the stage directions allow for her exit and re-entry in women's clothing. That Fenisa quickly returns to her con games and free life is explicitly spelled out in this version as, in the closing line, she tells Celia "Trae mis anzuelos, . . . que a pescar vamos al puerto . . ." [Bring my lines, . . . for we're going to the port to fish] (104). Thus the ending reproduces two of the three likely endings for the picaresque as described by Babcock: the *pícaro* is both punished and also continues her adventures.[14] This latest version shows greater awareness of and respect for the original structure of the text, seeking to innovate through staging and interpretation, but keeping close to the original spirit.

How were these adaptations received? The opening night review of Cristóbal de Castro's 1912 adaptation begins with a complaint that "We need to be instructed in the atmosphere and nature of these classical works." Nevertheless the reviewer adds

"por la finura de su trama, la verdad de su ambiente y la frescura de su diálogo, parece una comedia por la que no pasó la patina de los siglos. Ha sido su labor, inteligente y culta, la de un hábil restaurador que nos descubriese en toda su pureza un lienzo de Velásquez."

[for the fineness of its plot, the truth of its atmosphere and the freshness of its dialogue, it seems to be a play which has not undergone the passage of centuries. It has been the learned and intelligent work of a skillful restorer who has discovered for us in all its purity a canvas of Velásquez.]

Of the 1961 version the reviewer comments

". . . una auténtica delicia y maravilla para los ojos. . . el director saludó con el adaptador y el escenógrafo, al final de la obra, entre bravos y ovaciones, mientras se alzaba diez o doce veces el telón en justificada apoteosis de triunfo . . . todo en *El anzuelo de Fenisa* es delicioso y cautivador, divertido y gozoso: el verso lozano, jugoso y fresco; la réplica intencionada y aguda; el diálogo, llevado con un juego centelleante de esgrima poética, como el plateado batir de los espadas . . . ¿Quién ha dicho que nuestros clásicos son pesados y farragosos, triviales o insubstanciales? Esta farsa lopesca da ciento y raya a los más divertidos y atrevidos vodeviles, a la más osada comedia de enredo, dentro de una elegancia insuperable y de un verdo sin daño . . ."[15]

[an authentic delight for the eyes . . . the director bowed with the adaptor and the set designer at the end of the work amid bravos and ovations, while the curtain was raised ten or twelve times in a justified apotheosis of triumph . . . everything in *El anzuelo de Fenisa* is delightful, captivating, entertaining and pleasurable; the juicy, clever, fresh verse, the intentional and witty reply, the dialogue, carried along with a scintillating play of poetic fencing, like the silvery striking of the swords, who said our classics are heavy and dull, trivial or insubstantial? This Lopesque farse keeps up with the most entertaining and daring vaudeville presentations, with the most daring comedy of errors, with in an insuperable elegance and a harmless risque wit.]

As James Mandrell has pointed out in his recent discussion in *Hispania* of Don Juan Tenorio as *Refundición,* this form is "a rewriting in which aspects of one literary text are reworked so as to admit the claims of both inclusion and originality within another text."[16] He says they were made with two purposes in mind: to bring Golden Age *Comedias* in line with different dramatic precepts, such as the unities, and to resolve difficulties with language and staging. The process of adaptation constituted a critical and aesthetic re-evaluation, not just a reworking but also a refurbishing of what has previously been judged outmoded or inappropriate. The end result was that they succeeded "in the important task of keeping alive an active interest in a national theater" (22). The play under consideration here has provided an excellent opportunity for the study of these issues involved in adaptation: the changes and their rationale in response to requirements in the society for which they were produced, and how the productions of the adaptations were finally received. In the adaptations studied there did take place a critical and aesthetic re-evaluation, and changes based on these produced an altered text acceptable to the society for which it was intended. As Henry Sullivan points out in his study of the historical reception of Calderon's theater, "Since the life of a work of art begins only when it leaves its creator's hands, adaptations and translations form part of the widening river of its progress through history."[17] Given the original text and the demands of the twentieth-century audience, the texts produced presented a meeting of minds between text and society of a different era. The "keeping alive an active interest in a national theater" is one result of the synthesis of a historically viable text and a receptive audience. And most specifically in the case of the play studied, the universal human need for "kicking over the traces" that is served with the spirit of carnival and that is present in this play of Lope's (and represented by the unforgettable Fenisa) and in its adaptations keep alive for the audience the spirit of freedom and play.

Notes

1. Two important articles on this subject are Helen F. Grant's "The World Upside-down" in *Studies in Spanish Literature of the Golden Age Presented to E. M. Wilson*, ed. R. O. Jones (London: Tamesis, 1973), 114; and Dawn Smith's "Women and Men in a World Turned Upside-Down: an Approach to Three Plays by Tirso," *Revista Canadiense de Estudios Hispánicos* 10, no. 2 (Invierno, 1986): 247–60.

2. The earliest is the reworking by Cándido María Trigueros, published as *La buscona* (Madrid: Librería González, 1803). There are also two twentieth-century versions. Cristóbal de Castro's version (Madrid: Sociedad de Autores Españoles) dates from 1912. The third, by Juan-Germán Schroeder, was published in 1916. David Gitlitz has prepared an English translation, *Fenisa's Hook*, published by Trinity University Press, 1989.

3. Melveena McKendrick, *Woman and Society in the Spanish Drama of the Golden Age: A Study of the "Mujer Varonil"* (Cambridge: Cambridge University Press, 1974), x.

4. McKendrick, *Woman and Society,* 208.

5. All page references, hereafter referred to in the text, are from the version published in 1617 in *Parte VIII* of Lope's plays; this quote is from page 28. For further information on the use of risqué material in Golden Age Drama, see David Gitlitz's article *"El galán Castrucho:* Lope in the Tradition of the Bawdy" *Bulletin of the Comediantes* 32 (Spring 1980): 3–11.

6. Nancy D'Antuono has studied this play in her book *Boccaccio's "Novelle" in the Theater of Lope de Vega* (Madrid: José Porrúa Turanzas, 1983).

7. Barbara Babcock, "Liberty's a Whore: Inversions, Marginalia, and Picaresque Narrative," in *The Reversible World: Symbolic Inversion in Art and Society*

(Ithaca: Cornell University Press, 1978). She explains that the inversions of norms have the effect of "rendering ambiguous . . . primary categories which are usually distinguished, such as good and evil, fidelity and treason, life and death, "high" and "low" style, and to negate these disjunctions. . ." (110).

8. Mikhail Bakhtin, *Rabelais and His World,* trans. Helen Iswolsky (Bloomington, Indiana, 1984), 7.

9. Babcock, "Liberty's a Whore," 32.

10. This is consonant with the idea which Bruce Wardropper outlines in his *La comedia española del Siglo de Oro:*

> [La comedia] No sólo constituye la reclamación de un cambio, sino la de una inversión: se pide lo saturnal, se pide el mundo al revés. Al insistir sobre la prioridad de los derechos del individuo sobre los derechos de la sociedad, la comedia española desdeña la concepión masculina de la forma de alcanzar la felicidad en una sociedad ordenada. Exhorta, si no a olvidar, sí a soslayar la primacía de la sociead. Y pregunta: ¿para qué existe la sociedad si no para la felicidad individual? El mensaje de la comedia es el de que los individuos tienen derechos que exceden a los de la sociedad. Este mensaje era, y es, revolucionario. (235)

> [It not only constitutes the demand for change, but also for an inversion: the saturnalian, the world upside down, is sought. By insisting on the priority of the individual's rights over the rights of society, the Spanish comedia disdains the masculine conception of the way to obtain happiness in an ordered society. It exhorts one to overlook, if not to forget, the primacy of society. And it asks: why does society exist if not for individual happiness? The message of the comedy is that individuals have rights which exceed those of society. This message was, and is, revolutionary.]

11. *La buscona* (Madrid: Librería González, 1803), 25. All further pages references are found in the text. The *Advertencia* is paginated "A" and page number.

12. Alfredo Marquerie's review in *El mundo,* 4 March 1961.

13. Schroeder, *El Anzuelo de Fenisa* 15.

14. The third possibility is ". . . the pícaro reenters society, sometimes through marriage, and is apparently reintegrated into the social structure" (111).

15. *El mundo,* 4 March 1961.

16. James Mandrell, *"Don Juan Tenorio* as Refundición," *Hispania* 70 (1987): 22–30.

17. Henry Sullivan, *Calderón in the German Lands and the Low Countries: His Reception and Influence. 1654–1980* (Cambridge: Cambridge University Press, 1983), 5.

Works Cited

Babcock, Barbara A. "Liberty's a Whore": Inversion, Marginalia, and Picaresque Narrative." In *The Reversible World: Symbolic Inversion in Art and Society,* edited by Barbara A. Babcock, 1–34 and 95–116. Ithaca: Cornell University Press, 1978.

Bakhtin, Mikhail. *Rabelais and His World.* Translated by Helene Iswolsky. Bloomington: Indiana University Press, 1984.

D'Antuono, Nancy. *Boccaccio's "Novelle" in the Theater of Lope de Vega.* Madrid: José Porrúa Turanzas, 1983.

El Mundo, Madrid, 25 November, 1912.

Gitlitz, David. *"El galán Castrucho:* Lope in the Tradition of the Bawdy," *Bulletin of the Comediantes* 32 (Spring 1980): 3–11.

Grant, Helen F. "The World Upside-down." In *Studies in Spanish Literature of the Golden Age Presented to E. M. Wilson,* edited by R. O. Jones, 103–35. London: Tamesis, 1973.

Mandrell, James. *"Don Juan Tenorio* as Refundición." *Hispania* 70 (1987): 22–30.

Marquerie, Alfredo. In *El mundo,* Madrid, 4 March 1961.

Olson, Elder. *Teoría de la comedia.* In Bruce W. Wardropper, *La comedia española del Siglo de Oro.* Barcelona-Caracas-Mexico: Editorial Ariel, 1978.

Sullivan, Henry. *Calderón in the German Lands and the Low Countries: His Reception and Influence. 1654–1980.* Cambridge: Cambridge University Press, 1983.

Vega Carpio, Lope de. *El anzuelo de Fenisa.* Madrid, 1617.

———. *La buscona. (El anzuelo de Fenisa).* Edited by José María Trigueros. Madrid: Librería González, 1803.

———. *El anzuelo de Fenisa.* Edited by Juan Germán Schroeder. Madrid: Ediciones Alfa, 1963.

Sexual Inversion: Carnival and *La mujer varonil* in *La fénix de Salamanca* and *La tercera de sí misma*

AMY R. WILLIAMSEN

Despite the number of studies devoted to the exploration of *la mujer vestida de hombre* [the woman dressed as a man] and *la mujer varonil* [the manly, or virile woman] in the *comedia,* at least one crucial aspect—the connection between sexual inversion and the carnival—has not yet been completely examined. Although Melveena McKendrick claims that "the possibilities for investigation of . . . the *disfraz varonil* [male disguise] have been virtually exhausted," I would argue that we need to re-examine the possible sources that may have influenced the development of *la mujer vestida de hombre* and the *mujer varonil* in order to reach a fuller understanding of their significance.[1]

In the past, critical evaluation of the possible origins of the figure has ranged from insisting on her emergence as a purely artistic creation to the search for inspiration among various historical figures. M. Romera-Navarro categorically denies the possibility of any "real-life" precedents for the *mujer vestida de hombre,* arguing that nature prevents a woman from being able to pass for a man.[2] He concludes that "no fue el ejemplo de la vida sino la gracia del arte la que puso calzas varoniles a una mujer española" [it was not real life examples but rather the spirit of art that put male breeches on a Spanish woman].[3] Carmen Bravo-Villasante, while she acknowledges the existence of a few "extraordinary" women throughout the course of history, also perceives the *disfraz varonil* as a fundamentally literary creation that enters Spain by way of Italy. B. B. Ashcom, in his ascerbic review of her study, counters this assertion by first citing examples from other literary traditions and, then, enumerating historical cases of women in male attire from the Renaissance to the Civil War years. He concludes: "It is time to make up Miss Bravo's mind for her. In light of the long history of transvestism, . . . one cannot consider the theme merely 'una creación literaria' [a literary creation]. It is doubtful that real-life cases have ever been lacking in a society in which male costume differs from female."[4]

McKendrick's study provides a much needed equilibrium between these extreme positions. After careful consideration, she suggests that: "The *mujer varonil* of the Golden Age drama represents a fusion, in time and place, of nearly all manifestations of extraordinary women which history, mythology, and literature from the days of classical antiquity down to the seventeenth century can offer."[5] Throughout her study, she defines the *mujer varonil* as "the woman who departs in any significant way from the feminine norm of the sixteenth and seventeenth centuries, . . . the woman who is masculine not only in her dress, but also in her acts, her speech or even her attitude of mind."[6] She identifies part of the fundamental appeal of the character as stemming from her embodiment of the "the requisite Baroque tension . . . Appearances deceive—the *mujer varonil* is not what she seems to be nor what she is expected to be. Either her sex hides her masculine characteristics or her masculine characteristics (clothes, actions) hide her sex. In other words, the reality she seems to present is an illusion, and this is the essence of the conceit."[7]

As McKendrick intimates, the figure captures the tension between the feminine and the masculine so aptly conveyed by the juxtaposition within the term *mujer varonil*. As a woman who displays male behavior, the *mujer varonil* belongs to the realm of the *mundo al revés* [world upside down] in which the established social order is inverted. In essence, she embodies the coalescence of two polar opposites. If one accepts Bakhtin's definition of carnival as "the inversion of binary opposition," the connection between the two is evident.[8] Furthermore, carnival "celebrates temporary liberation from the prevailing truth and the established order—it mark[s] the suspension of all hierarchical rank, privileges, norms, and in essence, prohibitions."[9] Within the extremely hierarchical society of Golden Age Spain, women were considered completely subordinate to men. In this context, McKendrick accurately defines the "revolt" of *la mujer varonil* as directed against "society and convention, and woman's inferior role in them."[10] Yet, the brief period of liberation afforded by her revolt against hierarchy usually ends, as does carnival, with her reintegration into the established social order.[11] A great deal of theoretical and empirical evidence, in fields ranging from anthropology to literary criticism, exists to support the claim of the carnival's influence on the figure of

the *mujer varonil*. Natalie Zemon Davis attests that: "In hierarchical and conflictive societies, which loved to reflect on the
world upside down, the topos of the "woman on top" was one of
the most enjoyed. Indeed, sexual inversion—that is, switches in sex
roles—was a widespread form of cultural play in literature, art and
in festivity."[12] In her study of *el mundo al revés,* Helen F. Grant observes the frequent recurrence within the Spanish tradition of this
topos, "usually associated with the Roman Saturnalia and Kalen-
dae, but [that] goes back much further, at least as far as Dionysius
and Aphrodite."[13] The carnivalesque festivities involving the inversion of sexual roles that evolved from these early traditions continue to exist throughout Europe today, as Julio Caro Baroja has
demonstrated in his discussion of the relationship between pagan
rite and Christian forms of celebration associated with carnival or
Carnestolendas [Mardi Gras or pre-Lenten festivities].[14] Not the
least of these is the carnival celebration held in Zamarramala,
Segovia, on the feast of Saint Agueda (5 February). During the
festivities, men and women exchange roles. Even the *alcade*
[mayor] surrenders his post to a female counterpart in a symbolic
act that signifies the complete dominance of women.

Frequently, characters in the *comedia* make direct references to
the connection between *Carnestolendas* and the *mujer varonil*. In
El vergonzoso en palacio, Serafín, dressed as a man, proclaims
"Fiestas de Carnestolendas, / todas paran en disfraces" [Mardi-
Gras festivities all end up with disguises].[15] In an even more explicit
passage, the father in Francisco Villegas's *Lo que puede la crianza*
mentions the carnival as he tries to convince his daughter to return
to female dress:

> "Pues ser quien eres es fuerza
> piensa que representaste
> por Pascua o Carnestolendas
> una comedia entre amigos
> donde a ti, por más dispuesta
> te dieron el de hombre
> y se acabó la comedia.[16]

> [Since to be who you are is imperative,
> think that you represented
> for Easter or Lent
> a play among friends
> where they gave you, as the most well-suited,
> the role of a man,
> and the play has ended.]

Clearly, the carnival's influence on the development of the *mujer varonil* complements that of the literary prototypes and extraordinary historical figures.

The *mujer varonil* who dresses as a man is doubly indebted to the carnivalesque. Ivanov explains that "transvestism (as other carnival rituals) is considered to be an instance of ritual neutralization of semiotically significant oppositions, in this case, the opposition male/female."[17] One means he cites of achieving this equilibrium between binary polar oppositions is the unification of two opposite poles in a single whole, as in the example of the Chinese yin (feminine) and yang (masculine). The Spanish term *mujer/varonil"* provides a striking analogy.

The temporary inversion of sexual roles, even when not accompanied by transvestism, provides not only a brief period of liberation from social constraints but also the opportunity to criticize the existing social order. Nevertheless, scholars usually agree that sexual inversions function as other carnivalesque inversions in that they "pose no real threat to the established norm;" rather, they serve to affirm order and stability in a hierarchical society by providing an accepted form of release of tension.[18] "They can clarify the structure by the process of reversing it," thereby exposing its faults without endangering the system.[19]

In this study I employ the carnival as a framework for the analysis of the *mujer varonil* in two plays by Mira de Amescua, *La fénix de Salamanca* [The phoenix of Salamanca) and *La tercera de sí misma* [Her own go-between]. Both female protagonists demonstrate their quick wits [ingenio] and use their wiles [industria] to carry them through many potentially volatile situations as they seek to secure their respective loves. I will demonstrate how, as embodiments of the carnival inversion of male and female, the two fulfill "the carnivalesque functions of mocking and unmasking the truth."[20]

Doña Mencía, the principal character of *La fénix de Salamanca,* is a beautiful young widow who dresses herself as a man and sets forth on her quest accompanied by her maid who also masquerades as a male.[21] She vows to find Don Garcerán who, after courting her persistently, disappeared without a trace. She insists that, while she need not find him to avenge her irreproachable honor, she must appease her curiosity. Once in Madrid, she becomes involved in Doña Alejandra's struggle to escape an impending marriage to her aging uncle, Capitán Beltrán, that her brother, Don Juan, has arranged despite his sister's wish to marry Conde Horacio. In the end,

Mencía not only secures Garcerán's hand in marriage, she also helps assure Alejandra's future with Horacio.

From her first appearance on stage, she is identified as a *viuda varonil* [virile widow] (32). Her disguise itself underscores her stance as a symbol of sexual inversion—the unification of two polar opposites. As Byron P. Palls has noted in his insightful essay, the habit of San Juan she wears (a long, black robe adorned with a white cross on the chest), suggests

un panorama de asociaciones y fuerzas opuestas que a su vez componen el ciclo de la entidad del símbolo 'yin-yan.' Tanto la antítesis cromática como la resultante del intercambio del traje (hombre-mujer) apuntan a una ambivalencia que se introduce en el mismo título de la obra"

[a panorama of associations and oppositions that, at the same time, constitute the cycle of the entity of the "yin-yang" symbol. The chromatic antithesis as well as that resulting from the exchange of costume (man-woman) signal an ambivalence that the title of the work itself introduces.]

The rest of his essay discusses how the vacillation in the gender ascribed to "Fénix"—alternately masculine and feminine—highlights the *hermafroditismo* [hermaphroditism] of the mythological creature and, by extension, that of Mencía as well. Consequently, a barrage of signs, visual and auditory, combine to strengthen the carnivalesque sexual inversion Mencía represents.

The comic treatment of Leonor, Mencía's maid, underscores the presence of sexual inversion in a manner consistent with the carnival folk tradition that celebrates bodily functions and scurrilous humor. "Earthy" elements pervade the presentation of her relationship with Solano, Garcerán's manservant. The two actually sleep together for two months without his realizing that Jaramillo (Leonor's alias) is, in fact, a woman. After the first night, however, he accuses his bedmate of suffering from some disease:

Déjola; mas, Jaramillo,
si no es sarna, yo soy muerto,
que algún contagio encubierto
debe de ser, no hay sufrillo:

porque cuando te acostaste
cierto olorcillo me diste,

con que el alma me encendiste
las entrañas me helaste;

y tras esto, un comezón,
un fuego vivo, una llama,
que ni yo cabía en la cama,
ni en el cuerpo el corazón,

y si acaso me extendía
y con los pies te tocaba,
un no sé que me picaba
que como pulga mordía;

y con aquesta inquietud
tuve noche toledana.

(1237–54)

[I'll drop it; but Jaramillo,
if it's not mange, I'm a dead man;
it must be some unmentionable contagion,
it's unbearable:

because when you came to bed,
a certain little scent came my way,
that inflamed my soul
and froze my innards;

and then, an itch
a raging fire, a flame
that would neither allow me to rest in bed
nor my heart in my body,
and if by accident I stretched out
and touched you with my feet
a *je ne sais quoi* stung me
that bit like a flea;
and with this inquietude
I spent a sleepless night.]

Later, still plagued by misgivings, he confesses his doubts to Don Garcerán,

Lo que temo;
que es hermafrodito . . .
que una de dos ha de ser:
que es Jaramillo mujer,
y si no mujer, potroso

(2693–94, 2720–21)

[I am afraid that
he's a hermaphrodite . . . one of two things must be:
that Jaramillo is a woman,
and if not a woman, a hernia sufferer.]

In addition to these examples, the cross-dressing of the two female characters creates many humorous moments throughout the play. Mencía, acting as don Carlos, assumes female attire in order to persuade don Juan to permit Alexandra to marry the count. She manages to capture his romantic interest, to the great amusement of his opponents and to the bewilderment of his allies—all of whom believe Juan is being seduced by a man in drag.

Nevertheless, as a truly carnivalesque figure, Mencía's significance surpasses the purely ludic. She represents temporary liberation from the established norm as she moves freely among the men, participating in a sphere normally inaccessible to women. Moreover, she criticizes the extant social order with respect to two central issues: the custom of dueling and the practice of arranged marriages, especially those between an elderly man and a young woman.

During her first encounter with don Garcerán on stage, she intervenes and convinces four men who are on the brink of a duel to sheathe their swords. Later, when the Count receives a note from the Captain, Alejandra's uncle, challenging him, she persuades the men to talk rather than engage in combat. When she learns the men have decided to fight anyway, she takes Alejandra to the site of the duel and eloquently argues that their violent actions have the potential to endanger Alejandra's honor more that any past incident possibly could. Her aversion to dueling does not stem from cowardice. Numerous passages attest to her bravery and willingness to fight when necessary (979–84, 3168–72, for example). The attitude she conveys clarifies the contradiction inherent in the system that accepts dueling as a way to remedy damage to one's honor: dueling does not silence rumors; indeed, it generates them. Thus she demonstrates the absurdity of this behavior.

Mencía also fulfills the carnivalesque function of criticism of the established order with respect to forced marriages between partners of disparate ages. She consistently intercedes on Alejandra's behalf to ensure that she not be forced to marry the Captain. At one time or another, almost all characters in the play, including Alejandra's brother, acknowledge that her failing uncle is a poor match for the young woman. When, in the last scene, the papal dispensation petitioned by the Captain is denied, Mencía entreats him to bless the marriage of Alejandra and the Count. She acts, in accordance with the mythological role of the god Hermaphrodite, as the protector of physical love between the young couple. The date, 1 May, that appears on the letter Mencía sends to Garcerán accepting his love, further strengthens her connection with the forces protecting sensual love. As the only specific day mentioned in the entire play, it carries special significance. May Day, the carnivalesque celebration of spring traditionally practiced among Latin and Germanic peoples, originated from rites in honor of Maia, the Roman goddess of human and natural fertility. Consistent with this spirit of carnival, Mencía helps liberate Alejandra from the *cautiverio* [captivity] and enables her to enjoy the Count's love.

In *La fénix de Salamanca,* Mencía's temporary liberation ends with her reintegration into the social order, but not before she has obtained don Garcerán's hand in marriage and helped join the Count and Alejandra. She succeeds, not only in unmasking the absurdity and injustice of two social conventions, but also in her search for love.

In contrast, Lucrecia, the protagonist of *La tercera de sí misma,* ultimately fails in her conquest of the Duque de Mantua. She witnesses the Duke's participation in the "juegos de Nápoles" [games of Naples] and, although she only sees him once, falls desperately in love with him. She dons male attire and the pseudonym César as she embarks upon her quest to Mantua to secure his love, thus acting as "la tercera de sí misma" [her own go-between]. Upon her arrival in Mantua, she learns that the Duke has sent for his betrothed, Porcia, Condesa de la Flor. Immediately, César (Lucrecia) bursts on stage, claiming that he is being pursued. The Duke grants him his protection. César then invents a story that enables him to praise Lucrecia (herself) and slander Porcia. He declares that while in service at the court of Flor, Porcia attempted to seduce him. This alleged breach of honor enrages the Duke, who sends word to his manservant, Fisberto, to return the Countess to her home.

Meanwhile, on the way to Mantua, Fisberto has fallen in love with Porcia. He tells her that he is really the Duke disguised as a servant. Porcia laments that her betrothed seems so unattractive and so unworthy. Undaunted, Fisberto entrusts her to Lisardo, a rustic peasant, in the hope that she will eventually relent and accept him. Porcia and her servant, Marcela, adopt rustic dress and christen themselves Nise and Pascuala in an attempt to escape the impending marriage to the false Duke. To complicate matters further, the real Duke encounters Nise/Porcia in the woods. He loves her instantly and, in order not to frighten the woman he believes to be a peasant, assumes Fisberto's identity.

Lucrecia, under the assumed identity of a peasant maiden named Laura, also seeks refuge in Lisardo's home. The proliferation of aliases results in several very humorous scenes. Finally, after a series of complex maneuvers, all identities are revealed. The Duke pardons Fisberto and offers to marry Lucrecia, not out of love for her, but because he feels obliged to do so out of gratitude for her devotion. Although this represents the resolution Lucrecia sought so avidly, she declines because she prefers to marry the Count, the Duke's younger brother, who loves her deeply. Her decision frees the Duke to marry Porcia, his true love.

Lucrecia epitomizes the figure of the *mujer varonil*. Even when dressed as a woman, her virility remains apparent. In one scene, the Duke and Count discuss a portrait of her. The Count praises her spirit: "Que tiene ingenio sutil / y el ánimo varonil" [She has a subtle genius and a masculine spirit] (1101–2). The Duke responds that "Ser / de altiva naturaleza / y varonil gentileza "(To be of proud nature and masculine gentility] (1130–32) seems to him a defect— he wants a woman

> hermosa afeminada,
> y tímida y delicada. Tras garza ni jabalí
> no la quiero; en casa sí
> y un ratón la ha de espantar
>
> (1111–15)

> [a feminine beauty,
> meek and delicate. Chasing after either bird or boar
> I do not want her; but at home,
> and a mouse should frighten her.]

The protagonist avails herself of many of the same stratagems as Mencía, yet, while the latter strives to create harmony, Lucrecia sows discord through repeated false accusations, first against Porcia and then against the Duke. She will use any means to secure her end. Elenora R. Sabin, reacting to this characteristic she terms "ruthlessness," sustains that the presentation of Lucrecia represents a flawed recreation of the *mujer varonil,* Amalasunta, from *Las lises de Francia.*[23] I would contend that the failure Sabin perceives does not result from a flawed character portrayal as she argues, but from the portrayal of a flawed character. Lucrecia certainly has faults, but they are crucial to the development of the play. If she were a perfect, completely admirable heroine, it would reduce the comic possibilities of the work.

As stated earlier, most researchers agree that one of the functions of carnival is to clarify structures and their inherent flaws—sometimes through the process of reversal. In *La tercera de sí misma,* Lucrecia's role reversal serves to illuminate the absurd consequences of the blind acceptance of "amor a primera vista [love at first sight] and "amar sin saber a quien" [to fall in love not knowing with whom]. Within the tradition of the *comedia,* a *galán* [courtier] may fall in love upon seeing a woman. As Matthew Stroud notes, this perpetuates the perception of woman as a mere object of sexual desire.[24] In this instance, the tables are reversed, thus enabling the audience to perceive the ridiculousness of this accepted convention.

The exploration of "amor a primer vista" and "amar sin saber a quien," extremely popular themes during Mira's period, prevails throughout the play. All four main characters offer observations regarding the plausibility of such love. The Duke admits he has chosen to marry Porcia, even though he has only heard of her, yet he questions Lucrecia's confession of love; "Notable facilidad / que pueda haber voluntad / donde no se comunica" [Notable facility that there can exist feeling where there is no communication] (1063–65). Porcia worries that she may have erred by agreeing to marry the Duke without having met him first: "Dame cuidado / el pensar que me he casado / sin haber visto con quién" [It worries me to think that I have married without having seen to whom] (518–20). The Count claims to have fallen in love with Lucrecia's portrait, and although attracted to Laura (really Lucrecia in disguise), refuses to submit to his feelings for her as his heart already belongs to another.

Porcia's mistrust of "amar sin saber a quien" proves well founded. Because the Duke and she have never met, their relationship falls prey to Lucrecia's false accusations that could not have succeeded as easily if the couple had known one another. Only when Porcia and the Duke actually meet and speak with one another does their love have a chance to develop. Lucrecia's failure itself presents the best argument against "amar sin saber a quien." Her earlier faith in the power of "amor, ingenio y mujer" [love, wit, woman] is eventually tempered by the realization that "No hay arte para querer / si no inclinan las estrellas / poco aprovechan sin ellas/ amor, ingenio y mujer" [There's no way to inspire love / if the stars are not so inclined, / without them, little comes of / love, wit and woman] (2161–64). The play emphasizes the importance of "amor correspondido" [requited love]—love cannot be forced, nor can it be built on the unstable foundation provided by a passing glimpse.

By allowing her to assume the role traditionally played by a man, Lucrecia's sexual inversion serves to mock the convention of "amar sin saber a quien." Even though she succeeds in eliciting the Duke's offer of marriage, she realizes that it does not represent a victory because he still does not love her. The love that motivated her quest had no sound foundation and, therefore, she cannot succeed in obtaining her desires. In the final scene, her brief period of dominion, during which she manipulates the actions of the other characters, comes to an end when she accepts the Count as her husband. After temporary liberation from the norms of expected behavior, she rejoins the established social order.

Both Lucrecia and Mencía embody the inversion of female and male roles, symbolically represented by their use of male dress. Both enjoy a period of temporary liberation during which they fulfill the carnivalesque mission of revealing flaws within the established order. Thus, the significance of the bond between the carnival and the protagonists transcends the purely ludic, for the characters fulfill "the carnivalesque function of mocking and unmasking the truth." Moreover, the established relationship between theatre and ritual [both religious and carnivalesque] supports the hypothesis of the impact of the carnival on the development of *la mujer varonil*. As the analysis of these two *comedias* demonstrates, the carnival's influence extends beyond the comic elements associated with the *mujer varonil* to the questioning of existing societal norms. An understanding of the crucial link between carnival and the *mujer varonil* not only enhances the appreciation of isolated works, but also lends new insight into the complex nature of the challenge to the dominant order posed by this recurring female icon.

Notes

1. Melveena McKendrick, *Woman and Society in the Spanish Drama of the Golden Age: A Study of the Mujer Varonil* (Cambridge: Cambridge University Press, 1974), xi.

2. M. Romera-Navarro, "Las disfrazadas de varón en la comedia," *Hispanic Review* 2, no. 4 (1934): 279.

3. Romera-Navarro, "Las disfrazadas de varón," 286.

4. B. B. Aschom, "Concerning 'La mujer en hábito de hombre' in the Comedia" *Hispanic Review* 28 (1960): 62.

5. McKendrick, *Woman and Society,* 276.

6. Ibid., ix–x.

7. Ibid, 323.

8. As cited in V. V. Ivanov's "The Semiotic Theory of Carnival as the Inversion of Bipolar Opposites," in *Carnival,* ed. Thomas A. Sebeok and Marcia E. Erickson (Berlin: Walter de Gruyter, 1984), 11.

9. Mikhail Bakhtin, *Rabelais and His World,* trans. Helen Iswolsky (Cambridge: M.I.T. Press, 1968), 10.

10. McKendrick, *Woman and Society,* 317.

11. See discussions in Matthew Stroud, "The Resocialization of the Mujer Varonil in Three Plays by Vélez," in *Antigüedad y Actualidad de Luis Vélez de Guevara,* ed. C. George Peale (Philadelphia: John Benjamin, 1983), 111–26; and Dawn L. Smith, "Women and Men in a World Turned Upside Down: An Approach to Three Plays by Tirso" *Revista Canadiense de Estudios Hispánicos* 10, no. 2 (1968): 257.

12. Natalie Zemon Davis, "Women on Top: Symbolic Sexual Inversion and Political Disorder in Early Modern Europe," in *The Reversible World: Symbolic Inversion in Art and Society,* ed. Barbara A. Babcock (Ithaca: Cornell University Press, 1978): 152.

13. Helen F. Grant, "The World Upside-Down" in *Studies in Spanish Literature of the Golden Age Presented to E. M. Wilson,* ed. R. O. Jones (London: Tamesis, 1973), 114.

14. Julio Caro Baroja, *El carnaval* (Madrid: Taurus, 1965).

15. As cited in Carmen Bravo Villasante's *La mujer vestida de hombre en el teatro español* (Madrid: Revista de Occidente, 1955), 195.

16. As cited in Bravo Villasante, *La mujer vestida de hombre,* 194–95.

17. Ivanov, "Semiotic Theory," 14.

18. Davis, "Women on Top," 153.

19. Stroud, "Resocialization of the Mujer Varonil," 113.

20. Davis, "Women on Top," 163.

21. All references to the plays will be cited parenthetically in the text. Mira de America, *La fénix de Salamanca,* ed. Angel Valbuena Prat (Madrid: Espasa-Calpe, 1957). I was fortunate to be able to work with an unpublished edition of *La tercera de sí misma* by Vern G. Williamsen.

22. Bryon P. Palls, "Una justificación del título de la comedia de Mira de Amesuca *La fénix de Salamanca,"* *Hispanófila* 47 (1973): 62.

23. Elenora R. Sabin, "Lucrecia of Mira de Amescua's *La tercera de sí misma:* A Flawed Recreation," *Bulletin of the Comediantes,* 33, no. 2 (1981): 121–28.

24. Stroud, "Resocialization of the Mujer Varonil," 113.

Works Cited

Amescua, Mira de. *La fénix de Salamanca.* Edited by Angel Valbuena Prat. Madrid: Espasa-Calpe, 1957.

———. *La tercera de sí misma.* Edited by Vern G. Williamsen. Unpublished.

Aschom, G. G. "Concerning 'La mujer en hábito de hombre' in the Comedia." *Hispanic Review* 28 (1960): 43–62.

Bakhtin, Mikhail. *Rabelais and His World.* Translated by Helen Iswolsky. Cambridge: M.I.T. Press, 1968.

Bravo Villasante, Carmen. *La mujer vestida de hombre en el teatro español.* Madrid Revista de Occidente, 1955.

Caro Baroja, Julio. *El carnaval*. Madrid: Taurus, 1965.

Davis, Natalie Zemon. "Women on Top: Symbolic Sexual Inversion and Political Disorder in Early Modern Europe." *The Reversible World: Symbolic Inversion in Art and Society*. Edited by Barbara A. Babcock, 147–90. Ithaca: Cornell University Press, 1978.

Grant, Helen F. "The World Upside-down." In *Studies in Spanish Literature of the Golden Age Presented to E. M. Wilson,* Edited by R. O. Jones, 103–35. London: Támesis, 1973.

Ivanov, V. V. "The Semiotic Theory of Carnival as the Inversion of Bipolar Opposites." *Carnival*. Edited by Thomas A. Seboek and Marcia E. Erickson. Berlin: Walter de Gruyter, 1984: 11–35.

McKendrick, Melveena. *Woman and Society in the Spanish Drama of the Golden Age: A Study of the Mujer Varonil*. Cambridge: Cambridge University Press, 1974.

Palls, Bryon P. "Una justificación del título de la comedia de Mira de Amescua *La fénix de Salamanca.*" *Hispanófila* 47 (1973): 59–71.

Romera-Navarro, M. "Las disfrazadas de varón en la comedia" *Hispanic Review,* 2, no. 4. (1934): 269–86.

Sabin, Elenora R. "Lucrecia of Mira de Amescua's *La tercera de sí misma*: A Flawed Recreation." *Bulletin of the Comediantes* 33, no. 2 (1981): 121–28.

Smith, Dawn L. "Women and Men in a World Turned Upside Down: An Approach to Three Plays by Tirso." *Revista Canadiense de Estudios Hispánicos* 10, no. 2 (1986): 247–60.

Stroud, Matthew. "The Resocialization of the Mujer Varonil in Three Plays by Vélez," In *Antigüedad y Actualidad de Luis Vélez de Guevara,* edited by C. George Peale, 111–26. Philadelphia: John Benjamin, 1983.

Index

273